The South East Bus Handbook

British Bus Publishing

Body codes used in the Bus Handbook series:

Type:
A	Articulated vehicle
B	Bus, either single-deck or double-deck
BC	Interurban - high-back seated bus
C	Coach
M	Minibus with design capacity of 16 seats or less
N	Low-floor bus (*Niederflur*), either single-deck or double-deck
O	Open-top bus (CO = convertible; PO = partial open-top)

Seating capacity is then shown. For double-decks the upper deck capacity is followed by the lower deck.

Door position:
C	Centre entrance/exit
D	Dual doorway.
F	Front entrance/exit
R	Rear entrance/exit (no distinction between doored and open)
T	Three or more access points

Equipment:
L	Lift for wheelchair	TV	Training vehicle.
M	Mail compartment	RV	Used as tow bus or engineer's vehicle.
T	Toilet	w	Vehicle is withdrawn and awaiting disposal.

e.g. - B32/28F is a double-deck bus with thirty-two seats upstairs, twenty-eight down and a front entrance/exit.
N43D is a low-floor bus with two or more doorways.

Re-registrations:
Where a vehicle has gained new index marks, the details are listed at the end of each fleet showing the current mark, followed in sequence by those previously carried starting with the original mark.

Regional books in the series:
The Scottish Bus Handbook
The Ireland & Islands Bus Handbook
The North East Bus Handbook
The Yorkshire Bus Handbook
The North West Bus Handbook
The East Midlands Bus Handbook
The West Midlands Bus Handbook
The Welsh Bus Handbook
The Eastern Bus Handbook
The London Bus Handbook
The South East Bus Handbook
The South West Bus Handbook

Annual books are produced for the major groups:
The Stagecoach Bus Handbook
The Go-Ahead Bus Handbook
The First Bus Handbook
The Arriva Bus Handbook
The National Express Handbook (bi-annual)
Most editions for earlier years are available direct from the publisher.

Associated series:
The Hong Kong Bus Handbook
The Malta Bus Handbook
The Leyland Lynx Handbook
The Model Bus Handbook
The Postbus Handbook
The Overall Advertisement Bus Handbook - Volume 1
The Toy & Model Bus Handbook - Volume 1 - Early Diecasts
The Fire Brigade Handbook (fleet list of each local authority fire brigade)
The Police Range Rover Handbook

Some earlier editions of these books are still available. Please contact the publisher on 01952 255669.

Contents

ASD Bus	5		Kent Coach Tours	77
Accord Operations	6		Kent County Council	78
Airport Parking	70		The Kings Ferry	80
Altonian	8		Kingsman	83
Amberlee	9		Lucketts	84
Autocar	11		M K Metro	85
Autopoint	12		McLeans	89
Avis	13		Marchwood Motorways	90
Bailey's	14		Menzies	92
Banstead	15		Mervyns Coaches	94
Black & White	16		Motts Travel	95
Brijan	17		Newnham Coaches	97
British Airways	18		Nu-Venture	98
Buddens	22		OFJ Connections	100
Buzzlines	24		Parking Express	102
C & S Coaches	26		Pearces	103
Cardinal	27		Poynter's	104
Carousel	28		RDH Services	105
Centra	30		Rambler	106
Chalkwell	36		Reading Buses	108
Charlton Services	38		Rebound	113
Cheney	39		Red Rose	114
Coastal Coaches	41		Redroute	115
Coliseum	42		Regent Coaches	116
Compass Travel	43		Renown Travel	117
Countryliner	45		Richardson Travel	119
County Rider	47		Safeguard	120
Countrywide Travel	48		Scotland & Bates	122
Courtney	49		Seaview Services	123
Crawley Luxury	51		Solent Blue Line	124
Crosskeys	53		Souls	126
Cruisers	54		Southern Vectis	128
Eastbourne Buses	55		Tappins	130
Eastonways	57		Thames Travel	133
Edward Thomas & Son	58		Timetrak	134
Empress of Hastings	59		Tourex	135
Emsworth & District	60		Truemans Travel	136
Farleigh Coaches	61		W & H Motors	137
Fleetwing	62		Warrens	138
Flights-Hallmark	33		Weavaway	139
Grayline	63		West Kent Buses	141
Ham's Travel	64		Wheelers Travel	142
Hellyers	66		White Bus Services	143
Heritage Travel	68		Wight Bus	144
Hertz Rent-a-Car	70		Wiltax	145
Heyfordian	71		Woottens	146
Hodges	74		Worth's	147
Horseman	75			
Hotelink	70			
John Pike	76		Vehicle index	148

The South East Bus Handbook

The South East Bus Handbook

This third edition of the South East Bus Handbook covers the South East region of England, an area surrounding much of the London Region, and is part of a series that details the fleets of bus and express coach operators from across Britain. A list of current editions is shown on page 2. The operators included in this edition are those who provide tendered and commercial services in the counties and unitary boroughs within the region. We have also included a number of operators who provide significant coaching activities, particularly at London Heathrow and Gatwick airports.

Quality photographs for inclusion in the series are welcome, for which a fee is payable. The publishers unfortunately cannot accept responsibility for any loss and request you show your name on each picture or slide.

To keep the fleet information up to date we recommend the Ian Allan publication, *Buses,* published monthly, or for more detailed information, the PSV Circle monthly news sheets.

The writer and publisher would be glad to hear from readers should any information be available which corrects or enhances that given in this publication.

Series Editor: Bill Potter
Principal editors for *The South East Bus Handbook:* David Donati and Bill Potter.

Acknowledgments:
We are grateful to Dave Heath, Tom Johnson, Mark Lyons, Stuart Martin, the PSV Circle and the operating companies for their assistance in the compilation of this book.

The cover photographs are by Mark Lyons and Bill Potter.

Earlier editions of the area covered by the South East Bus Handbook:

1st Edition - South Central Bus Handbook - 1-897990-43-X
2nd Edition - South Central Bus Handbook - 1-897990-65-0

Some earlier editions of the Bus Handbook series are still available. Please contact the publisher on 01952 255669.

ISBN 1 904875 51 3
Published by *British Bus Publishing Ltd*
16 St Margaret's Drive, Telford, TF1 3PH

Telephone: 01952 255669 - Facsimile 01952 222397 - www.britishbuspublishing.co.uk
© British Bus Publishing Ltd, October 2005

A S D BUS

AS HS & RS Dosanjh, Neptune Close, Medway City Estate, Strood, Rochester, ME2 4LT

FTN708W	Leyland National 2 NL116AL11/1R		B49F	1981	Go-Ahead Northern, 2003
C113CHM	Leyland Olympian ONLXB/1R	Eastern Coach Works	B42/26D	1986	Arriva London, 2005
D156FYM	Leyland Olympian ONLXB/1R	Eastern Coach Works	B42/26D	1986	Arriva London, 2005
H220LOM	Scania N113DRB	Alexander RH	B45/31F	1990	The Kings Ferry, Gillingham, 2004
J8ASD	Mercedes-Benz 814D	Cunliffe	BC32FL	1992	W Midlands Special Needs, 2001
K864ODY	Mercedes-Benz 709D	Alexander Sprint	B25F	1993	Stagecoach South, 2001
K874ODY	Mercedes-Benz 709D	Alexander Sprint	B25F	1993	Stagecoach South, 2001
L881MWB	Mercedes-Benz 609D	Cunliffe	BC15FL	1994	Derbyshire CC, 2002
M429RDC	Volvo B6	Alexander Dash	B40F	1994	Go-Ahead Northern, 2003
M432RDC	Volvo B6	Alexander Dash	B40F	1994	Go-Ahead Northern, 2003
N411DRH	Ford Transit VE6	Ford	M14	1996	
N662FLR	Ford Transit VE6	PVB	BC10FL	1996	LB Barnet, 2002
N669FLR	Ford Transit VE6	PVB	BC10FL	1996	LB Barnet, 2002
N572GRH	Ford Transit VE6	Ford	M11	1996	private owner, 1998
N531RJR	Ford Transit VE6	Ford	M11	1996	private owner, 1998
T789KNW	Optare Solo M920	Optare	N30F	1999	LB Waltham Forest, 2004
T816RVA	LDV Convoy	LDV	M16	1999	Global SD, 2004

Previous registrations:
D156FYM   D156FYM, 656DYE

ASD Bus operates a pair of Volvo B6 midibuses that carry Alexander Dash bodies. This model was produced in the mid-1990s for the final normal-floor height chassis, and was succeeded on low-floor chassis by the ALX200 model.
Dave Heath

ACCORD OPERATIONS

UNI-LINK - CITY-LINK

Accord Operations Ltd, University of Southampton, Waterfront Campus, European Way, Southampton, SO14 3ZH; Accord Operations Ltd, Drayton Lane, Chichester, PO20 6BN

10-18			Dennis Dart SLF		Caetano Compass		N26F	2001		
10	HX51LPJ	12	HX51LPL	14	HX51LPO	16	HX51LPV	18	HX51LPZ	
11	HX51LPK	13	HX51LPN	15	HX51LPU	17	HX51LPY			
40	FJ04SNF		TransBus Dart		Caetano Compass		N37F	2004		
31	YN04YJR		Scania OmniDekka N94UD		East Lancs		N51/25D	2004		
32	YN04YJS		Scania OmniDekka N94UD		East Lancs		N51/25D	2004		
33	YN04YJT		Scania OmniDekka N94UD		East Lancs		N51/25D	2004		
34	YN04YJU		Scania OmniDekka N94UD		East Lancs		N51/25D	2004		
AV11	N178OUT		Bluebird CSRE2700		Bluebird Q-Bus		BC60F	1995	West Sussex CC, 1999	
AV12-22			Bluebird CSRE2700		Bluebird Q-Bus		BC60F	1996	West Sussex CC, 1999	
AV12	N729EOT	AV15	N732EOT	AV17	N734EOT	AV19	P36JCR	AV21	P38JCR	
AV13	N730EOT	AV16	N733EOT	AV18	N735EOT	AV20	P37JCR	AV22	P39JCR	
AV14	N731EOT									
	AUP356W		Leyland Atlantean AN68B/1R		Roe		B43/30F	1980	Go-Ahead Northern, 1999	
	GIL5976		Volvo B10M-61		LAG		C53F	1984	Woods, Bognor Regis, 2001	
	M618YGH		Iveco Daily 49-10		Pilcher Green		B15FL	1994	West Sussex CC, 1999	
	M212EGF		Dennis Dart 9m		Plaxton Pointer		B35F	1995	London General, 2004	
	M43AOT		LDV 400		LDV		M16	1995	West Sussex CC, 2000	
	P827MTR		LDV Convoy		LDV		M16	1997	West Sussex CC, 2000	
	R670EWV		Mercedes-Benz Vario 412D		UVG		B16FL	1997	West Sussex CC, 1999	
	R348FYJ		Mercedes-Benz Sprinter 312D		Mellor		B15FL	1998	West Sussex CC, 1999	
	R351FYJ		Mercedes-Benz Sprinter 312D		Mellor		B15FL	1998	West Sussex CC, 1999	
	R355FYJ		Mercedes-Benz Vario 412D		Mellor		B15FL	1998	West Sussex CC, 1999	

Accord Operations is the name of the commercial unit that operates buses, which initially were for the benefit of Southampton University students. The company has expanded recently with further minibuses and double-decks. Pictured in Southampton is Dart 12, HX51LPL, which was operating route U1 when seen. *Dave Heath*

Accord took over the operation of Southampton 'City Link' shuttle service in September 2005 from Firstgroup. Pictured in the city is 32, YN04YJS, one of four Scania OmniDekka buses. It is seen here in *uni-link* colours. *Dave Heath*

R125CMY	Mercedes-Benz Sprinter 614D	Whitacre	M16L	1998		
R127CMY	Mercedes-Benz Sprinter 614D	Whitacre	M16L	1998		
R128CMY	Mercedes-Benz Sprinter 614D	Whitacre	M16L	1998		
R685HGX	Mercedes-Benz Sprinter 612D	Whitacre	M16L	1998		
R686HGX	Mercedes-Benz Sprinter 612D	Whitacre	M16L	1998		
S844BUF	Mercedes-Benz 412D	UVG	B16FL	1998	West Sussex CC, 1999	
T781LNT	LDV Convoy	LDV	M16	1999	West Sussex CC, 1999	
W126YOR	LDV Convoy	LDV	M16	2000	private owner, 2001	
W552PPC	Renault Master	Euromotive	M11L	2000	West Sussex CC, 2000	
X203APY	Irisbus 50C11	Mellor Dailybus	M16L	2000	TLS, 2004	
LX51OPC	Volkswagen LT35D	Stanford	M12L	2001		
LX51OPD	Volkswagen LT35D	Stanford	M12L	2001		
CE02MDJ	Mercedes-Benz 413cdi	UVG	B16FL	2002		
KN52KOH	Volkswagen LT35D	Stanford	M12L	2002		
GK52KLA	Renault Master	Rohill Harrier	B15F	2002		
GK52KLC	Renault Master	Rohill Harrier	B15F	2002		
GK52OKU	Citroën Relay	Rohill	B16F	2002		
	Mercedes-Benz 311 CDi	Frank Guy	M16	2003		
YR52OGY	YR52OHA	YR52OHC	YR52OHE		YR52OHF	
YR52OGZ	YR52OHB	YR52OHD				
	Mercedes-Benz 411 CDi	Frank Guy	BC16FL	2003		
YN03LUE	YN03LUH	YN03LUL	YN03LUR		YN03LUT	
YN03LUF	YN03LUJ	YN03LUP				
HX04JLV	Mercedes-Benz 411 CDi	Stanford	M15FL	2004		
HX04VRT	Mercedes-Benz 411 CDi	Stanford	M15FL	2004		
HX04VRU	Mercedes-Benz 411 CDi	Stanford	M15FL	2004		
HX04VRW	Mercedes-Benz 411 CDi	Stanford	M15FL	2004		
HX04VRY	Mercedes-Benz 411 CDi	Stanford	M15FL	2004		
WX04GXB	Mercedes-Benz 413 CDi	UV Modular	BC16FL	2004		

Previous Registrations:
GIL5976   A136GJT

On order: Three Alexander Dennis Darts with East Lancs high capacity bodies and another Scania OmniDekka.
Depots: Worthing Road, Broadbridge Heath; Drayton Lane, Drayton, Chichester; London Road, Hassocks; University of Southampton, European Way, Southampton and Long Furlong, Clapham Village, Worthing.

The South East Bus Handbook

ALTONIAN

Warrens Transport Ltd, 1 Westbrook Walk, Alton, GU34 1HZ

YIB9078	Dennis Javelin 12m	Plaxton Paramount 3200 III	C53F	1988	East Surrey, 1996
997GAT	Van Hool T815H	Van Hool Van Hool Alizée	C53FT	1988	Midland Fox, 1991
F548WGL	Dennis Javelin 12m	Duple 320	C51FT	1989	Darley Ford Coaches, 1994
YIB9079	Volvo B10M-61	Plaxton Paramount 3200 III	C57F	1989	Turner, Bristol, 1996
G960ATP	Dennis Javelin 8.5m	Plaxton Paramount 3200 III	C35F	1989	B Kavanagh, Urlingford, 1997
H929DRJ	Scania K93CRB	Plaxton Paramount 3200 III	C55F	1991	Holmeswood Coaches, 2003
H758DTM	Leyland Swift ST2R44C97T5	Reeve Burgess Harrier	C37F	1990	Ralph's, Langley, 1994
J528WTW	Mercedes-Benz 709D	Wadham Stringer Wessex	B24F	1992	Javelin, Battersea, 1997
M579RCP	DAF SB3000	Van Hool Alizée HE	C55F	1994	Holmeswood Coaches, 2003
P545RBX	Renault Master	Cymric	M15	1997	Bostocks, Congleton, 2001
R180BDT	Scania K124IB	Irizar Century 12.35	C49FT	1998	
S131SET	Dennis Javelin GX	Neoplan Transliner	C49FT	1998	
T571JND	Ford Transit	Ford	M7	1999	private owner, 2003
W382KBE	Mercedes-Benz Vario O814	Autobus Nouvelle 2	C29F	2000	
X293AKW	Dennis Javelin GX 12m	Neoplan Transliner	C53F	2000	
X294AKW	Dennis Javelin GX 12m	Neoplan Transliner	C53F	2000	
Y63RBK	Dennis Javelin 12m	Caetano Cutlass	C70F	2001	

Previous registrations:

997GAT	E445MMM	XIL9631	H523SWE
G960ATP	89D31617(EI)	YIB9078	E132PLJ
H929DRJ	H929DRJ, YTY867	YIB9079	F326SHU, 2170MV, F326SHU

Depots: Mill Lane, Alton and Willis Lane, Four Marks.

Purchased principally for school duties, Altonian's Y63RBK is a Dennis Javelin with Caetano Cutlass bodywork. Caetano took over the Waterlooville factory from UVG in 1998 and has been building the Cutlass and Nimbus models in small numbers since. These models were designed in the company's main drawing office in Portugal. *Dave Heath*

AMBERLEE

Amberlee UK Ltd, 56 Holly Road, Wainscott, Rochester, ME2 4LH

	JJD535D	AEC Routemaster R2RH1	Park Royal	B40/32R	1966	Go-Ahead London, 2005
	GOG138W	MCW Metrobus DR102/18	MCW	B43/30F	1980	ASD, Strood, 2005
	GYE586W	MCW Metrobus DR102/14	MCW	B43/31F	1981	Arriva Southern Counties, 2005
	ORJ72W	MCW Metrobus DR102/21	MCW	B43/30F	1981	ASD, Strood, 2005
	B120WUL	MCW Metrobus DR101/17	MCW	B43/28D	1984	Trustline, Potters Bar, 2002
	B213WUL	MCW Metrobus DR101/17	MCW	B47/28F	1985	Trustline, Potters Bar, 2002
	B743GCN	London Olympian ONCL10/1RV	Eastern Coach Works	B45/32F	1985	Go-Ahead Northern, 2004
	B747GCN	London Olympian ONCL10/1RV	Eastern Coach Works	B45/32F	1985	Go-Ahead Northern, 2004
	C650LJR	London Olympian ONCL10/1RV	Eastern Coach Works	B45/32F	1985	Go-Ahead Northern, 2004
	C665LJR	London Olympian ONCL10/1RV	Eastern Coach Works	B45/32F	1985	Go-Ahead Northern, 2004
w	C391BUV	MCW Metrobus DR101/17	MCW	B47/28D	1985	Trustline, Potters Bar, 2002
	C286LOX	Leyland Tiger TRCTL11/3RH	Plaxton Paramount 3500 II	C49FT	1986	Millership, Tipton, 2003
w	MIL4690	Leyland Tiger TRBTL11/2RP	Plaxton Derwent 2	BC54F	1988	Camden, West Kingsdown, 2001

Based in Rochester, Amberlee has several contracts in the Medway area, including some for the Medway campus of the University of Greenwich. In 2003, the entire batch of low floor Dennis Lance buses, initially purchased by Stagecoach for its Ribble subsidiary contracts in Salford, was acquired. These carry Berkhof 2000 bodywork and one of these, N1777CK, is shown here, though currently out of service. *Dave Heath*

Amberlee operates several Metrobuses on local service. Pictured in Chatham is B120WUL, one of many that were new to London Buses, and an example that has retained its centre exit doors. *Dave Heath*

w	E61MDT	Leyland Lynx LX112TL11ZR1	Leyland Lynx	B45F	1988	Lancashire United, 2003
w	F239CNY	Leyland Lynx LX112L10ZR1R	Leyland Lynx	BC47F	1989	Camden, West Kingsdown, 2001
	F77DDA	Leyland Lynx LX2R11C15Z4R	Leyland Lynx 2	B49F	1989	Blue Triangle, Rainham, 2003
w	K848EEC	Scania K113TRA	Berkhof Excellence 2000 HD	C57/19DT	1993	Galleon, Hunsdon, 2004
	K589SUP	Volvo B10M-60	Plaxton Paramount 3500 III	C49FT	1993	Go-Ahead Northern, 2003
	P712RWU	DAF SB3000	Ikarus Blue Danube 350	C53F	1996	North Kent Express, 2003
	P713RWU	DAF SB3000	Ikarus Blue Danube 350	C53F	1996	North Kent Express, 2003
	P714RWU	DAF SB3000	Ikarus Blue Danube 350	C53F	1996	North Kent Express, 2003
	P715RWU	DAF SB3000	Ikarus Blue Danube 350	C53F	1996	North Kent Express, 2003
	N176LCK	Dennis Lance SLF 11m	Berkhof 2000	N35F	1996	Lancashire United, 2003
w	N177LCK	Dennis Lance SLF 11m	Berkhof 2000	N35F	1996	Lancashire United, 2003
	N178LCK	Dennis Lance SLF 11m	Berkhof 2000	N35F	1996	Lancashire United, 2003
	N179LCK	Dennis Lance SLF 11m	Berkhof 2000	N35F	1996	Lancashire United, 2003
w	N180LCK	Dennis Lance SLF 11m	Berkhof 2000	N35F	1996	Lancashire United, 2003
	W367EOL	Mercedes-Benz O404	Hispano Vita	C49FT	2000	Centra, Hounslow, 2005
	W368EOL	Mercedes-Benz O404	Hispano Vita	C49FT	2000	Centra, Hounslow, 2005
	X482AHE	Scania L94IB4	Irizar Century 12.35	C49FT	2000	Bus Eireann, 2003
	X491AHE	Scania L94IB4	Irizar Century 12.35	C49FT	2000	Bus Eireann, 2003
	X493AHE	Scania L94IB4	Irizar Century 12.35	C49FT	2000	Bus Eireann, 2003
	Y338FNH	Scania L94IB4	Irizar Century 12.35	C49FT	2001	Bus Eireann, 2003

Previous registrations:

C286LOX	C922HYA, 90RYD, C443WUT, MIL2273	X491AHE	00D83688
K589SUP	K2VOY	X493AHE	00D83679
X482AHE	00D83722	Y338FNH	01D72090

Depot: Lower Road, Northfleet

AUTOCAR

Autocar Bus & Coach Services Ltd, The Bus Garage, 64 Whetsted Road, Five Oak Green, Tonbridge, TN12 6RT

WIB1118	Leyland Tiger TRCLXC/2RH	Plaxton Paramount 3200 E	C53F	1984	Highland Scottish, 1998
B108KPF	Leyland Tiger TRCTL11/3RH	East Lancs (1991)	B61F	1984	Arriva Midlands, 2002
E31UNE	Leyland Tiger TRBTL11/3ARZA	Alexander N	BC69F	1988	Arriva Midlands, 2003
E32UNE	Leyland Tiger TRBTL11/3ARZA	Alexander N	BC69F	1988	Arriva Midlands, 2004
IAZ8156	Volvo B10M-60	Plaxton Paramount 3200 III	C53F	1989	Accord, Southampton, 2005
G456MGG	Dennis Dart 9m	Duple Dartline	B35F	1990	Quantock, Norton Fitzwarren, '03
944BKT	Dennis Dart 9m	WS Coachbuilders	BC39F	1995	LB Redbridge, 2005
V7PCL	DAF SB3000	Plaxton Première 320	C55F	1999	Pullman, Crofty, 2004
OSJ1X	Scania N113DRB	East Lancs Cityzen	BC47/31F	2000	

Previous registrations:

944BKT	L298URV	WIB1118	A182UGB
IAZ8156	NXI9003, F256BHF		

Pictured at Tonbridge Castle, G456MGG, with body number D8900/0001 has the distinction of being the very first production Dartline bus built by Blackpool coachbuilder Duple. While initially it operated for the Scottish operator, Hutchinsons, the bus now sees service with the small fleet of Autocar in whose livery it is shown here. *Martin Smith*

The South East Bus Handbook   **11**

AUTOPOINT

BP Rodemark, Causeway Yard, Bodle Street, Hailsham, BN27 4UA

Fleet No.	Chassis	Body	Seating	Year	Previous Owner
8903AP	Volvo B10M-61	Van Hool Alizée H	C49F	1983	Smiths Shearings, Wigan, 1989
5501AP	Bedford YNT	Plaxton Paramount 3200	C57F	1984	New Enterprise, Tonbridge, 1998
7693AP	Leyland Royal Tiger B50	Plaxton Paramount 3500	C53F	1986	Armchair, Brentford, 1994
1509AP	Mercedes-Benz 609D	North West	BC24F	1989	
3442AP	Mercedes-Benz 709D	Reeve Burgess Beaver	B25F	1989	Armchair, Brentford, 1997
2317AP	Volvo B10M-60	Plaxton Paramount 3200 III	C53F	1990	Capital, West Drayton, 1999
1108AP	Mercedes-Benz 811D	Wright NimBus	B26F	1990	Stagecoach Transit, 2000
2779AP	Mercedes-Benz 811D	PMT Ami	BC33F	1991	Creighton, Annan, 2001
9925AP	Dennis Dart 8.5m	Plaxton Pointer	B40F	1992	Metroline, 2002
7634AP	Mercedes-Benz 811D	UVG Citi Star	BC33F	1996	
5752AP	Mercedes-Benz 811D	UVG Citi Star	BC33F	1996	
5536AP	Marshall Minibus	Marshall MM	B29F	1996	Glyn Williams, Pontllanfraith, 2002
9415AP	Marshall Minibus	Marshall MM	B29F	1996	Glyn Williams, Pontllanfraith, 2002
3069AP	Optare Solo M850	Optare	N29F	2004	

Previous registrations:

1108AP	HDZ2609	4058AP	-	7693AP	C758FMC
1509AP	F255KDM	5501AP	A222DRM	8903AP	ENF578Y, SPR124, GNF470Y
2779AP	J701USF			9163AP	-
2317AP	G81BLD	5536AP	P409KAV	9415AP	R116VLX
3069AP	GX04AWR	5752AP	From new	9925AP	J823GGF, 33LUG, J823GGF
3442AP	G94VMM	7634AP	From new		

Depots: Windmill Hill Garage, Herstmonceux and Causeway Yard, Bodle Street.

Autopoint operates several services in East Surrey with a fleet that carries suitable AP index marks. Illustrating the fleet is 5252AP, one of the last UVG-bodied Mercedes-Benz minibuses built. During 1998 the UVG facility closed though the factory was subsequently purchased and reopened by Caetano. *Phillip Stephenson*

AVIS

Avis Rent-a-Car Ltd, Northrop Road, Heathrow Airport, TW8 2QA

1	W248OLA	Mercedes-Benz Sprint 310	Autobus	M10	2000
2	P202CAY	Toyota Coaster BB50R	Caetano Optimo IV	C14F	1997
3	R703XAL	Toyota Coaster BB50R	Caetano Optimo IV	C16F	1998
4	R704XAL	Toyota Coaster BB50R	Caetano Optimo IV	C16F	1998
5	W249OLA	Mercedes-Benz Sprint 310	Autobus	M10	2000
6	R706XAL	Toyota Coaster BB50R	Caetano Optimo IV	C14F	1998
7	W262OLA	Mercedes-Benz Sprint 310	Autobus	M10	2000
8	W263OLA	Mercedes-Benz Sprint 310	Autobus	M10	2000
9	P209CAY	Toyota Coaster BB50R	Caetano Optimo IV	C14F	1997
10	R710XAL	Toyota Coaster BB50R	Caetano Optimo IV	C14F	1998
11	P211CAY	Toyota Coaster BB50R	Caetano Optimo IV	C14F	1997
12	P212CAY	Toyota Coaster BB50R	Caetano Optimo IV	C14F	1997
14	P214CAY	Toyota Coaster BB50R	Caetano Optimo IV	C14F	1997
15	W261OLA	Mercedes-Benz Sprint 310	Autobus	M8	2000
16	W265OLA	Mercedes-Benz Sprint 310	Autobus	M10	2000
17	W264OLA	Mercedes-Benz Sprint 310	Autobus	M10	2000

Avis is one of the car hire companies at London Heathrow that requires as fleet of mini coaches to transfer customers from the passenger terminals to the car-hire sites. The Toyota Coaster with Caetano Optimo bodywork has been popular for this type of transport for many years. Now in its fifth version, it is available in two widths, 2 metres and 2.3 metres with the narrow model carrying up to 21 passengers. R704XAL is a Optimo IV that also provides additional luggage space.
Dave Heath

BAILEY'S

Baileys Buses (Portsmouth) Ltd, 38 Green Lane, Copnor, Portsmouth, PO3 5EZ

HPK504N	Leyland National 11351/1R		B49F	1975	White Rose, Staines, 2001
N986FWT	DAF SB220	Northern Counties Paladin	B32D	1996	Luton Airport, 2001
R977FNW	DAF SB220	Plaxton Prestige	B30D	1997	Flyerbus, Dublin, 2000
R979FNW	DAF SB220	Plaxton Prestige	B30D	1997	Flyerbus, Dublin, 2000

Previous registrations:

HPK504N	HPK504N, VLT23	R977FNW	R977FNW, 97D62301
R977FNW	R977FNW, 97D62302		

Depot: Walton Road North, Farlington, Portsmouth

The sole National in the small fleet of Bailey's carries the livery for the service it operates. This connects Portsmouth centre with the Ferry port. *Phillip Stephenson*

14   *The South East Bus Handbook*

BANSTEAD COACHES

Banstead Coaches Ltd, 1 Shrubland Road, Banstead, SM7 2ES

D72HRU	Bedford Venturer YNV	Plaxton Paramount 3200 III	C53F	1987	
L164PDT	Dennis Javelin 12m	Plaxton Première 320	C53F	1994	
M8BSL	Dennis Javelin 12m	Plaxton Première 320	C53F	1995	Alfa, Chieveley, 2000
M427WAK	Dennis Javelin 12m	Plaxton Première 320	C53F	1995	
MUI5922	Dennis Javelin 12m	Plaxton Première 320	C53F	1995	
N581GBW	Dennis Javelin 12m	Caetano Algarve 2	C53F	1996	
N30BAN	Dennis Javelin GX 12m	Berkhof Excellence 1000 LD	C53F	1996	
P4BAN	Dennis Javelin GX 12m	Berkhof Excellence 1000 LD	C53F	1997	
R2BAN	Dennis Javelin 12m	Plaxton Première 320	C53F	1998	
T50BAN	Dennis Javelin 12m	Plaxton Première 320	C53F	1999	
W7BAN	Dennis Javelin GX 12m	Berkhof Axial 50	C53F	2000	
Y6BAN	Dennis R	Berkhof Axial 50	C53F	2001	
MY02BAN	Dennis R	Plaxton Panther	C53F	2002	
MY52BAN	Dennis R	Plaxton Panther	C53F	2002	
GO04BAN	Mercedes-Benz Touro 1836RL	Mercedes-Benz	C53F	2004	
CH05BAN	Mercedes-Benz Touro 1836RL	Mercedes-Benz	C53F	2005	

Web: www.bansteadcoaches.co.uk

While the majority of the fleet comprises Dennis products, Banstead Coaches operates two Mercedes-Benz Touro coaches including CH05BAN which won the Mercedes-Benz Trophy at the British Coach Rally in Brighton during 2005. Illustrated here is Banstead's other Touro, GO04BAN. *Dave Heath*

The South East Bus Handbook

BLACK & WHITE

Black & White Motorways Ltd, 68 Kensington Road, Copnor, Portsmouth, PO2 0RJ

XYE101G	AEC Reliance 6MU4R	Plaxton Panorama Elite	C41F	1969	Hudson, Rowlands Castle, 2000
MBU534L	AEC Reliance 6U3ZR	Plaxton Elite III	C55F	1973	preservation, 2003
HTR557P	Leyland Atlantean AN68/1R	East Lancs	B45/31F	1975	Intech, Winchester, 2001
MUK739R	Bristol VRT/SL3/6LXB	Eastern Coach Works	B43/28F	1976	Duchy, Newton Abbot, 2003
RAN646R	Bristol VRT/SL3/6LXB	Eastern Coach Works	B43/28F	1977	Duchy, Newton Abbot, 2003
OSR197R	Bristol VRT/SL3/6LXB	Eastern Coach Works	B43/31F	1978	Hannell, Speke, 2004
BVR59T	Leyland Fleetline FE30AGR	Northern Counties	B43/32F	1979	Thamesdown, Swindon, 2002
TWH698T	Leyland Fleetline FE30AGR	Northern Counties	B43/32F	1979	Thamesdown, Swindon, 2003
WYW59T	MCW Metrobus DR101/9	MCW	B43/28D	1979	preservation, 2002
YRV256V	Leyland Atlantean AN68A/1R	East Lancs	B45/31F	1979	?, 2005
DBK264W	Leyland Atlantean AN68A/1R	East Lancs	B45/31F	1979	First, 2005
DK264W	Leyland Atlantean AN68A/1R	East Lancs	B45/31F	1981	First, 2004
447ECR	Leyland Tiger TRCTL11/2R	Plaxton Supreme V	C53F	1982	Thamesdown, Swindon, 2001
PMK106X	Volvo B10M-61	Plaxton Viewmaster IV	C53F	1982	Alexander, Eythorne, 2001
A385XGG	Neoplan Skyliner N122/3	Neoplan	C57/20CT	1984	Coaching International, 2003
LUA272V	Leyland Leopard PSU3F/4R	Plaxton Supreme IV	C57F	1984	Bryant, Wood Green, 2002
DCZ2316	Leyland Tiger TRCTL11/3R	Plaxton Paramount 3200	C57F	1985	Thamesdown, Swindon, 2001

Heritage fleet (original owners shows):

JHT122	Bristol K6A	Eastern Coach Works	B--/--R	1946	Bristol OC
HDD654	Bristol L6G	Duple	C35F	1948	Black & White Motorways
KLB596	AEC Regent III 0961	Weymann	B30/26R	1950	London Transport
NFM46	Bristol LL6B	Eastern Coach Works	B39R	1952	Crosville MS
NDG172	Guy Arab LUF	Duple	C37C	1954	Black & White Motorways
UHY374	Bristol KSW6B	Eastern Coach Works	B32/28R	1955	Cheltenham & District
SAD189	Guy Arab LUF	Willowbrook	C37C	1956	Black & White Motorways
MSV412	Albion Victor FT39AN	Heaver	B35F	1956	Guernsey Motors
NJV995	AEC Bridgemaster B3RA	Park Royal	O41/27R	1960	Grimby-Cleethorpes CT
6775DD	Leyland Leopard PSU3/1R	Plaxton Panorama	C47F	1962	Black & White Motorways
RDG304G	Daimler Roadliner SPR8	Plaxton Panorama	C47F	1969	Black & White Motorways

Previous registrations:
A385XGG   A133UFE, 4009SC, A385XGG, XHY378   MSV412   1463(GBG)

East Lancs bodywork has been a favourite of many municipal operators, especially those in north-west England, and the south coast. HTR557P was previously with Intech of Winchester, who acquired it from First's Southampton operation. Shwn is the black and white livery now carried by this former City of Portsmouth Atlantean.

BRIJAN

Brijan Tours Ltd, The Coach Station, 1 Abbey Mill, Bishops Waltham, Southampton, SO32 1DH

29	R9BJT	Dennis Javelin	Plaxton Première 320	C55F	1997	
35	S35KRV	Mercedes-Benz Vario O814	Plaxton Beaver 2	BC27F	1998	
36	P424PBP	Dennis Javelin	UVG 320	C57F	1997	Lewis's, Llanrhystyd, 1998
39	S9BJT	Dennis Javelin	Plaxton Première 320	C53F	1999	
53	UVY412	MCW Metrobus DR132/15	MCW	BC43/27F	1989	Stagecoach South, 2000
54	TIL4754	MCW Metrobus DR132/15	MCW	BC43/27F	1989	Stagecoach South, 2000
56	R83EDW	Mercedes-Benz Vario O814	Autobus Classique Nouvelle	BC33F	1998	Bebb, Llantwit Fardre, 2000
57	TIL4557	Leyland Titan TNLXB2RR	Leyland	B44/26D	1984	Vale of Ffestiniog, 2000
64	HT02BJT	Scania K114IB4	Irizar InterCentury 12.32	C53F	2002	
65	N5BJT	Mercedes-Benz 811D	Autobus Classique	BC29F	1996	Country Lion, Northampton, 2002
66	V66BJT	Mercedes-Benz Vario O814	Plaxton Beaver 2	B31F	2000	McQueen, Garelochhead, 2002
67	XJJ668V	Bristol VRT/SL3/6LXB	Eastern Coach Works	B43/31F	1980	Chennel, South Harting, 2002
68	P73VWO	Mercedes-Benz 814D	Autobus Classique	BC33F	1997	Bodman & Heath, Worton, 2002
70	G258TSL	Mercedes-Benz 709D	Alexander Sprint	B25F	1990	Dickson, Erskine, 2003
71	N129MBW	Scania K113CRB	Van Hool Alizée HE	C53F	1996	Pearce's, Berinsfield, 2004
73	Y252OHC	Volvo B7	Plaxton Prima	C57F	2001	Hallmark, Luton, 2005
74	Y253OHC	Volvo B7	Plaxton Prima	C57F	2001	Hallmark, Luton, 2005
75	R10APT	Volvo B9M	Van Hool T9 Alizée	C38F	1997	APT, Rayleigh, 2004
76	N356ETM	Mercedes-Benz 709D	Alexander Sprint	B27F	1995	Arriva The Shires, 2005
77	N917ETM	Mercedes-Benz 709D	Plaxton Beaver	B29F	1995	Monk, Heaton Chapel, 2005
78	BT05BJT	Mercedes-Benz Vario O814	Plaxton Cheetah	C33F	2005	
79	BEP968V	Bristol VRT/SL3/6LXB	Eastern Coach Works	B43/31F	1980	First, 2005

Previous registrations:

N5BJT	L10NCC, N428DVV		UVY412	F764EKM
TIL4557	A942SYE		Y252OHC	Y4APH
TIL4754	F765EKM		Y252OHC	Y4APH

Special livery: blue and yellow (Solent Blue Line) 35, 45/7, 53/6/7, 68/9.

Eight of Brijan's vehicles operate on Solent Blue Line services. Illustrating their livery scheme is Mercedes-Benz Vario 35, S36KRV, which has a Plaxton Beaver 2 body. It is seen in Bishops Waltham in July 2005. *Gerry Mead*

BRITISH AIRWAYS

British Airways plc, Building 470, North Perimeter Road West, Heathrow Airport, TW6 2JA

BU0401-0423		DAF SB220		Optare Delta		B40D*	1990		seating varies
BU0401 G191BLM	**BU0406** G196BLM		**BU0410** H312HLB		**BU0414** H317HLB			**BU0420** J855MLC	
BU0402 G192BLM	**BU0407** G197BLM		**BU0411** H313HLB		**BU0415** H319HLB			**BU0421** J856MLC	
BU0403 G193BLM	**BU0408** G198BLM		**BU0412** H314HLB		**BU0416** J851MLC			**BU0422** J857MLC	
BU0404 G194BLM	**BU0409** G199BLM		**BU0413** H315HLB		**BU0417** J852MLC			**BU0423** J858MLC	
BU0405 G195BLM									

BU0424-0445		DAF SB220		Optare Delta		B40T	1993	
BU0424 K809PLX	**BU0429** K814PLX		**BU0434** K819PLX		**BU0438** K823PLX			**BU0442** K316SLF
BU0425 K810PLX	**BU0430** K815PLX		**BU0435** K820PLX		**BU0439** K824PLX			**BU0443** K317SLF
BU0426 K811PLX	**BU0431** K816PLX		**BU0436** K821PLX		**BU0440** K825PLX			**BU0444** K318SLF
BU0427 K812PLX	**BU0432** K817PLX		**BU0437** K822PLX		**BU0441** K826PLX			**BU0445** K319SLF
BU0428 K813PLX	**BU0433** K818PLX							

BU0446 T172AUA	DAF SB220	Ikarus Citibus	B D	1999
BU0447 T173AUA	DAF SB220	Ikarus Citibus	B D	1999

BU0448-460		Optare Excel L1180		Optare		N27D	2001	
BU0448 Y675UUM	**BU0451** Y678UUM		**BU0454** Y537XNW		**BU0457** YJ51JXC			**BU0459** YJ51JXE
BU0449 Y676UUM	**BU0452** Y679UUM		**BU0455** YJ51JXA		**BU0458** YJ51JXD			**BU0460** YJ51JXF
BU0450 Y677UUM	**BU0453** Y536XNW		**BU0456** YJ51JXB					

British Airways operates a fleet of buses that service their aircraft activities at London Heathrow airport. These include staff transport as well as passenger services, both air-side and land-side. For air-side use, the main unit is the NAW Cobus represented by BU6034, L388ULX, shown here.

One of the models imported principally for crew transport is the integral Van Hool A308 midibus. Pictured here is CC0485, N183FLR, which carries the Benyhone World Art Livery for Scotland. While the tails of the aircraft have been repainted into *Trinity Flag* the ground vehicles continue to use the various representation of countries. *Gerry Mead*

BU6029	L392ULX	NAW Cobus	Contrac Cobus	B15T	1994
BU6030	L391ULX	NAW Cobus	Contrac Cobus	B15T	1994
BU6031	L389ULX	NAW Cobus	Contrac Cobus	B15T	1994
BU6032	L390ULX	NAW Cobus	Contrac Cobus	B15T	1994
BU6034	L388ULX	NAW Cobus	Contrac Cobus	B15T	1994
BU6035	N613FLR	NAW Cobus	Contrac Cobus	B15T	1995
BU6036	N614FLR	NAW Cobus	Contrac Cobus	B15T	1995
BU6037	N615FLR	NAW Cobus	Contrac Cobus	B15T	1995
BU6038	N616FLR	NAW Cobus	Contrac Cobus	B15T	1995
BU6039	P620MLE	NAW Cobus	Contrac Cobus	B15T	1997
BU6040	P619MLE	NAW Cobus	Contrac Cobus	B15T	1997
BU6041	P618MLE	NAW Cobus	Contrac Cobus	B15T	1997
BU6045	V365ECD	NAW Cobus	Contrac Cobus	B15T	1999
BU6046		NAW Cobus	Contrac Cobus	B15T	1997
BU6047	V803DDY	NAW Cobus	Contrac Cobus	B15T	1997
BU6048	V804DDY	NAW Cobus	Contrac Cobus	B15T	1997
BU6049	V805DDY	NAW Cobus	Contrac Cobus	B15T	1997
BU6050	V806DDY	NAW Cobus	Contrac Cobus	B15T	1997
BU9001	-	Toyota Coaster BB50L	Caetano Optimo	C12F	1999
BU9002	-	Toyota Coaster BB50L	Caetano Optimo	C12F	1999
BU9003	-	Toyota Coaster BB50L	Caetano Optimo	C12F	1999
CC436	FLY747T	Van Hool A308	Van Hool	N25F	1991
CC437	J248LLK	Van Hool A308	Van Hool	N25F	1991
CC438	J275LLK	Van Hool A308	Van Hool	N25F	1991
CC439	J311LLK	Van Hool A308	Van Hool	N25F	1991

CC440-459   Mercedes-Benz 711D   Wright NimBus   B13F   1995

CC440	M139MPL	CC444	M145MPL	CC448	M154MPL	CC452	M157MPL	CC456	M158MPL
CC441	M144MPL	CC445	M143MPL	CC449	M151MPL	CC453	M150MPL	CC457	M152MPL
CC442	M138MPL	CC446	M142MPL	CC450	M156MPL	CC454	M140MPL	CC458	M149MPL
CC443	M146MPL	CC447	M141MPL	CC451	M148MPL	CC455	M153MPL	CC459	M159MPL

The South East Bus Handbook

CC460-487   Van Hool A308   Van Hool   N23F   1995

CC0460 M566BLC	CC0466 M579BLC	CC0472 M595BLC	CC0478 N134FLR	CC0483 N204FLR
CC0461 M565BLC	CC0467 M580BLC	CC0473 M596BLC	CC0479 N137FLR	CC0484 N184FLR
CC0462 M572BLC	CC0468 M592BLC	CC0474 N123FLR	CC0480 N138FLR	CC0485 N183FLR
CC0463 M573BLC	CC0469 M591BLC	CC0475 N121FLR	CC0481 N149FLR	CC0486 N182FLR
CC0464 M574BLC	CC0470 M593BLC	CC0476 N122FLR	CC0482 N198FLR	CC0487 N196FLR
CC0465 M578BLC	CC0471 M594BLC	CC0477 N133FLR		

CC6017-6030   Mercedes-Benz 811D   Wright NimBus   B21F   1996

CC6017 N179UPG	CC6020 N470VPJ	CC6023 N475VPJ	CC6027 N452VPM	CC N388VPB
CC6018 N115VPJ	CC6021 N477VPJ	CC6025 N473VPJ	CC6028 N453VPM	CC6030 P849BPB
CC6019 N469VPJ	CC6022 N478VPJ	CC6026 N114VPJ	CC6029 N472VPJ	

Code	Reg	Chassis	Body	Type	Year	Notes
CC6031	V963ENJ	Mercedes-Benz O405N	Caetano	B31D	2000	
CC6032	W302NUF	Mercedes-Benz O405N	Caetano	B31D	2000	
CC6033	V962ENJ	Mercedes-Benz O405N	Caetano	B31D	2000	
CC6034	V625ENJ	Mercedes-Benz O405N	Caetano	B31D	2000	
CC6035	V626ENJ	Mercedes-Benz O405N	Caetano	B31D	2000	
CC90--	T883JBC	MAN 13.220	Marcopolo Explorer	C37FT	1999	Newby, Backbarrow, 2002
EV6003	N974WJH	Renault Master T35D	Crystals	M12L	1996	
EV6005	N976WJH	Renault Master T35D	Crystals	M12L	1996	
EV6007	N692YJB	Renault Master T35D	Crystals	M12L	1996	
IN1009	N347UJB	Renault Master T35D	Crystals	M10L	1996	
IN1010	N348UJB	Renault Master T35D	Crystals	M10L	1996	
IN1011	N349UJB	Renault Master T35D	Crystals	M10L	1996	
MB857	E65ELT	Renault-Dodge S46	Wadham Stringer	BC15F	1987	
MB952	K320SLF	Ford Transit VE6	Ford	M8	1993	
MB953	K321SLF	Ford Transit VE6	Ford	M8	1993	

MB954-967   Ford Transit VE6   Ford   M11   1993

MB954 L221ULU	MB957 L225ULU	MB960 L228ULU	MB963 L231ULU	MB966 L234ULU
MB955 L223ULU	MB958 L226ULU	MB961 L229ULU	MB964 L232ULU	MB967 L235ULU
MB956 L224ULU		MB962 L230ULU	MB965 L233ULU	

MB969-995   Ford Transit VE6   Ford   M11*   1996   *971/2 M8

MB969 N279HLA	MB972 N272HLA	MB979 N303HLA	MB992 N284HLN	MB994 N278HLN
MB970 N284HLA	MB973 N288HLA	MB980 N278HLA	MB993 N285HLN	MB995 N286HLN
MB991 N283HLN				

Code	Reg	Chassis	Body	Type	Year
MB	N273HLN	Ford Transit VE6	Ford	M11	1996
MB	N274HLN	Ford Transit VE6	Ford	M11	1996
MB	N283HLN	Ford Transit VE6	Ford	M11	1996
MB986	N342HLN	Ford Transit VE6	Ford	M11	1996
MB	N343HLN	Ford Transit VE6	Ford	M11	1996
MB1003	N349HLN	Ford Transit VE6	Ford	M11	1996
MB1004	P433LLU	Ford Transit VE6	Ford	M11	1996
MB1005	P417LLU	Ford Transit VE6	Ford	M11	1996
MB1006	P480LLU	Ford Transit VE6	Ford	M8	1996
MB1010	P631MLD	Ford Transit VE6	Ford	M11	1996
MB1012	W977ULD	Ford Transit VE6	Ford	M11	1996
MB1013	P321MLY	Ford Transit VE6	Ford	M11	1996
MB1015	P143NLR	Ford Transit VE6	Ford	M11	1996
MB1019	P142NLR	Ford Transit VE6	Ford	M11	1996
MB1020	P144NLR	Ford Transit VE6	Ford	M11	1996
MB1021	P138NLR	Ford Transit VE6	Ford	M11	1996
MB1022	P148NLR	Ford Transit VE6	Ford	M8	1996
MB1025	P170NLA	Ford Transit VE6	Ford	M11	1997
MB1026	R440TLB	Ford Transit VE6	Ford	M14	1998
MB1027	R246YLL	Ford Transit VE6	Ford	M11	1997
MB1028	S417RLH	Ford Transit VE6	Ford	M11	1997
MB1029	S129LLN	Ford Transit VE6	Ford	M11	1998
MB1031	S130LLN	Ford Transit VE6	Ford	M8	1998
MB1032	S132LLN	Ford Transit VE6	Ford	M8	1998
MB1033	S133LLN	Ford Transit VE6	Ford	M8	1998
MB1034	S134LLN	Ford Transit VE6	Ford	M8	1996
MB1035	S135LLN	Ford Transit VE6	Ford	M8	1998
MB1036	S136LLN	Ford Transit VE6	Ford	M8	1998
MB1038	T87LJC	Ford Transit VE6	Ford	M14	1998
MB	T92LJC	Ford Transit VE6	Ford	M14	1998
MB	R173YLL	Ford Transit VE6	Ford	M11	1996

Photographed while on inter-terminal transport is CC6034, V625ENJ, a Mercedes-Benz O405N with bodywork finished by Caetano. The rear-end image here is called *Nami Tsuru*.

MB1043	T497KLF	Ford Transit VE6	Ford	M14	1998	
MB1045	T981LLB	Ford Transit VE6	Ford	M11	1998	
MB1047	T972LLB	Ford Transit VE6	Ford	M11	1998	
MB1050	W67RLA	Ford Transit VE6	Ford	M11	1998	
MB1051	W38RLA	Ford Transit VE6	Ford	M11	1998	
MB1055	W876ULH	Ford Transit VE6	Ford	M11	1998	
MB1056	W298ULY	Ford Transit VE6	Ford	M11	1998	
MB1060	X643DLH	Ford Transit VE6	Ford	M11	1998	
MB6070	M995ALR	Ford Transit VE6	Ford	M11	1995	
MB6072	N205HLN	Ford Transit VE6	Ford	M11	1996	
MB6073	N203HLN	Ford Transit VE6	Ford	M11	1996	
MB6074	N246HLN	Ford Transit VE6	Ford	M11	1996	
MB6076	N348HLN	Ford Transit VE6	Ford	M11	1996	
MB6080	P288MLY	Ford Transit VE6	Ford	M11	1998	
MB6084	W989PLA	Ford Transit VE6	Ford	M11	1998	
MB60	W928PLA	Ford Transit VE6	Ford	M11	1998	
MB6088	W954PLA	Ford Transit VE6	Ford	M11	1998	
MB	T504KLF	Ford Transit VE6	Ford	M11	1996	
MB	T962LLB	Ford Transit VE6	Ford	M11	1996	
MB	P490LLU	Ford Transit VE6	Ford	M8	1996	
	L697CNR	Toyota Coaster HZB50R	Caetano Optimo III	C18F	1994	Wheadon Greyhound, Cardiff, 00
	L58YJF	Toyota Coaster HZB50R	Caetano Optimo III	C18F	1994	Wheadon Greyhound, Cardiff, 00
	N209WMS	Toyota Coaster HZB50R	Caetano Optimo III	C18F	1994	Hancock, Sheffield, 2000

Depots: North Perimeter Road West, Heathrow Airport, London and Longridge House, North Terminal, Gatwick Airport

The South East Bus Handbook

BUDDENS COACHES

Buddens Coaches - Phoenix Band Services

Romsey Coaches Ltd, 29 Premier Way, Romsey, SO51 9AQ

SJI8124	Scania K113CRB	Jonckheere Deauville P50	C16FT	1991	
J35UHP	Scania K113TRB	Van Hool Astrobel	C57/17CT	1992	Harry Shaw, Coventry, 1995
K55PBS	Scania K113TRA	Berkhof Excellence 3000HD	C6/10FT	1995	
K66PBS	Scania K113TRB	Irizar Century 12.37	C12FT	1996	
K77PBS	Scania K113TRB	Irizar Century 12.37	C16FT	1996	
S370SET	Scania L94IB	Irizar InterCentury 12.32	C57F	1999	
T728JHE	Scania K124IB4	Irizar Century 12.35	C49FT	1999	
T729JHE	Scania K124IB4	Irizar Century 12.35	C49FT	1999	
T730JHE	Scania K124IB4	Irizar Century 12.35	C49FT	1999	
T731JHE	Scania K124IB4	Irizar Century 12.35	C49FT	1999	
K88PBS	Neoplan Starliner N516/3	Neoplan	C44FT	2000	Parry, Cheslyn Hay, 2003
K99PBS	Neoplan Starliner N516/3	Neoplan	C14FT	2000	Parry, Cheslyn Hay, 2003
K44PBS	Neoplan Starliner N516/3	Neoplan	C14FT	2000	Parry, Cheslyn Hay, 2003
W908MDT	Neoplan Starliner N516/3	Neoplan	C44FT	2000	Parry, Cheslyn Hay, 2003
X3PBS	Scania K124IB6	Irizar Century 12.37	C16FT	2000	
X4PBS	Scania K124IB6	Irizar Century 12.37	C16FT	2000	
X698AGM	Volvo B10M-62	Berkhof Axial 50	C49FT	2000	
X799AGM	Volvo B10M-62	Berkhof Axial 50	C49FT	2000	
X636GJU	Iveco EuroMidi CC80E.18	Indcar Maxim	C29F	2000	

Buddens operates eight Setra coaches which have left-hand drive and are used under the Phoenix Band Services name. Meanwhile, the latest right-hand drive coaches are from Scania with the higher Irizar Century model. While the InterCentury is 3.2 metres high, the Century is available in 3.5 metre (on K114 chassis) and 3.7 metre (on K124 chassis) high bodies. Shown here is Y82HHE. *Dave Heath*

Buddens was an early operator of Scania Irizar coaches and seen passing Waterloo is X424WVO, a L94 with the lower Irizar InterCentury body. The Irizar is built in Spain and was launched into British market in 1993. It is available only on 12-metre Scania chassis. The InterCentury is designed for interurban work and is less common than the Century.
Colin Lloyd

X424WVO	Scania L94IB4	Irizar InterCentury 12.32	C53F	2001
Y5PBS	Setra Imperial S328DT	Setra	C16/0FT	2001
Y82HHE	Scania K124IB4	Irizar Century 12.35	C49FT	2001
Y83HHE	Scania K124IB4	Irizar Century 12.35	C49FT	2001
Y84HHE	Scania K124IB4	Irizar Century 12.35	C49FT	2001
HS51PBS	Setra Imperial S328 DT-HD	Setra	C7/7CT	2002
JS51PBS	Setra Imperial S328 DT-HD	Setra	C9/7CT	2002
KS51PBS	Setra Imperial S328 DT-HD	Setra	C7/7CT	2001
LS51PBS	Setra Imperial S328 DT-HD	Setra	C9/7CT	2001
ES05PBS	Setra S431 DT-HD	Setra	C9/7CT	2004
FS05PBS	Setra S431 DT-HD	Setra	C9/7CT	2004
GS54PBS	Setra S431 DT-HD	Setra	C9/7CT	2004

Previous registrations:

K33PBS	W902MDT	K77PBS	N918DWJ
K44PBS	W907MDT	K88PBS	K544EHE
K55PBS	M15BUD	K99PBS	W904MDT
K66PBS	N917DWJ	SJI8124	H399ERP

Note: Setra coaches in purple are left hand drive.
Livery: Silver, yellow and brown (Phoenix Band Services - all PBS index marks)

The South East Bus Handbook

BUZZLINES

Buzzlines Ltd, G1 Lympne Industrial Estate, Hythe, CT21 4LR

NBZ2248	Toyota Coaster HZB50R	Caetano Optimo III	C18F	1996	Advantage Travel, Gorebridge, 00
S36UBO	Volvo B10M-62	Plaxton Première 350	C44FT	1998	Bebb, Llantwit Fardre, 2001
S45UBO	Volvo B10M-62	Plaxton Première 350	C44FT	1998	Bebb, Llantwit Fardre, 2001
S46UBO	Volvo B10M-62	Plaxton Première 350	C44FT	1998	Bebb, Llantwit Fardre, 2001
S47UBO	Volvo B10M-62	Plaxton Première 350	C44FT	1998	Bebb, Llantwit Fardre, 2001
S48UBO	Volvo B10M-62	Plaxton Première 350	C44FT	1998	Bebb, Llantwit Fardre, 2001
T130AUA	DAF DB250 10.5m	Plaxton President 4.4m	N45/19D	1999	London Sovereign, 2005
T132AUA	DAF DB250 10.5m	Plaxton President 4.4m	N45/19D	1999	London Sovereign, 2005
T133AUA	DAF DB250 10.5m	Plaxton President 4.4m	N45/19D	1999	London Sovereign, 2005
T134AUA	DAF DB250 10.5m	Plaxton President 4.4m	N45/19D	1999	London Sovereign, 2005
T137AUA	DAF DB250 10.5m	Plaxton President 4.4m	N45/19D	1999	London Sovereign, 2005
T138AUA	DAF DB250 10.5m	Plaxton President 4.4m	N45/19D	1999	London Sovereign, 2005
T139AUA	DAF DB250 10.5m	Plaxton President 4.4m	N45/19D	1999	London Sovereign, 2005
V387SVV	Dennis Dart SLF	Plaxton Pointer 2	N37F	1999	Centra, Heathrow, 2005
W252UGX	Setra S315 GT-HD	Setra	C53F	2000	Redwing, Herne Hill, 2004
W253UGX	Setra S315 GT-HD	Setra	C53F	2000	Redwing, Herne Hill, 2004
W258UGX	Setra S315 GT-HD	Setra	C53F	2000	Redwing, Herne Hill, 2004
W259UGX	Setra S315 GT-HD	Setra	C53F	2000	Redwing, Herne Hill, 2004
Y637AVV	Mercedes-Benz Vario O814	Plaxton Cheetah	C18FT	2001	
Y638AVV	Mercedes-Benz Vario O814	Plaxton Cheetah	C18FT	2001	
Y639AVV	Mercedes-Benz Vario O814	Plaxton Cheetah	C18FT	2001	
Y8BUS	Mercedes-Benz Sprinter 413CDi	Excel	M16	2001	Fletcher, Newport Pagnall, 2002
OK51BUZ	Mercedes-Benz Citaro O530	Mercedes-Benz	N38F	2001	
KX5UDG	Dennis Dart SLF	Plaxton Pointer 2	N37F	2001	Centra, Heathrow, 2005
KY51BUZ	Ford Transit	Ford	M16	2001	
BU51BUZ	Scania K114EB4	Irizar Century 12.35	C42FT	2001	
UN02BUZ	Scania K114EB4	Irizar Century 12.35	C49FT	2002	
WO02BUZ	Volkswagen Caravelle	Cotrim	M7	2002	
LO02BUZ	Mercedes-Benz Sprinter 413CDi	Excel	M16	2002	
PO02BUZ	Mercedes-Benz Sprinter 413CDi	Excel	M16	2002	
AP52SET	Mercedes-Benz Touro 1836RL	Mercedes-Benz	C49FT	2002	Streamline, Maidstone, 2005
RP03SET	Mercedes-Benz Touro 1836RL	Mercedes-Benz	C49FT	2002	Streamline, Maidstone, 2005

Buzzlines is one of the first British operators to take the 70-seat S-Kool version of the Irizar model. Two entered service in 2004 with SC04OOL seen in Ashford. *Rob Hawkes*

Additions to the Buzzlines' fleet during 2005 were seven double-deck DAF DB250 buses. These were latterly with London Sovereign and T132AUA is shown here in its new colours. *Dave Heath*

NE03BUZ	Neoplan Starliner N516/2	Neoplan		C48FT	2003
NB03BUZ	Neoplan Starliner N516/2	Neoplan		C48FT	2003
NU03BUZ	Neoplan Starliner N516/2	Neoplan		C48FT	2003
DD53BUZ	Neoplan Skyliner N122/3	Neoplan		C57/17CT	2003
MD53WKB	Mercedes-Benz Sprinter 413CDi	Olympus		M16	2003
MV53CXC	Mercedes-Benz Sprinter 413CDi	-		M16	2003
MX53WDA	Mercedes-Benz Sprinter 413CDi	-		M16	2004
VX53AVF	Mercedes-Benz Sprinter 413CDi	-		M16	2004
DB04BUZ	Toyota Coaster BB50R	Caetano Optimo V		C26F	2004
SB04BUZ	Toyota Coaster BB50R	Caetano Optimo V		C26F	2004
JB04BUZ	Toyota Coaster BB50R	Caetano Optimo V		C26F	2004
KB04BUZ	Neoplan Starliner N516/2	Neoplan		C48FT	2004
AK04KZY	Ford Transit	Ford		M16	2004
AK04LFL	Ford Transit	Ford		M16	2004
AK04LWK	Ford Transit	Ford		M16	2004
GJ04WKU	SEAT Alhambra	SEAT		M6	2004
SC04OOL	Scania K94IB4	Irizar S-Kool		C70F	2004
SK04OOL	Scania K94IB4	Irizar S-Kool		C70F	2004
YN54JTV	Neoplan Skyliner N122/3	Neoplan		C57/19CT	2005
EV05BUZ	Setra S415 HD	Setra		C49FT	2005
GO05BUZ	Setra S415 HD	Setra		C49FT	2005
GX05AVV	Alexander Dennis Dart 8.8m	Alexander Dennis Mini Pointer		N29F	2005
YN05WEU	Scania K124EB6 12.9m	Irizar PB		C48T	2005
YN05WEV	Scania K124EB6 12.9m	Irizar PB		C48FT	2005
PB05BUZ	Scania K124EB6 12.9m	Irizar PB		C48FT	2005
UF05BUZ	Scania K124EB6 12.9m	Irizar PB		C48FT	2005

Previous registrations:
NBZ2248   P773BJF   Y8BUS   Y471EDA

Web: www.buzzlines.co.uk

The South East Bus Handbook

C & S COACHES

CL Hicks & GJ Shaw, Station Road, Heathfield, TN21 8DF

58DAF	Scania K112TRS	Jonckheere Jubilee P99	C55/18CT	1988	Bailey, Sutton in Ashfield, 1995
JIL7705	Leyland Leopard PSU5D/4R	Plaxton Supreme IV	C57F	1981	Simmonds, Letchworth, 1996
JIL6399	Leyland Swift LBM6T/2RS	Reeve Burgess Harrier	C28F	1989	Cook, Sampford Moor, 1996
JIL6396	Scania K113CRB	Jonckheere Deauville P599	C57F	1989	Scancoaches, North Acton, 1996
JIL6397	Scania K113CRB	Jonckheere Deauville P599	C57F	1989	Scancoaches, North Acton, 1996
JIL3969	Volvo B10M-61	Van Hool Alizée H	C49FT	1989	Ron's, Washington, 2000
G79BLD	Volvo B10M-61	Plaxton Paramount 3500 III	C57F	1990	Marshall's, Baillieston, 2000
G887VNA	Scania K113CRB	Plaxton Paramount 3500 III	C53F	1990	Allison's, Dunfermline, 1998
H787RWJ	Scania K113CRB	Plaxton Paramount 3500 III	C53F	1991	Ideal Services, Watford, 1995
H185DVM	Volvo B10M-61	Van Hool Alizée H	C53F	1991	Ron's, Washington, 2000
J223XKY	Scania K113CRB	Plaxton Paramount 3500 III	C51FT	1992	Slattery, Kentish Town, 1997
J224XKY	Scania K113CRB	Plaxton Paramount 3500 III	C51FT	1992	Astons, Kempsey, 1997
NKZ8970	DAF MB230	Van Hool Alizée	C51FT	1993	Wise, Hailsham, 2004
MKZ2030	DAF SB3000	Van Hool Alizée HE	C49FT	1994	Selwyn's, Runcorn, 2005
J823KRH	DAF SB2305	Van Hool Alizée H	C53F	1994	Arriva Bus & Coach, 2005
J246NNC	Volvo B10M-61	Van Hool Alizée H	C57F	1994	Shearings, 1999
J247NNC	Volvo B10M-61	Van Hool Alizée H	C57F	1995	Shearings, 1999
J248NNC	Volvo B10M-61	Van Hool Alizée H	C57F	1995	Shearings, 1999
J252NNC	Volvo B10M-61	Van Hool Alizée H	C57F	1995	Shearings, 1999
J254NNC	Volvo B10M-61	Van Hool Alizée H	C57F	1995	Shearings, 1999
J256NNC	Volvo B10M-61	Van Hool Alizée H	C57F	1995	Shearings, 1999
M572RCP	DAF SB3000	Van Hool Alizée HE	C55F	1995	Arriva Bus & Coach, 2002
M615RCP	DAF SB3000	Van Hool Alizée HE	C51FT	1995	Arriva Bus & Coach, 2002
M619RCP	DAF SB3000	Van Hool Alizée HE	C51FT	1995	Arriva Bus & Coach, 2002
M628RCP	DAF SB3000	Van Hool Alizée HE	C51FT	1995	Arriva Bus & Coach, 2002
M633RCP	DAF SB3000	Van Hool Alizée HE	C55F	1995	Arriva Bus & Coach, 2002
M636RCP	DAF MB230	Van Hool Alizée HE	C51FT	1995	Arriva Bus & Coach, 2002
M650RCP	DAF SB3000	Van Hool Alizée HE	C55F	1995	Voyager Int', Greenock, 2005
M745RCP	DAF SB3000	Van Hool Alizée HE	C55F	1995	Arriva Bus & Coach, 2002
M802RCP	DAF MB230	Van Hool Alizée HE	C53FT	1995	Arriva Bus & Coach, 2002
M803RCP	DAF MB230	Van Hool Alizée HE	C53FT	1995	Arriva Bus & Coach, 2002
M804RCP	DAF MB230	Van Hool Alizée HE	C51FT	1995	Arriva Bus & Coach, 2002
M809RCP	DAF MB230	Van Hool Alizée HE	C51FT	1995	Bennetts, Gloucester, 2005
N81FWU	DAF SB3000	Van Hool Alizée HE	C51FT	1996	Holt, Swinefleet, 2005
N84FWU	DAF SB3000	Van Hool Alizée HE	C51FT	1996	Voyager Int', Greenock, 2005
N86FWU	DAF SB3000	Van Hool Alizée HE	C51FT	1996	Bradshaw, St Anne's, 2005
P208RWR	DAF SB3000	Van Hool Alizée HE	C49FT	1997	Airport Travel, Morriston, 2005
P209RWR	DAF SB3000	Van Hool Alizée HE	C51FT	1997	Airport Travel, Morriston, 2005

Recently, C&S Coaches has been replacing older coaches with Van Hool-bodied DAF models similar to M615RCP, which was acquired from hire fleet of dealer Arriva Bus & Coach.
Dave Heath

Previous registrations:

58DAF	E216GNV, NJI8869, A20NPT, E839JHJ
238JUO	E39JRF, 4327PL, E548NVT
G79BLD	G79BLD, WIW3627
J638JAB	B894CFV, LSB83, B378DBV, WDM193
JIL3969	G869RNC
JIL6396	F948RNV
JIL6397	F949RNV
JIL6399	G828UMU
JIL7705	XGS763X
KIB7891	ONV639Y
LIL6610	D25ORO
MKZ2030	L544EHD, SEL133
NKZ8970	K536RJX, MKZ2030
N84FWU	N84FWU, 6RED
TIB8565	D883ANH, TSU648, D409HPO

Depots: Station Road, Heathfield and East Sussex CC Yard, Heathfield
Web: www.candscoaches.co.uk

CARDINAL

AB Troth-Alexander, 43 Cherry Tree Avenue, Dover, CT16 2NL

XXI8968	Scania K112CRS	Jonckheere Jubilee P599	C51FT	1984	Dailybus, Standish, 2004
C348DND	Volvo B10M-61	Plaxton Paramount 3200 II	C53F	1986	Johnson Bros, Hodthorpe, 2002
809AOU	DAF SB2305	Jonckheere Jubilee	C51FT	1989	Bailey, Biddisham, 2000
K631GVX	Mercedes-Benz 709D	Plaxton Beaver	BC25F	1993	Dawson, Heywood, 2004
L813SAE	Mercedes-Benz 709D	Plaxton Beaver	BC25F	1993	First, 2004
ANA3T	Scania K113CRB	Berkhof Excellence 2000	C51FT	1994	Ayling, Shipley, 2003
P244WWX	Mercedes-Benz 611D	Mellor	BC18FL	1997	MB Leeds, 2004
GK02WCY	Renault Master	Rohill	BC18F	2002	
YF02SKN	Optare Solo M850	Optare	N27F	2002	

Previous registrations:

809AOU	G470JNH, SJI8131, G344ATP, 866VNU	C348DND	C348DND, GIL5109
ANA3T	L337DTG	XXI8968	B69MLT, C892WEA

Cardinal's newest bus is YF02SKN, one of the shorter Solo models, the M850. Ther are over 1500 such buses now in service, including many assembled for export, the Solo's main benefit is a step-free entry and flat floor which make it more like a scaled-down big bus. *Dave Heath*

CAROUSEL

Carousel Buses Ltd; J L Robinson, Westbourne Street, High Wycombe, HP11 2PX

	CUV198C	AEC Routemaster R2RH	Park Royal	B36/28R	1965	London Traveller, Neasden, 2002
M57	WYW57T	MCW Metrobus DR101/9	MCW	B43/28D	1979	preservation, 2003
M258	BYX258V	MCW Metrobus DR101/12	MCW	B43/28D	1980	Nostalgia Bus, Mitcham, 2002
M283	BYX283V	MCW Metrobus DR101/12	MCW	B43/28F	1980	Arriva Southern Counties, 2002
M336	EYE336V	MCW Metrobus DR101/12	MCW	B43/28F	1980	Arriva Southern Counties, 2002
M524	GYE524W	MCW Metrobus DR101/14	MCW	B43/28D	1981	Metroline, 2002
M598	GYE598W	MCW Metrobus DR101/14	MCW	B43/32F	1981	Abbey Cars, High Wycombe, 2002
M703	KYV703X	MCW Metrobus DR101/14	MCW	B43/28D	1981	Aventa, Crawley, 2002
M737	KYV737X	MCW Metrobus DR101/14	MCW	B43/28D	1982	Abbey Cars, High Wycombe, 2002
M758	KYV758X	MCW Metrobus DR101/14	MCW	B43/28D	1982	Abbey Cars, High Wycombe, 2002
M1092	B90WUL	MCW Metrobus DR134/1	MCW	B43/28D	1984	Arriva London, 2004
M1100	B100WUL	MCW Metrobus DR134/1	MCW	B43/28D	1984	Arriva London, 2004
M1101	B101WUL	MCW Metrobus DR134/1	MCW	B43/28D	1984	Arriva London, 2004
M1272	B272WUL	MCW Metrobus DR101/17	MCW	B43/28D	1985	NuVenture, Aylesford, 2003
M1386	C386BUV	MCW Metrobus DR101/17	MCW	B43/28D	1985	Abbey Cars, High Wycombe, 2002
M1345	C345BUV	MCW Metrobus DR101/17	MCW	B43/28D	1985	London United, 2004
M1351	C351BUV	MCW Metrobus DR101/17	MCW	B43/28D	1985	London United, 2004
M1356	C356BUV	MCW Metrobus DR101/17	MCW	B43/28D	1985	London United, 2004
M1393	C393BUV	MCW Metrobus DR101/17	MCW	B43/28F	1985	Metroline, 2004
M1432	C432BUV	MCW Metrobus DR101/17	MCW	B43/28D	1985	Abbey Cars, High Wycombe, 2002
LX75	F75DDA	Leyland Lynx LX2R11C15Z4S	Leyland	B49F	1989	Blue Triangle, Rainham, 2002
LX78	F78DDA	Leyland Lynx LX2R11C15Z4S	Leyland	B49F	1989	Blue Tangle, Rainham, 2002
LX558	F558NJM	Leyland Lynx LX112L10ZR1S	Leyland	B52F	1988	Arriva The Shires, 2002
LX559	F559NJM	Leyland Lynx LX112L10ZR1S	Leyland	B49F	1988	Arriva The Shires, 2002
LX283	G283EOG	Leyland Lynx LX2R11C15Z4R	Leyland	B49F	1990	McHugh, Garston, 2003
L554	H554GKX	Leyland Olympian ON2R50C13Z4	Leyland	B47/31F	1991	Armchair, 2003
L556	H556GKX	Leyland Olympian ON2R50C13Z4	Leyland	B47/31F	1991	Armchair, 2003
L563	H563GKX	Leyland Olympian ON2R50C13Z4	Leyland	B47/31F	1991	Armchair, 2002
L564	H564GKX	Leyland Olympian ON2R50C13Z4	Leyland	B47/31F	1991	Armchair, 2003

Carousel operates route A40, which links High Wycombe with Heathrow. Three Mercedes-Benz Citaro integral buses are used in a livery of silver and red. Seen leaving its northern terminus is MB52, CB52BUS. *Colin Lloyd*

During 2005, Carousel added this VDL Bus SB120 to the fleet which carries one of the CB-BUS index marks owned by the operator. This Wrightbus Cadet, CB54BUS, is seen operating route 74 in High Wycombe. *Dave Heath*

	J310WHJ	Dennis Dart 9m	Plaxton Pointer	B35F	1991	Arriva Southern Counties, 2005
	K323CVX	Dennis Dart 9m	Plaxton Pointer	B35F	1992	Arriva Southern Counties, 2005
	L153WAG	Dennis Dart 9m	Plaxton Pointer	B34F	1993	Arriva London, 2005
	L109HHV	Dennis Dart 9m	Northern Counties Paladin	B34F	1994	Ensign, Rainham, 2005
DAF976	R976FNW	DAF SB220	Plaxton Prestige	B30D	1998	NCP Birmingham, 2005
DAF984	R984FNW	DAF SB220	Plaxton Prestige	B40F	1998	Heathrow Express, 2005
DAF986	R986FNW	DAF SB220	Plaxton Prestige	B40F	1998	Heathrow Express, 2005
DAF988	R988FNW	DAF SB220	Plaxton Prestige	B40F	1998	NCP Birmingham, 2005
DAF991	R991FNW	DAF SB220	Plaxton Prestige	B40F	1998	Heathrow Express, 2005
MB51	CB51BUS	Mercedes-Benz Citaro O530	Mercedes-Benz	N42F	2003	
MB52	CB52BUS	Mercedes-Benz Citaro O530	Mercedes-Benz	N42F	2003	
MB53	CB53BUS	Mercedes-Benz Citaro O530	Mercedes-Benz	N42F	2003	
	CB54BUS	VDL Bus SB120	Wrightbus Cadet 2	N30F	2005	

Previous registrations:

C432BUV	C432BUV, WLT432	R981FNW	R981FNW, 97D62303

Special livery: green (service 336) R984/6FNW.

Depot: Abbey Business Centre, Desborough Road, HIgh Wycombe.

CENTRA

Centra London - Centra Coaches

Central Parking System of UK Ltd, Unit 18 Heathrow International Trading Estate, Green Lane, Hounslow, TW4 6HB

Single-deck Buses

DC4-33			Dennis Dart SLF 10.5m		Caetano Nimbus		N31D	2002		Mitcham Belle, 2004
4	MC	KM51BFO	12	MC	KM02BEO	20	MC	HV52WSJ	27	MC	HV52WSX
5	MC	KM51BFU	13	MC	KU02YBA	21	MC	HV52WSK	28	MC	HV52WSY
6	MC	KM51BFX	14	MC	KU02YBB	22	MC	HV52WSL	29	MC	HV52WSZ
7	MC	KM51BFL	15	MC	KU02YBC	23	MC	HV52WSN	30	MC	HV52WTA
8	MC	KM51BFP	16	MC	KU02YBD	24	MC	HV52WSO	31	MC	HV52WTG
9	MC	KM51BFN	17	MC	KU02YBE	25	MC	HV52WSU	32	MC	HV52WTJ
10	MC	KM51BFV	18	MC	KU02YBF	26	MC	HV52WSW	33	MC	HV52WTK
11	MC	KM51BFY	19	MC	KU02YBG						

DC34	MC	KX53SHJ	TransBus Dart SLF 10.5m		Caetano Compass		N31D	2004	Mitcham Belle, 2004
DPS1	MC	V540JBH	Dennis Dart SLF		Plaxton Pointer 2		N31F	1999	Frank Thorpe, 2004
DPS4	MC	V544JBH	Dennis Dart SLF		Plaxton Pointer 2		N31F	1999	Frank Thorpe, 2004
DPS6	MC	V546JBH	Dennis Dart SLF		Plaxton Pointer 2		N31F	1999	Frank Thorpe, 2004
DPS7	MC	V547JBH	Dennis Dart SLF		Plaxton Pointer 2		N31F	1999	Frank Thorpe, 2004
DPS9	MC	V549JBH	Dennis Dart SLF		Plaxton Pointer 2		N31F	1999	Frank Thorpe, 2004

DPS12-49			Dennis Dart SLF 10.1m		Plaxton Pointer 2		N31D	2000		Mitcham Belle, 2004
12	MC	W112WGT	22	MC	W122WGT	33	MC	W133WGT	42	MC	W142WGT
14	MC	W114WGT	24	MC	W124WGT	34	MC	W134WGT	43	MC	W143WGT
16	MC	W116WGT	26	MC	W126WGT	36	MC	W136WGT	44	MC	W144WGT
17	MC	W117WGT	27	MC	W127WGT	37	MC	W137WGT	46	MC	W146WGT
18	MC	W118WGT	28	MC	W128WGT	38	MC	W138WGT	47	MC	W147WGT
19	MC	W119WGT	32	MC	W132WGT	41	MC	W141WGT	49	MC	W149WGT

During the second half of 2005 Centra segregated and sold the coaching operations of Flights - Hallmark. In this edition we show the two parts of the organisation at the time of separation, which feature two distinct numbering systems. Now part of the coaching operation is Transbus Enviro 42001, SN04EFH. *Dave Heath*

Centra has exchanged many buses in recent months to update the fleet. Pictured on route 426 to Woking is Dart 34103, HX51LPE, now operating in the new Flights-Hallmark fleet. Also used are similar Darts that were acquired with the Mitcham Belle and Frank Thorpe services. *Dave Heath*

DPL51-80

Dennis Dart SLF 10.7m   Plaxton Pointer 2   N33D   1999   Mitcham Belle, 2004

51	MC	T151OGC	54	MC	T154OGC	58	MC	T158OGC	76	MC	T876HGT
52	MC	T152OGC	56	MC	T156OGC	59	MC	T159OGC	77	MC	T877HGT
53	MC	T152OGC	57	MC	T157OGC	75	MC	T875HGT	80	MC	T880HGT

OS1-4

Optare Solo M850   Optare   N29F   2001   Mitcham Belle, 2004

1	MC	KX51UCS	2	MC	KX51UCT	3	MC	KX51UCU	4	MC	KX51UCV

OS5	MC	X385VVY	Optare Solo M850	Optare	N30F	2001	Thames Travel, 2004
OS	BR	LA02WMZ	Optare Solo M850	Optare	N30F	2002	
OS	BR	MX03EHC	Optare Solo M850	Optare	N30F	2003	

Double-deck buses

DA1	MC	T131AUA	DAF DB250 10.5m	Plaxton President 4.4m	N45/19D	1999	London Sovereign, 2005
NV29	MC	N529LHG	Volvo Olympian YN2RV18Z4	Northern Counties Palatine	B48/27D	1996	Go-Ahead London, 2004
NV31	MC	N531LHG	Volvo Olympian YN2RV18Z4	Northern Counties Palatine	B48/27D	1996	Go-Ahead London, 2004
NV32	MC	N532LHG	Volvo Olympian YN2RV18Z4	Northern Counties Palatine	B48/27D	1996	Go-Ahead London, 2004

Coaches

	SR	Y3HMC	Dennis R310	Plaxton Panther	C34FT	2001	Hallmark, 2004
	SR	Y11HMC	Dennis R310	Plaxton Panther	C34FT	2001	Hallmark, 2004
	SR	Y12HMC	Dennis R310	Plaxton Panther	C34FT	2001	Hallmark, 2004
	SR	Y15HMC	Dennis R310	Plaxton Panther	C34FT	2001	Hallmark, 2004
S	SR	W845UVV	Scania K114IB4	Irizar Century 12.351	C49FT	2001	Bus Eireann, 2004
V	SR	YN03WYH	Volvo B7	TransBus Prima	C53F	2003	
V	SR	L275HJD	Volvo B10M-60	Plaxton Première 350	C49FT	1994	Redwing, Herne Hill, 2005
V	SR	X216AWB	Volvo B10M-60	Plaxton Paragon	C49FT	2001	2Travel, Swansea, 2005
VP24	SR	Y334AUT	Volvo B10M-62	Plaxton Paragon	C49F	2001	
VP25	SR	Y335AUT	Volvo B10M-62	Plaxton Paragon	C49F	2001	

The South East Bus Handbook

Minibuses

-	MC	BU53POV	BMC Probus 850 RE	BMC	C35F	2003
FTC1	PF	A12GPS	Ford Transit VE6	Ford	M12	19
FTC2	PL	A14GPS	Ford Transit VE6	Ford	M12	19
IM4	w	M618DPN	Iveco Daily 49.10	Devon Conversions	B15FL	1995
IM5	w	M619DPN	Iveco Daily 49.10	Devon Conversions	B15FL	1995
	PF	T75WGH	Mercedes-Benz Vario O814	Plaxton Beaver 2	BC20F	1999
	PF	T95GGO	Mercedes-Benz Vario O814	Plaxton Beaver 2	BC20F	1999
	PF	T805FGT	Mercedes-Benz Vario O814	Plaxton Beaver 2	BC20F	1999
	PF	T806FGT	Mercedes-Benz Vario O814	Plaxton Beaver 2	BC20F	1999
	SR	V308DHC	Iveco Daily 40.10	Euromotive	M15L	1999
LDV6	SR	W918XGH	LDV Convoy	Euromotive	M15L	2000
LDV7	SR	W919XGH	LDV Convoy	Euromotive	M8L	2000
VW106	EU	X106MGN	Volkswagen LT35	Frank Guy	M8	2000
VW109	EU	X109MGN	Volkswagen LT35	Frank Guy	M8	2000
VW113	EU	X113MGN	Volkswagen LT35	Frank Guy	M8	2000
MUT1	SR	KF02ZWH	Mercedes-Benz Sprinter	UV Trekker	BCl6FL	2002
MUT3	SR	KF02ZWS	Mercedes-Benz Sprinter	UV Trekker	BCl6FL	2002
MUT4	SR	KF02ZWT	Mercedes-Benz Sprinter	UV Trekker	BCl6FL	2002
MUT5	SR	KF52TZV	Mercedes-Benz Sprinter	UV Trekker	BCl6FL	2002
MUT6	SR	KF52TZW	Mercedes-Benz Sprinter	UV Trekker	BCl6FL	2002
	PF	KE03ZFB	Mercedes-Benz Sprinter 413CDi	UV Modular	BCl6FL	2003
	PF	KE03ZFC	Mercedes-Benz Sprinter 413CDi	UV Modular	BCl6FL	2003
	PF	KE03ZFD	Mercedes-Benz Sprinter 413CDi	UV Modular	BCl6FL	2003
MUT7	SR	KE04DZM	Mercedes-Benz Sprinter	UV Trekker	BCl6FL	2004
	PF	KE04OLK	Mercedes-Benz Sprinter 413CDi	UV Modular	BCl6FL	2004
VW	EU	KX54NKJ	Volkswagen LT55	VDL Kusters	M8	2004
VW	EU	KX54NKK	Volkswagen LT55	VDL Kusters	M8	2004
VW	EU	KX54NKL	Volkswagen LT55	VDL Kusters	M8	2004
VW	EU	KX54NKM	Volkswagen LT55	VDL Kusters	M8	2004
VW	EU	KX54NKN	Volkswagen LT55	VDL Kusters	M8	2004
VW	EU	KX54NKO	Volkswagen LT55	VDL Kusters	M8	2004
VW	EU	KX54NKP	Volkswagen LT55	VDL Kusters	M8	2004
VW	EU	KX54NKR	Volkswagen LT55	VDL Kusters	M8	2004
VW	EU	KX54NKT	Volkswagen LT55	VDL Kusters	M8	2004
VW	EU	KX54NKU	Volkswagen LT55	VDL Kusters	M8	2004
TB1	MC	HN54OBE	Ford Transit	Ford	M	2004
TB2	MC	HN54WMO	Ford Transit	Ford	M	2004
TB3	MC	HN54WMP	Ford Transit	Ford	M	2004

Ancillary vehicle:

T1	.	E21ECH	Scania K92CRB	Alexander PS	TV	1988	Thames Bus, New Haw, 2004

Depots: Bristol Airport (BR); Europcar Site, Heathrow Airport (EU); Beddington Lane, Croydon (MC); Scylla Road, Heathrow Airport (PF); Streatham Road, Mitcham (SR).

Several of the Centra coaches are in a white livery, including this Dennis R310 with Plaxton Panther bodywork. It is one of four which now carry HMC plates and is seen heading for Heathrow.
Dave Heath

FLIGHTS - HALLMARK

Flights - Hallmark - Jet Coach

Flights Hallmark Ltd, Long Acre, Birmingham, B7 5JJ

12101	HX	BW03ZUD	Mercedes-Benz Sprinter	UV Modular	BC16FL	2003	
12102	HX	BW03UWH	Mercedes-Benz Sprinter	UV Modular	BC16FL	2003	
12103	HX	BW03UWJ	Mercedes-Benz Sprinter	UV Modular	BC16FL	2003	
20201	WY	X151NGK	Mercedes-Benz Vario O814	Plaxton Beaver 2	B31F	2001	
20202	WY	KF02ZXB	Mercedes-Benz Vario O814	Plaxton Beaver 2	B31F	2002	Menzies, Heathrow, 2004
21002	HX	KE05KXX	Mercedes-Benz Vario O814	Plaxton Cheetah	C29F	2005	
21003	HX	KE05KXZ	Mercedes-Benz Vario O814	Plaxton Cheetah	C29F	2005	
21004	HX	KE05MMF	Mercedes-Benz Vario O814	Plaxton Cheetah	C29F	2005	
21005	HX	KE05MMJ	Mercedes-Benz Vario O814	Plaxton Cheetah	C29F	2005	
21006	HX	KE05MPX	Mercedes-Benz Vario O814	Plaxton Cheetah	C29F	2005	
22001	LA	P70FTG	Toyota Coaster BB50R	Caetano Optimo V	C18F	1997	Dunn-Line, 2004
22002	LA	P77FTG	Toyota Coaster BB50R	Caetano Optimo V	C18F	1997	Dunn-Line, 2004
30401	WY	N401SPA	Dennis Dart 9.8m	Plaxton Pointer	B40F	1996	
30578	LA	M78HHB	Volvo B6 9.9m	Alexander Dash	BC40F	1993	2Travel, Swansea, 2004
30662	WY	L662MSF	Volvo B6 9.9m	Alexander Dash	BC40F	1993	Stagecoach, 2004
30667	WY	L667MSF	Volvo B6 9.9m	Alexander Dash	BC40F	1993	Stagecoach, 2004
31001	WY	W361ABD	Dennis Dart SLF 8.5m	Plaxton MPD	N28F	2000	Dawson Rentals, 2004
31002	WY	KV51KZC	Dennis Dart SLF 8.5m	Plaxton MPD	N28F	2002	
31004	LA	X171BNH	Dennis Dart SLF 8.5m	Plaxton Pointer MPD	N29F	2001	
31101	GW	KP02BVA	Dennis Dart SLF 8.5m	Plaxton Pointer MPD	N29F	2002	

32001-32010   Dennis Dart SLF 10.6m   Plaxton Pointer 2   N40F   1996   Dunn-Line, 2004

32001	EC	P1FTG	32004	EC	P4FTG	32007	EC	P7FTG	32009	EC	P9FTG
32002	EC	P2FTG	32005	EC	P5FTG	32008	EC	P8FTG	32010	EC	P10FTG
32003	EC	P3FTG	32006	EC	P6FTG						

Carrying Hallmark colours, 81208, YR02UMV, is a Neoplan Starliner N516SHD, seen in central London. Flights Hallmark Coaches has its main base off the dual carriageway at Long Acre in Birmingham. *Colin Lloyd*

Based at the Gatwick coach centre, 71006, KX04HTE, is a Volvo B12B with TransBus Panther bodywork. It is seen with Centra names as it rounds Hyde Park Corner while on contract to gta touring. The Panther (swept-back front) and the Paragon (upright front) were launched by Plaxton in 1999, a name dropped in favour of parent TransBus in 2003. However, following the collapse of Transbus, a new Plaxton company has been formed and current production again uses the Plaxton name and the Scarborough factory. *Colin Lloyd*

32012	HX	X212ONH	Dennis Dart SLF 10.7m	Plaxton Pointer 2	N43F	2001	
32013	HX	X213ONH	Dennis Dart SLF 10.7m	Plaxton Pointer 2	N43F	2001	
32015	HX	X215ONH	Dennis Dart SLF 10.7m	Plaxton Pointer 2	N43F	2001	
32016	HX	KX51UCR	Dennis Dart SLF 10.7m	Plaxton Pointer 2	N43F	2002	
32021	WY	S396HVV	Dennis Dart SLF 10.7m	Plaxton Pointer 2	N43F	1999	

31201-7   Alexander Dennis Dart 8.5m   Alexander Dennis Mini Pointer   N29F   2005

31201	HX	KP54BYO	31203	HX	KP54BYT	31205	HX	KP54BYV	31207	HX	KP54BYX
31202	HX	KP54BYR	31204	HX	KP54BYU	31206	HX	KP54BYW			

31208	HX	T5BUS	Dennis Dart SLF 8.5m	Plaxton Pointer MPD	N28F	2001	Norbus, Kirby, 2004

32401-8   Alexander Dennis Dart 10.7m   Alexander Dennis Pointer   N37F   2005

32401	HX	KP54BYJ	32403	HX	KP54BYL	32405	HX	KP54BYN	32407	HX	KP54BYZ
32402	HX	KP54BYK	32404	HX	KP54BYM	32406	HX	KP54BYY	32408	HX	KP54BZA

32409	HX	KX05KFC	Alexander Dennis Dart 10.7m	Alexander Dennis Pointer	N37F	2005	
32410	HX	KX05KFD	Alexander Dennis Dart 10.7m	Alexander Dennis Pointer	N37F	2005	
32411	HX	KX05KFE	Alexander Dennis Dart 10.7m	Alexander Dennis Pointer	N37F	2005	
32412	HX	KX05KFF	Alexander Dennis Dart 10.7m	Alexander Dennis Pointer	N37F	2005	
34103	WY	HX51LPE	Dennis Dart SLF 10.7m	Caetano Nimbus	N31D	2002	
42001	WY	SN04EFH	TransBus Enviro 300	TransBus	N44F	2004	Alexander-Dennis, 2004
40001	GW	BU04EXS	Mercedes-Benz Citaro O530	Mercedes-Benz	N32F	2004	Evobus demonstrator, 2004
40002	WY	BU53AYA	Mercedes-Benz Citaro O530	Mercedes-Benz	N32F	2004	Evobus demonstrator, 2004
40003	GW	KX05KDZ	Mercedes-Benz Citaro O530	Mercedes-Benz	N32F	2005	
40004	GW	BW05LGW	Mercedes-Benz Citaro O530	Mercedes-Benz	N32F	2005	Evobus demonstrator, 2005
50020	WY	C820BYY	Leyland Olympian ONLXB1/RH	Eastern Coach Works	B42/24D	1986	Arriva London, 2004
50055	WY	D255FYM	Leyland Olympian ONLXB1/RH	Eastern Coach Works	B42/24D	1987	Arriva London, 2004
50125	GW	TPD125X	Leyland Olympian ONTL11/1R	Roe	B45/33F	1982	Eastville, Bristol, 2004
52082	GW	M82MYM	Volvo Olympian YN2RC16Z4	Alexander Royale	B45/33F	1995	Go-Ahead London, 2004
52083	GW	M83MYM	Volvo Olympian YN2RC16Z4	Alexander Royale	B45/33F	1995	Go-Ahead London, 2004
52119	WY	G119NGN	Volvo Citybus B10M-50	Northern Counties	B46/35F	1989	Renown, Bexhill, 2004

52339	WY	P339ROO	Volvo Olympian	East Lancs	B43/31D	1997	Sullivan, South Mimms, 2004
58432	-	SVS617	AEC Routemaster R2RH	Park Royal	B36/28R	1960	Arriva London, 2005
60008	LA	A8FTG	Volvo B10M-62	Plaxton Excalibur	C36FT	1998	Dunn-Line, 2004
60051	LA	S51UBO	Volvo B10M-62	Plaxton Expressliner 2	C49FT	1998	Bebb, Llantwit Fardre, 2004
60295	LA	S295WOA	Volvo B10M-SE	Plaxton Expressliner 2	C44FT	1999	Dunn-Line, 2004
60296	LA	S296WOA	Volvo B10M-SE	Plaxton Expressliner 2	C44FT	1999	Dunn-Line, 2004
60297	LA	S297WOA	Volvo B10M-SE	Plaxton Expressliner 2	C44FT	1999	Dunn-Line, 2004
60298	LA	S298WOA	Volvo B10M-SE	Plaxton Expressliner 2	C44FT	1999	Dunn-Line, 2004
60364	LA	S364OOB	Volvo B10M-SE	Plaxton Expressliner 2	C44FT	1998	Dunn-Line, 2004
60365	LA	S365OOB	Volvo B10M-SE	Plaxton Expressliner 2	C44FT	1998	Dunn-Line, 2004
60447	LA	V447EAL	Volvo B10M-SE	Plaxton Expressliner 2	C44FT	1999	Dunn-Line, 2004
60448	LA	V448EAL	Volvo B10M-SE	Plaxton Expressliner 2	C44FT	1999	Dunn-Line, 2004
68332	WY	MIL8332	Volvo B10M-60	Plaxton Paramount 3500 III	C49F	1991	Dunn-Line, 2004
70008	LA	FE02FBF	Volvo B10M-62	Plaxton Panther	C53F	2002	Dunn-Line, 2004
70009	LA	FE02FBG	Volvo B10M-62	Plaxton Panther	C53F	2002	Dunn-Line, 2004
70010	LA	FE02FBJ	Volvo B10M-62	Plaxton Panther	C53F	2002	Dunn-Line, 2004
70011	LA	FE02FBK	Volvo B10M-62	Plaxton Panther	C53F	2002	Dunn-Line, 2004
70012	LA	FE02FBL	Volvo B10M-62	Plaxton Panther	C53F	2002	Dunn-Line, 2004
70013	LA	FE02FBN	Volvo B10M-62	Plaxton Panther	C53F	2002	Dunn-Line, 2004
70461	LA	X461KUT	Volvo B10M-62	Plaxton Paragon	C32FT	2000	Dunn-Line, 2004
70462	GW	X462KUT	Volvo B10M-62	Plaxton Paragon	C32FT	2000	Dunn-Line, 2004
71001	HX	KV03ZFZ	Volvo B12B	TransBus Panther	C53F	2003	
71002	LA	KV03ZGA	Volvo B12B	TransBus Panther	C49FT	2003	
71003	LA	KV03ZGB	Volvo B12B	TransBus Panther	C49FT	2003	
71004	HX	KV03ZGC	Volvo B12B	TransBus Panther	C49FT	2003	
71005	HX	KX04HTD	Volvo B12B	TransBus Panther	C49FT	2004	
71006	GW	KX04HTE	Volvo B12B	TransBus Panther	C49FT	2004	
71007	HX	KX53SJV	Volvo B12B	TransBus Panther	C34FT	2003	
71008	LA	KX04HRC	Volvo B12B	TransBus Panther	C49FT	2004	
71214	LA	FE02FBO	Volvo B12M	Sunsundegui Sideral	C53F	2002	Dunn-Line, 2004
71215	LA	FE02FBU	Volvo B12M	Sunsundegui Sideral	C53F	2002	Dunn-Line, 2004
71316	LA	FE51RDO	Volvo B12T	Jonckheere Mistral 70	C53FT	2001	Dunn-Line, 2004
79005	WY	Y5HMC	Dennis R310	Plaxton Panther	C34FT	2001	Hallmark, 2004
79006	LA	YR02ZKV	Dennis R310	Plaxton Panther	C34FT	2002	Hallmark, 2004
79007	WY	YR02ZKW	Dennis R310	Plaxton Panther	C34FT	2002	Hallmark, 2004
79008	WY	YR02ZKX	Dennis R310	Plaxton Panther	C34FT	2002	Hallmark, 2004
79009	WY	YR02ZKY	Dennis R310	Plaxton Panther	C34FT	2002	Hallmark, 2004
79010	LA	YR02ZKZ	Dennis R310	Plaxton Panther	C34FT	2002	Hallmark, 2004
79014	LA	YR52MDX	Dennis R310	Plaxton Panther	C49FT	2002	Hallmark, 2004
80001	HX	BU53AXH	Mercedes-Benz Touro 1836RL	Mercedes-Benz	C34FT	2003	
80002	LA	BU53AXJ	Mercedes-Benz Touro 1836RL	Mercedes-Benz	C34FT	2003	
81207	LA	FOR35T	Neoplan Starliner N516SHD	Neoplan	C32FT	2002	Hallmark, 2004
81208	LA	YR02UMV	Neoplan Starliner N516SHD	Neoplan	C32FT	2002	Hallmark, 2004
81209	LA	YR02UOE	Neoplan Starliner N516SHD	Neoplan	C32FT	2002	Hallmark, 2004
81301	LA	Y1HMC	Neoplan Starliner N516SHD	Neoplan	C32FT	2001	Hallmark, 2004
81302	LA	HC6422	Neoplan Cityliner N116/3	Neoplan	C32FT	1999	Hallmark, 2004
81303	LA	YN51XMS	Neoplan Starliner N513SHD	Neoplan	C34FT	2001	Hallmark, 2004
81304	LA	T4HMC	Neoplan Cityliner N116/2	Neoplan	C32FT	1999	
81306	GW	T6HMC	Neoplan Cityliner N116/3	Neoplan	C32FT	1999	Hallmark, 2004
81310	LA	1FTO	Neoplan N516SHD	Neoplan EuroStar	C27FT	2000	Dunn-Line, 2004
83001	LA	491NFC	EOS E180Z (MAN)	EOS 200	C32FT	1998	

Ancillary vehicles:

93001	HX	W991XGH	LDV Convoy	Euromotive	Staff	2000	
93002	GW	W992XGH	LDV Convoy	Euromotive	Staff	2000	
93009	HX	X109MGN	Volkswagen LT35	Frank Guy	Staff	2000	
93014	WY	X114MGN	Volkswagen LT35	Frank Guy	Staff	2000	
93017	HX	X117MGN	Volkswagen LT35	Frank Guy	Staff	2000	
93018	HX	X118MGN	Volkswagen LT35	Frank Guy	Staff	2000	

Previous registrations:

491NFC	R6HMC	G119NGN	G119NGN, 619DYE
BW05LGW	BU05UWK	HC6422	T5HMC
FOR35T	YR02UMW	MIL8332	H948DRG
		T5BUS	KV51KZH

Depots: Gatwick Coach Centre, Lowfield Heath, Crawley (GW); Green Lane, Hounslow (HX); Flights Coach Station, Long Acre, Birmingham (LA); National Exhibition Centre, Birmingham (EC) and Byfleet Road, Addlestone (WY).

The South East Bus Handbook

CHALKWELL

Chalkwell Garage & Coach Hire Ltd, 195 Chalkwell Road, Sittingbourne, ME10 1BJ

VIB5241	Leyland Olympian ONLXB/2R	East Lancs	B51/37F	1982	Warrington BT, 2005	
VIB5237	Leyland Olympian ONLXB/2R	East Lancs	B51/37F	1982	Warrington BT, 2005	
YIL7734	Volvo B10M-61	Plaxton Paramount 3200 III	C53F	1988	Eastbourne Buses, 1998	
CSU960	Volvo B10M-61	Plaxton Paramount 3500 III	C53F	1988	Motts, Stoke Mandeville, 1996	
F94KDS	Mercedes-Benz 814D	Alexander Sprint	BC33F	1989	IBT, 2001	
F349TSX	Mercedes-Benz 814D	Alexander Sprint	BC33F	1989	IBT, 2001	
E93MRF	Mercedes-Benz 609D	Reeve Burgess	BC25F	1988	Bassetts, Tittensor, 2003	
H847DKL	Mercedes-Benz 814D	Phoenix	BC33F	1990		
433SKO	Volvo B10M-61	Plaxton Paramount 3500 III	C53F	1991	Arriva Southern Counties, 1999	
347KKP	Volvo B10M-60	Plaxton Paramount 3500 III	C50F	1991	Maidstone & District (NE), 1998	
H651ENK	Leyland-DAF 400	Jubilee (1993)	M16L	1991	van, 1993	
H922FEW	Iveco Daily 45.10	Videotech	M15L	1991	Bassetts, Tittensor, 2003	
J27UNY	Leyland Tiger TRCL10/3ARZM	Plaxton 321	BC70F	1992	Arriva Southern Counties, 2005	
M291UKM	Mercedes-Benz 814D	Wadham Stringer Wessex	BC25F	1995	MoD, 2004	
M969AGO	LDV 400	Jubilee	M16	1994	Mercury, Weybridge, 2002	
M457OVM	LDV 400	Concept	M16L	1994		
N353OBC	Mercedes-Benz 709D	Alexander Sprint	B27F	1995	Arrive Fox County, 2003	
N355OBC	Mercedes-Benz 709D	Alexander Sprint	B27F	1995	Arrive Fox County, 2003	
N210ESF	Mercedes-Benz 711D	Alexander Sprint	B29F	1996	Iqbal, Accrington, 2003	
N755GBF	Mercedes-Benz 711D	Plaxton Beaver	BC25F	1996	Bassetts, Tittensor, 2003	
P834LOK	LDV Convoy	LDV	M16	1997	Mercury, Weybridge, 2002	
577HLU	Volvo B10M-62	Plaxton Première	C49FT	1997	Steel's, Skipton, 2004	
187NKN	Volvo B10M-62	Plaxton Excalibur	C49FT	1997	City of Nottingham, 2004	
P848YGB	Mercedes-Benz Vario O810	Plaxton Beaver 2	B31F	1997	NCP, Glasgow Airport, 2005	
P850YGB	Mercedes-Benz Vario O810	Plaxton Beaver 2	B31F	1997	NCP, Glasgow Airport, 2005	

Situated in Sittingbourne, Chalkwell provides coach tours and private hire along with local services that use minibuses and a commuter service to London. Pictured in the capital is Volvo B10M 433SKO which carries a Plaxton Paramount 3500 body. *Colin Lloyd*

COLISEUM

Coliseum Coaches Ltd, Botley Road, West End, Southampton, SO30 3JA

WCR474	MAN 18.350	Neoplan Transliner	C53F	2001
MIB651	MAN 18.350	Neoplan Euroliner	C48FT	2001
MIB650	MAN 18.350	Neoplan Euroliner	C48FT	2002
VFJ687	Neoplan Euroliner N316 SHD	Neoplan	C48FT	2002
636VHX	Neoplan Euroliner N316 SHD	Neoplan	C49FT	2002
MIB652	Neoplan Euroliner N316 SHD	Neoplan	C48FT	2003
435SFC	Neoplan Starliner N516 SHD	Neoplan	C48FT	2003
KEN959	Neoplan Starliner N516 SHD	Neoplan	C30FT	2003
JIL8230	Neoplan Euroliner N316 SHD	Neoplan	C48FT	2004
MFX778	Neoplan Euroliner N316 SHD	Neoplan	C48FT	2004
HIL7978	Neoplan Euroliner N316 SHD	Neoplan	C49FT	2005
WCR833	Neoplan Euroliner N316 SHD	Neoplan	C48FT	2005

Previous registration:
KEN959   6KAE

Web: www.coliseumcoaches.co.uk

Coliseum employs a fleet of coaches sourced entirely from Neoman, the company established to produce Neoplan and MAN buses and coaches. Illustrating the fleet is the latest Euroliner WCR833, pictured in October at the Coach and Bus Live, 2005. Developed with an eye on the British and Irish markets, the integral Euroliner evolved from the Transliner, a body fitted to the Dennis Javelin. The N316 is the 12-metre version while a shorter version is also sold as the N313. *BBP*

COASTAL COACHES

PH Jenkins, 18 West Point, Newick, Lewes, BN8 4NU

115	GU52HAO	Dennis Dart SLF 8.5m	Plaxton MPD	N29F	2002
116	GU52HAX	Dennis Dart SLF 8.5m	Plaxton MPD	N29F	2002
117	XS2210	Dennis Dart SLF 10.7m	Plaxton Pointer 2	N38F	2002
118	GU52HJY	Dennis Dart SLF 10.7m	Plaxton Pointer 2	N38F	2002
119	GU52HKA	Dennis Dart SLF 10.7m	Plaxton Pointer 2	N38F	2002
120	GU52HKB	Dennis Dart SLF 10.7m	Plaxton Pointer 2	N38F	2002
121	GU52HKC	Dennis Dart SLF 10.7m	Plaxton Pointer 2	N38F	2002
122	GU52HKD	Dennis Dart SLF 10.7m	Plaxton Pointer 2	N38F	2002
123	GX04ASU	TransBus Dart 8.8m	TransBus Mini Pointer	N29F	2004
124	GX05AOP	Alexander Dennis Dart 10.7m	Alexander Dennis Pointer	N37F	2005

Previous registration:
XS2210   GU52HJX

Depot: Coppards Lane, Northiam

Coastal's fleet now comprises entirely low-floor Darts, with the latest, 124, GX05AOP, seen here carrying the badge of Alexander Dennis. This new company was established by a group of Scottish businessmen to purchase the assembly plants of Alexander and Dennis from the administrators of TransBus. To avoid re-tooling, the new badge fits neatly over the lozenge-shaped one of TransBus. *Dave Heath*

Established in 1976 by the present Chairman and his wife, the business has grown from a Chauffeur Car Service to being one of the largest coach operators in the area, and the only one in the historic town of Banbury. Seen at one of the shows is 137, UIL2720, a Volvo B10M with low-driving position Jonckheere Deauville P599 bodywork. *Dave Heath*

201	A864SUL	Leyland Titan TNLXB2RR	Leyland	B44/26D	1983	Blue Triangle, Rainham, 2000
202	A916SYE	Leyland Titan TNLXB2RR	Leyland	B44/26D	1983	London Central, 2000
203	RIL1024	Leyland Titan TNLXB2RR	Leyland	B44/30F	1983	London Central, 1999
301	H562FLE	Mercedes-Benz 609D	North West	C19FL	1990	Magpie, High Wycombe, 1996
302	H971FKE	Ford Transit VE6	Ford	M14	1991	Carotti, High Wycombe, 1998
303	K373HHK	Ford Transit VE6	Ford	M14	1993	
304	N399LEW	LDV Convoy	Jubilee	M16	1996	private owner, 1998
405	KUI5160	Mercedes-Benz 811D	Alexander Sprint	B28F	1988	Stagecoach Red & White, 2000
407	X94FOR	Dennis Dart SLF	Caetano Compass	N44F	2000	

Previous registrations:

820GXC	M626FNS	UIL2720	L724JUD
9785SM	88G1507 (EI), E340FNU	UIL2721	G744BCV
B8NEO	T850JWB	UIL2722	88C4700, E658FNU
IIL1355	F55HNC	UIL2723	F428RRY
KUI5160	F617XMS	UIL2725	E43JRF
NSU914	G652ONH, B4BCL, G705UFM, MJI2364, G814VUE, NIL4162	UIL2726	H839AHS, NIW1461, H839AHS
		UIL7821	H183EJF
NIW6518	C532DND	UIL7822	H184EJF
OGL849	F706ENE	UIL7823	H194DVM
RIL1024	A947SYE	UIL7824	F978HGE, 820GXC
RIL7974	L218ETG	URT682	?
RIL4956	E450MMM, VPF742	WXI5864	G729XHY
SIL6719	G373REG	YSU975	N819NHS
SIL8756	F248OFP		
TAZ4988	F794TBC, DSK558, F199UPC, YSU975, F189UPC		

Web: www.cheneycoaches.co.uk

CHENEY TRAVEL

Cheney Coaches Ltd, Cheney House, Thorpe Mead, Banbury, OX16 8SW

Fleet	Reg	Chassis	Body	Seating	Year	History
110	NIW6518	Volvo B10M-61	Van Hool Alizée	C53F	1986	Rossendale (Ellen Smith), 1997
111	OGL849	Leyland Tiger TRCL10/3ARZM	Plaxton Paramount 3500	C53F	1989	Pontefract Coachways, 1999
112	PDN873	Leyland Tiger TRCTL11/3RZ	Plaxton Paramount 3200	C55F	1988	Coastal Country, Whitby, 1999
113	RIL4956	Leyland Tiger TRCL10/3ARZM	Duple 320	C59F	1988	Nesbit, Somerby, 2000
116	TAZ4988	TAZ D3200	TAZ Dubrava	C49FT	1989	Safeguard, Guildford, 1993
117	UIL2725	Leyland Tiger TRCTL11/3RZ	Plaxton Paramount 3200 III	C49F	1988	R Bullock, Cheadle, 2001
118	UIL7824	Volvo B10M-60	Plaxton Paramount 3500 III	C53F	1989	Ron's, Lancing, 2002
121	IIL1355	Leyland Tiger TRCL10/3ARZM	Duple 320	C55F	1989	Maynes, Manchester, 1997
122	URT682	Volvo B10M-60	Jonckheere Deauville	C53F	19	?,
124	NSU914	Volvo B10M-60	Jonckheere Deauville	C51FT	1990	Ron's, Lancing, 2002
126	9785SM	Volvo B10M-61	Plaxton Paramount 3500 III	C53F	1988	Cummer, Galway, 2000
128	SIL6719	Volvo B10M-61	Plaxton Paramount 3500 III	C51FT	1990	Owen's, Oswestry, 2000
129	SIL8757	Volvo B10M-61	Plaxton Paramount 3200 III	C53F	1989	Reliant, Citroën, 2000
130	SIL8756	Volvo B10M-61	Plaxton Paramount 3500 III	C53F	1989	Norfolk CC, 2000
131	UIL2721	DAF SB2305	Caetano Algarve II	C53F	1989	Reliant, Heather, 2001
132	UIL2723	DAF SB2305	Caetano Algarve II	C53F	1989	Reliant, Heather, 2001
133	UIL2722	Van Hool T815	Van Hool Alizée	C55F	1988	Island Coach, Yarmouth, 2001
134	WXI5864	Van Hool T815	Van Hool Alizée	C47FT	1990	Merlyn's, Skewen, 2001
136	UIL2726	Volvo B10M-60	Plaxton Paramount 3500 III	C53F	1991	Summerfield, Southampton, 2001
137	UIL2720	Volvo B10M-60	Jonckheere Deauville P599	C49FT	1994	Lepick, South Mimms, 2002
138	UIL7822	Volvo B10M-60	Caetano Algarve II	C55F	1991	Reliant, Heather, 2002
139	UIL7821	Volvo B10M-60	Caetano Algarve II	C55F	1991	Reliant, Heather, 2002
140	UIL7823	Volvo B10M-60	Van Hool Alizée H	C53F	1991	McCarthy, Macclesfield, 2003
141	820GXC	Volvo B10M-62	Jonckheere Mistral 50	C53F	1995	Gale, Haslemere, 2003
143	M603ORJ	Volvo B10M-62	Jonckheere Mistral 50	C53F	1995	Shearings, 2003
144	M604ORJ	Volvo B10M-62	Jonckheere Mistral 50	C53F	1995	Shearings, 2003
145	M609ORJ	Volvo B10M-62	Jonckheere Mistral 50	C53F	1995	Shearings, 2003
146	M610ORJ	Volvo B10M-62	Jonckheere Mistral 50	C53F	1995	Shearings, 2003
147	M614ORJ	Volvo B10M-62	Jonckheere Mistral 50	C53F	1995	Shearings, 2003
1	YSU975	Volvo B10M-62	Jonckheere Mistral 50	C53F	1996	Gale, Haslemere, 2003
1	RIL7974	Dennis Javelin GX 12m	Berkhof Excellence 1000 L	C50FT	1994	Ron's, Lancing, 2002
1	L565FND	Scania K113CRB	Van Hool Alizée	C49FT	1994	Timeline, Bolton, 2004
1	B8NEO	Neoplan Cityliner N116/3H	Neoplan	C48FT	1999	Z Cars, Bristol, 2005

Following on from the Deauville, Jonckheere's current model is the Mistral. Pictured in Lambeth, Cheney Travel's M604ORJ was new to Shearings. *Colin Lloyd*

CHARLTON SERVICES

NGJ & PD Holder, The Garage, High Street, Charlton-on-Otmoor, Kidlington, OX5 2UQ

Reg	Chassis	Body	Type	Year	History
BBW217Y	Leyland Olympian ONLXB/1R	Eastern Coach Works	B47/32F	1982	Oxford Bus Company, 1999
OJI3907	Leyland Tiger TRCTL11/3R	Plaxton Paramount 3200	C57F	1983	B J, Abbey Wood, 1988
GAZ8573	Leyland Tiger TRCTL11/3R	Plaxton Paramount 3500	C53F	1983	Lee, Rowlands Gill, 1995
YJI5277	Leyland Tiger TRCTL11/3R	Plaxton Paramount 3500	C51FT	1984	Den Caney, Birmingham, 2000
GJI7173	Leyland Tiger TRCTL11/3RH	Plaxton Paramount 3500 II	C49F	1985	Cheltenham & Gloucester, 1993
OXI9100	Leyland Royal Tiger RT	Plaxton Paramount 3500	C55F	1986	Horseman, Reading, 1992
TJI6278	Leyland Tiger TRCTL11/3RH	Plaxton Paramount 3500 II	C51F	1986	Brighton & Hove, 1995
FIL6689	Leyland Tiger TRCTL11/3RH	Van Hool Alizée	C53F	1986	Stokes, Carstairs, 1999
NJI4304	Leyland Tiger TRCTL11/3RH	Duple 340	C53F	1987	Primrose, Ryton, 1999
PIL3400	Mercedes-Benz 410D	G&M	M15	1993	van, 1998
K7GPH	Volvo B10M-60	Jonckheere Deauville 50	C50F	1993	Wootton, Northampton, 2001
K9NGH	Volvo B10M-62	Jonckheere Deauville	C53F	1994	Clarkes of London, 2002
N1VWL	Mercedes-Benz 711D	Plaxton Beaver	BC25F	1995	Boulton, Peterborough, 2002
3103PH	Volvo B10M-62	Van Hool Alizée HE	C53F	1996	Martin, Spean Bridge, 2003
N4PUS	Volvo B10M-62	Van Hool T9 Alizée	C49FT	1996	Edinburgh Castle Coaches, 2004
M40BUS	Volvo B10M-62	Jonckheere Mistral 50	C50F	1998	Shearings, 2005

Previous registrations:

3103PH	KSK984, L717ADS, 3786AT, L544PSB		N1VWL	N108BHL
CSU243	FJO603Y		N4PUS	LSK871, N621PUS, 99KK2861
FIL6689	C180EME, WSU209		NJI4304	D224YBB
GAZ8573	10RU, GNF980Y		OJI3907	YFG366Y
GJI7173	B215NDG, 511OHU, B177SFH, 3103PH		OXI9100	C801FMC
K7GPH	K829HUM		PIL3400	K709UFJ
K9NGH	L600CLA		TJI6278	C378PCD
M40BUS	R943YNF		YJI5277	A690WOM, DEN69D, A690WOM

The Jonckheere Deauville was the forerunner of the Mistral and is a popular import to the British market on Volvo chassis. Illustrating the model is Charlton Services' K7GPH, seen passing through Trafalgar Square. *Colin Lloyd*

Chalkwell has been serving the Swale area of Kent for over 70 years since Harry Eglington's Island Luxury Coaches ran the first express service to London from the Isle of Sheppey. Pictured on local service is Plaxton Beaver N755GBF, a Mercedes-Benz 711 which as seen here features high-back seating. *Martin Smith*

P101MKK	Dennis Javelin	Plaxton Première 320	C53F	1997	
P102MKK	Dennis Javelin	Plaxton Première 320	C53F	1997	
P103MKK	Dennis Javelin	Plaxton Première 320	C53F	1997	
P104NKL	Dennis Javelin	Plaxton Première 320	C53F	1997	
R105CKN	Dennis Javelin	UVG S320	C53F	1997	
R107GKN	Dennis Javelin	UVG S320	C53F	1997	
R26TKO	Mercedes-Benz Vario 0814D	Autobus Nouvelle 2	C25F	1997	
R108AKP	Dennis Javelin	Plaxton Première 320	C53F	1998	
R109AKP	Dennis Javelin	Plaxton Première 320	C53F	1998	
R110JKP	Dennis Javelin	Plaxton Première 320	C53F	1998	
R884HEJ	Dennis Javelin	UVG S320	C57F	1998	Lewis, Llanrhystyd, 2005
GJ52LUY	Mercedes-Benz Vario 0814	Plaxton Beaver 2	BC33F	2003	
GN54SVF	Mercedes-Benz Vario 0814	Plaxton Beaver 2	BC31F	2005	
GN54SVG	Mercedes-Benz Vario 0814	Plaxton Beaver 2	BC31F	2005	

Previous registrations:

187NKN	R929LAA, A13XEL		TIW9962	OES342Y, 220BSR, TAY71X
347KKP	H637UWR		VIB5230	D271XRG
433SKO	H618UWR		VIB5237	A210DTO
820YKE	E805DPN		VIB5241	A206DTO
CSU960	E486BFM		VIL8799	C347GSD, 187NKN
			YIL7734	E805DPN, 820YKE

Web: www.chalkwell.co.uk
Depot: Eurolink Commercial Park, Sittingbourne.

The South East Bus Handbook

COMPASS TRAVEL

Compass Travel (Sussex) Ltd, Faraday Close, Durrington, Worthing, BN13 3RB

	Reg	Chassis	Body	Seating	Year	History
	B42KAL	Volvo B10M-61	Jonckheere Jubilee P50	C53F	1985	Lianne Coaches, Windsor, 2001
w	HIL4415	Volvo B10M-60	Plaxton Paramount 3200 III	C53F	1991	Venture, Harrow, 2004
	J100SOU	DAF MB230	Van Hool Alizée	C51FT	1992	Galloway, Mendlesham, 2005
w	K725HUG	Optare MetroRider MR05	Optare	BC33F	1993	Arriva Yorkshire, 2001
	L542XUT	Volvo B10M-60	Plaxton Première 350	C49F	1994	The Coachmasters, Bala, 2003
	L717OMV	Dennis Dart 9.8m	Plaxton Pointer	B35F	1994	Metrobus, Crawley, 2004
	L718OMV	Dennis Dart 9.8m	Plaxton Pointer	B35F	1994	Metrobus, Crawley, 2004
	L719OMV	Dennis Dart 9.8m	Plaxton Pointer	B35F	1994	Metrobus, Crawley, 2004
	M440AVG	Optare MetroRider MR11	Optare	C31F	1994	Tillingbourne, Cranleigh, 2001
w	M292SBT	Mercedes-Benz 814D	Plaxton Beaver	BC33F	1995	Clarkson, South Elmsall, 2000
w	N150BOF	Optare MetroRider MR15	Optare	B31F	1996	Travel West Midlands, 2002
	N151BOF	Optare MetroRider MR15	Optare	BC33F	1996	Travel West Midlands, 2003
	N275DWY	Optare MetroRider MR11	Optare	BC23F	1996	Tillingbourne, Cranleigh, 2003
	N469WDA	Optare MetroRider MR15	Optare	BC33F	1995	Travel West Midlands, 2003
	N94WOM	Optare MetroRider MR15	Optare	BC33F	1995	Travel West Midlands, 2003
	N95WOM	Optare MetroRider MR15	Optare	BC33F	1995	Travel West Midlands, 2002
	N506LUA	DAF SB3000	Ikarus Blue Danube 350	C53F	1996	Holmeswood Coaches, 2004
	P6SYD	Mercedes-Benz 814D	Plaxton Beaver	BC33F	1997	Stringer, Pontefract, 2002
	R81EDW	Mercedes-Benz Vario O814	Autobus Nouvelle	BC33F	1998	Bebb, Llantwit Fardre, 1999
	T421ADN	Optare MetroRider MR	Optare	BC33F	1999	Optare demonstrator, 2001
	T422ADN	Optare MetroRider MR	Optare	BC33F	1999	Optare demonstrator, 2001

M440AVG is one of nine Optare MetroRiders in service with Compass Bus. Pictured at Worthing Pier, it is seen heading for Lancing on West Sussex route 13 that links Arundel with south Lancing. In additon, four services are operated for Surrey County Council. *Martin Smith*

Compass Travel operates four rare combination of 8.5-metre Darts with Alexander ALX200 bodies of which fewer than ninety were built and over half were sold to Stagecoach. Y252KNB is seen heading for the World's End. *Richard Godfrey*

T73JBO	Mercedes-Benz Vario 0814	Autobus Nouvelle 2	BC33F	1999	Hutchinson, Easingwold, 2003
T75JBO	Mercedes-Benz Vario 0814	Autobus Nouvelle 2	BC33F	1999	Hutchinson, Easingwold, 2003
T76JBO	Mercedes-Benz Vario 0814	Autobus Nouvelle 2	BC33F	1999	Bebb, Llantwit Fardre, 2004
V594DSM	Mercedes-Benz Vario 0814	Plaxton Beaver 2	BC33F	1999	Mathison, Inverness, 2003
Y251KNB	Dennis Dart SLF 8.5m	Alexander ALX200	N29F	2001	
Y252KNB	Dennis Dart SLF 8.5m	Alexander ALX200	N29F	2001	
Y253KNB	Dennis Dart SLF 8.5m	Alexander ALX200	N29F	2001	
Y254KNB	Dennis Dart SLF 8.5m	Alexander ALX200	N29F	2001	
GX02CGY	Mercedes-Benz Sprinter 411 CDi	Mercedes-Benz	M14	2002	
GX03AZJ	Dennis Dart SLF	Plaxton Pointer 2	N37F	2003	
GX03AZL	Dennis Dart SLF	Plaxton Pointer 2	N37F	2003	
SN53ETK	TransBus Dart 8.8m	TransBus Mini Pointer	N29F	2003	
SN53ETL	TransBus Dart 8.8m	TransBus Mini Pointer	N29F	2003	
SN53ETO	TransBus Dart 8.8m	TransBus Mini Pointer	N29F	2003	
SN53ETR	TransBus Dart 8.8m	TransBus Mini Pointer	N29F	2003	
GX04AZA	TransBus Dart 8.8m	TransBus Mini Pointer	N29F	2004	
GX04BXN	Mercedes-Benz Sprinter 411 CDi	Mercedes-Benz	M14	2004	
GX54AWH	Alexander Dennis SLF 8.8m	Alexander Dennis Minii Pointer	N29F	2004	

Previous registrations:

B497CBD	B497CBD, PSU631
HIL4415	H936DRJ
J100SOU	J100SOU, 5611PP
N275DWY	N275DWY, TIL1188
N506LUA	N506LUA, SBV703
V594DSM	V594DSM, YST738

Depots: Stairbridge Lane, Bolney; Faraday Close, Durrington; London Road, Hassocks; Pookbourne Lane, Hickstead; Henfiel Road, Upper Beeding and Staine Street, Pulborough.

Web: www.compass-travel.co.uk

COUNTRYLINER

Countryliner Coach Hire Ltd, GB House, Slyfield Industrial Estate, Guildford, GU1 1RR

MC2	BU03LXV	Mercedes-Benz Touro 1836RL	Mercedes-Benz	C49FT	2003	
MC3	BU03LXW	Mercedes-Benz Touro 1836RL	Mercedes-Benz	C49FT	2003	
MC4	BU04EXR	Mercedes-Benz Medio	Mercedes-Benz	C28F	2004	
MC5	BX54EBP	Mercedes-Benz Touro 1836RL	Mercedes-Benz	C49FT	2004	
MC6	LX03KPE	Mercedes-Benz Touro 1836RL	Mercedes-Benz	C49FT	2002	
VP40	R40TGM	Volvo B10M-62	Plaxton Première 350	C53F	1998	Tellings-Golden Miller, 2003
V511	R511WDC	Volvo B10M-62	Plaxton Première 350	C49FT	1998	Compass Royston, Stockton, 04
V710	P710ODA	Volvo B10M-62	Caetano Enigma	C53F	1997	Pat Kavanagh, Urlingford, 2004
VDP1	A11HOU	Volvo B10M-53	Plaxton Paramount 4000 III	C56/12DT	1990	, 2004
NSD1	FSK598	Neoplan Skyliner N122/3	Neoplan	C57/20CT	1992	Moffat & Williamson, 2005
DFC1	OYD693	DAF MB230	Van Hool Alizée SH	C53FT	1988	Horsham Buses, 1998
DFC3	776WME	DAF MB230	Van Hool Alizée SH	C53FT	1990	Horsham Buses, 1998
DJ621	G621CPS	Dennis Javelin 11m	Duple 300	B55F	1990	South Lancs, Atherton, 2005
RLH135	A135SMA	Leyland Olympian ONLXB/1R	Eastern Coach Works	BC40/32F	1983	Arriva Midlands, 2005
RLH681	A681KDV	Leyland Olympian ONLXB/1R	Eastern Coach Works	BC40/30F	1983	Stagecoach, 2005
RLH693	WDL693Y	Leyland Olympian ONLXB/1R	Eastern Coach Works	BC40/30F	1983	Southern Vectis, 2002
RLH695	WDL695Y	Leyland Olympian ONLXB/1R	Eastern Coach Works	BC40/30F	1983	Southern Vectis, 2002
RLH696	WDL696Y	Leyland Olympian ONLXB/1R	Eastern Coach Works	BC40/30F	1983	Southern Vectis, 2002

Countryliner can be traced back, in part, to 1911 with the formation of The East Surrey Bus Company based in Reigate. This later became part of the London General Omnibus Company, and then part of the country services of London Transport. Subsequently this area became London Country South West and under Arriva ownership Blue Saloon Coaches of Guildford was acquired. This company was later sold off as Countryliner Coach Hire Ltd. One of four Mercedes-Benz Touro coaches, BX54EBP carries fleet number MC6. *Dave Heath*

An interesting acquisition in 2005 was DLA116, J116WSC, seen here operating the North Heath Circular. New to London Buses, it passed to Stagecoach London on privatisation, the entire batch was transferred within Stagecoach to Ribble which then sold them to the Blazefield group along with its Lancashire operations. This batch remained intact when Bolton depot was sold to Blue Bus which is now part of Arriva. Here it carries what must be its seventh colour scheme.
Dave Heath

DLA116	J116WSC	Dennis Lance 11m	Alexander PS	B47F	1992	Blue Bus, Bolton, 2005
DP1	RL51CXB	Dennis Dart SLF 8.5m	Plaxton MPD	N29F	2002	
DP2	RL51CXC	Dennis Dart SLF 8.5m	Plaxton MPD	N29F	2002	
DP3	RL51CXD	Dennis Dart SLF 8.5m	Plaxton MPD	N29F	2002	
DP7	KU52RXX	Dennis Dart SLF 8.5m	Plaxton MPD	N29F	2002	
DP8	T72JBA	Dennis Dart SLF 8.5m	Plaxton MPD	N29F	1999	Rogers, Horden, 2002
DP9	W937JNF	Dennis Dart SLF 8.5m	Alexander ALX200	N29F	1999	Go-West, King's Lynn, 2002
DP10	W921JNF	Dennis Dart SLF 8.5m	Plaxton MPD	N29F	1999	Liskeard & District, 2002
DP11	T78JBA	Dennis Dart SLF 8.5m	Plaxton MPD	N29F	1999	M R Travel, Rochdale, 2003
DP12	T550HNH	Dennis Dart SLF 8.5m	Plaxton MPD	N29F	1999	Pink Elephant Parking, 2003
DP13	V247BNV	Dennis Dart SLF 8.5m	Plaxton MPD	N29F	1999	Nostalgiabus, Mitcham, 2003
DP14	P682RWU	Dennis Dart SLF 9.8m	Plaxton Pointer	N35F	1997	First PMT, 2003
DP15	P686RWU	Dennis Dart SLF 9.8m	Plaxton Pointer	N35F	1997	Tellings-Golden Miller, 2003
DP16	P688RWU	Dennis Dart SLF 9.8m	Plaxton Pointer	N35F	1997	First PMT, 2003
DP17	V257BNV	Dennis Dart SLF 8.5m	Plaxton Pointer MPD	N29F	1999	Dawson rentals, 2004
DP18	KV51KZJ	Dennis Dart SLF 8.5m	Plaxton Pointer MPD	N29F	2001	Menzies, Heathrow, 2003
DP19	W364ABD	Dennis Dart SLF 8.5m	Plaxton Pointer MPD	N29F	2000	
DP20	KP51SXU	Dennis Dart SLF 8.5m	Plaxton Pointer MPD	N29F	2001	
DP21	W773URP	Dennis Dart SLF 8.5m	Plaxton Pointer MPD	N29F	2000	
OT904	N904HWY	Optare MetroRider MR13	Optare	B26F	1996	Metrobus, Crawley, 2003
OT594	T594CGT	Optare MetroRider MR13	Optare	B24F	1999	Arriva Southern Counties, 2002

Previous registrations:
776WME   G974KJX   P710ODA   97W1
A11HOU   G717JOG, FTG5, A3FTG   OYD693   F618HGO

Depots: Slyfield Industrial Estate, Guildford (two locations)
Web: www.countryliner-coaches.com

COUNTY RIDER

East Sussex County Council, Transport & Environment, County Hall, St Annes Crescent, Lewes, BN7 1UE

	G91VMM	Leyland Swift LBM6T/2RA	Wadham Stringer Vanguard II	B34FL	1990	Metrobus, Orpington, 1999
B425	R84NNJ	Mercedes-Benz Vario 0814	Plaxton Beaver 2	B26F	1998	
B427	S794XUG	Optare Solo M850	Optare	N23F	1998	
B428	V931VUB	Optare Solo M850	Optare	N27F	1999	
B429	V932VUB	Optare Solo M850	Optare	N27F	1999	
B430	V933VUB	Optare Solo M850	Optare	N27F	1999	
B431	V934VUB	Optare Solo M850	Optare	N27F	1999	
B432	V935VUB	Optare Solo M850	Optare	N27F	1999	
	V101LKN	Iveco Daily 49.10	Mellor	B12F	1999	
	V241LKN	Iveco Daily 49.10	Mellor	B12F	1999	
	V951DKK	Iveco Daily 49.10	Mellor	B12FL	1999	
	V407KKM	Iveco TurboDaily 59-10	Mellor	B20FL	1999	
B434	W754URD	Mercedes-Benz 412D	Frank Guy	M16L	2000	
	W851VHB	Mercedes-Benz 412D	UVG	B16FL	2000	UVG demonstrator, 2003
B437	X657WYG	Optare Solo M850	Optare	N25F	2001	
	Y336UKN	Iveco TurboDaily 59-10	Mellor	B16FL	2001	
	YR02YTD	Optare Alero AL10	Optare	N16F	2002	
	YR02YTE	Optare Alero AL10	Optare	N16F	2002	
	YR02YTF	Optare Alero AL10	Optare	N16F	2002	
	YG52DHD	Optare Solo M850	Optare	N25F	2002	
	YV03UTX	Optare Solo M850	Optare	N27F	2003	
	YV03UTY	Optare Solo M850	Optare	N27F	2003	
	YN03WXZ	Mercedes-Benz Vario 0814D	TransBus Beaver	B22FL	2003	
	WX53OXZ	Mercedes-Benz Sprinter 413CDi	UV Modular	B16FL	2003	
	YN53ELU	Optare Solo M850	Optare	N25F	2003	
	YK05CDV	Optare Solo M850SL	Optare	N25F	2005	
	YJ05WCA	Optare Solo M850SL	Optare	N25F	2005	
	YJ05WCC	Optare Solo M850SL	Optare	N25F	2005	
	YJ05WCD	Optare Solo M850SL	Optare	N25F	2005	
	YJ05WCE	Optare Solo M850SL	Optare	N25F	2005	
	YJ05WCF	Optare Solo M850SL	Optare	N25F	2005	
	YJ05WCG	Optare Solo M850SL	Optare	N25F	2005	

Depot: The Broyle, Ringmer. Web: www.eastsussexcc.gov.uk

County Rider is the brand name for the local authority operations of East Sussex County Council. Many of the buses are allocated to operators who provide services on behalf of the council. Recent additions include six slim-line Optare Solo buses with YJ05WCG, the latest example, seen here. *Dave Heath*

COUNTYWIDE TRAVEL

Countywide Travel Ltd, 1 Clerken Green, Oakley, Basingstoke, RG21 6TA
Countywide Travel (Fleet) Ltd, 1 Foyle Park, Basingstoke, RG21 3HD

03	T696OCR	LDV Convoy	LDV	M16	1999	
04	HJ52OKK	LDV Convoy	Lonsdale	M16	2002	
05	HJ52OKL	LDV Convoy	Lonsdale	M16	2002	
11	H186EJF	Toyota Coaster HDB30R	Caetano Optimo II	C21F	1991	Marchwood Motorways, 1995
12	J137LLK	Toyota Coaster HDB30R	Caetano Optimo II	C18F	1991	Capital, West Drayton, 1996
31	N305FOR	Iveco TurboDaily 59-12	Mellor	B29F	1996	Marchwood Motorways, 1996
32	P616LTP	Iveco TurboDaily 59-12	Mellor	B29F	1997	
37	S377PGB	Mercedes-Benz Vario O814	Plaxton Beaver 2	B27F	1999	Weavaway, Newbury, 2003
38	W963JNF	Mercedes-Benz Vario O814	Plaxton Beaver 2	BC27F	2000	
39	W964JNF	Mercedes-Benz Vario O814	Plaxton Beaver 2	BC27F	2000	
40	Y113LTF	Mercedes-Benz Vario O814	Plaxton Beaver 2	B27F	2001	
41	Y133LTF	Mercedes-Benz Vario O814	Plaxton Beaver 2	B27F	2001	
42	RX51XXL	Mercedes-Benz Vario O814	Plaxton Beaver 2	B27F	2001	
43	RL51CVZ	Mercedes-Benz Vario O814	Plaxton Beaver 2	B31F	2002	
44	RL51CWA	Mercedes-Benz Vario O814	Plaxton Beaver 2	B31F	2002	
45	RL51ZLN	Mercedes-Benz Vario O814	Plaxton Beaver 2	B31F	2002	
46	RL51ZLO	Mercedes-Benz Vario O814	Plaxton Beaver 2	B31F	2002	
61	RX53LFH	MAN 14.200	East Lancs Myllennium	N35F	2004	
62	RX53LNH	MAN 14.200	East Lancs Myllennium	N35F	2004	
63	RX53LNJ	MAN 14.200	East Lancs Myllennium	N35F	2004	
71	M71AKA	Dennis Dart 9.8m	Marshall C37	B40F	1995	Halton Transport, 2001
73	M73AKA	Dennis Dart 9.8m	Marshall C37	B40F	1995	Halton Transport, 2001
74w	M74AKA	Dennis Dart 9.8m	Marshall C37	B40F	1995	Halton Transport, 2001
81	NIB7625	DAF SB2300	Plaxton Paramount 3200 III	C53F	1989	Marchwood Motorways, 1995
84	UDZ7334	DAF SB2300	Caetano Algarve	C53F	1989	Logan, Dunloy, 1996
85w	VFB617T	Bedford YMT	Caetano Alpha	C53F	1979	Marchwood Motorways, 1996
87w	SLJ387X	Leyland Leopard PSU3C/4R	Plaxton Supreme IV	C53F	1981	Wilson, Carnwath, 1999
88	R163GNW	DAF SB3000	Ikarus Blue Danube 350	C55F	1998	
89	R164GNW	DAF SB3000	Ikarus Blue Danube 350	C53F	1998	
90	R114GNW	DAF SB3000	Ikarus Blue Danube 350	C53F	1998	Eastbourne Buses, 2005

Previous registrations:
E613UGW   E613UGW, TAA68
NIB7625   F851YJX   UDZ7334   G745BCV

Depots: Andover Road, Basingstoke; Springwell Lane, Hartley Witney and Clerken Green, Oakley.

Countywide operates three East Lancs Myllennium-bodied MAN buses from its Oakley base. Seen on route 72 to Aldershot is 63, **RX53LNJ**. *Colin Lloyd*

COURTNEY

Courtney Coaches Ltd, 1 Berkshire Business Centre, Downmill Road, Bracknell, RG12 1QS

R672NFR	Scania L113CRL	East Lancs European	N49F	1997	Airparks, Birmingham, 2004
S847DGX	Volvo Olympian	East Lancs Pyoneer	B47/29F	1998	Metrobus, Crawley, 2004
S853DGX	Volvo Olympian	East Lancs Pyoneer	B47/29F	1998	Metrobus, Crawley, 2004
S854DGX	Volvo Olympian	East Lancs Pyoneer	B47/29F	1998	Metrobus, Crawley, 2004
S857DGX	Volvo Olympian	East Lancs Pyoneer	B47/29F	1998	Metrobus, Crawley, 2004
T2CCL	Mercedes-Benz Vario 0614	Autobus	C24F	1999	
W289EYG	Optare Solo M850	Optare	N24F	2000	HAD, Shotts, 2005
X906RHG	DAF SB220	East Lancs Myllennium	N46F	2000	Truronian, Truro, 2004
X9CCL	Mercedes-Benz Vario 614	Autobus	C26F	2000	
X751HVL	Mercedes-Benz Vario 614	Autobus	C26F	2001	
X752HVL	Mercedes-Benz Vario 614	Autobus	C26F	2001	
X753HVL	Mercedes-Benz Vario 614	Autobus	C26F	2001	
X754HVL	Mercedes-Benz Vario 614	Autobus	C26F	2001	
Y831HHE	Mercedes-Benz Vario 0814	Plaxton Cheetah	C33F	2001	Burgundy Cars, 2002
Y832HHE	Mercedes-Benz Vario 0814	Plaxton Cheetah	C25F	2001	Burgundy Cars, 2002
Y8CCL	Ayats Bravo A3E/BR1	Ayats	C57/18DT	2001	Keir, Kenmay, 2002
Y811KDP	Optare Solo M920	Optare	NC34F	2001	
Y812KDP	Optare Solo M920	Optare	NC34F	2001	
YG52DHJ	Optare Solo M850	Optare	N28F	2002	Docklands Minibuses, 2003
YG52DHK	Optare Solo M850	Optare	N28F	2002	Docklands Minibuses, 2003
YE52FGX	Optare Solo M850	Optare	N28F	2002	Zak's, Birmingham, 2005
YE52FHD	Optare Solo M850	Optare	N29F	2002	Edwards, Hailsham, 2004
YE52KPP	Optare Solo M920	Optare	N31F	2002	
YE52KPR	Optare Solo M920	Optare	N31F	2002	
YE52KPT	Optare Solo M850	Optare	N29F	2002	
YE52KPU	Optare Solo M850	Optare	N29F	2002	

Courtney's eye-catching double-deck coach is Y8CCL, an Ayats Bravo. This model is built in Spain with those for the UK featuring MAN engines. The type, without roofs, is starting to appear on open-top services in London. *Dave Heath*

Courtney's service operations use a large fleet of Solo buses, most of which are the larger M920 model. Pictured in Windsor, KX53SCV, carries the *borough bus* branding for buses operating routes in the Royal Borough of Windsor and Maidenhead unitary authority. Interestingly, sister bus KX53SBZ operates using biofuel (rapeseed oil) with one of the DAF buses also being converted. *Richard Godfrey*

CL52CCL	Optare Solo M850	Optare	N29F	2003
GU52HXM	Optare Solo M850	Optare	N29F	2003
RO03JVA	Renault Master	Frank Guy	M8L	2003
RO03JVD	Renault Master	Frank Guy	M8L	2003
RO03JVL	Renault Master	Frank Guy	M8L	2003
KX53SBY	Optare Solo M920	Optare	N33F	2004
KX53SBZ	Optare Solo M920	Optare	N33F	2004
KX53SCV	Optare Solo M920	Optare	N33F	2004
KX53SCZ	Optare Solo M920	Optare	N33F	2004
KX53SDO	Optare Solo M920	Optare	N33F	2004
KX04HRA	Optare Solo M920	Optare	N33F	2004
KX54NLA	DAF SB220	East Lancs Myllennium	N50F	2004
KX54NLC	Optare Solo M920	Optare	N33F	2004
KX54NLD	Optare Solo M920	Optare	N33F	2004
YJ54UXA	Optare Solo M920	Optare	N33F	2005
YJ05XMT	Optare Solo M920	Optare	N33F	2005
YJ05XNA	Optare Solo M920	Optare	N33F	2005
RX55AOT	Optare Solo M920	Optare	N33F	2005
SN55DUV	Alexander Dennis Enviro 300	Alexander Dennis	N60F	2005
SN55DUY	Alexander Dennis Enviro 300	Alexander Dennis	N60F	2005
SN55DVA	Alexander Dennis Enviro 300	Alexander Dennis	N60F	2005
SN55DVB	Alexander Dennis Enviro 300	Alexander Dennis	N60F	2005
	Alexander Dennis Enviro 300	East Lancs		On order
	Alexander Dennis Enviro 300	East Lancs		On order

Previous registrations:
Y8CCL   Y516SNA

Web: www.courtneycoaches.com

CRAWLEY LUXURY

J&M Brown Coaches Ltd, 32 Stephenson Way, Crawley, RH10 1TN

Reg	Chassis	Body	Type	Year	History
A4FPK	Mercedes-Benz 709D	Reeve Burgess	C15F	1979	Flightparks, Horley, 2000
HJB635K	Bedford YMQS	Dupe Dominant II	C31FT	1980	Ron, Lancing, 2002
B8JHN	Volvo B10M-61	Plaxton Paramount 3200 II	C53F	1984	Gatwick Parking, 2000
DJI654	Volvo B10M-56	Plaxton Paramount 3500 II	C47F	1985	Bell, Winterslow, 1994
LBZ2577	Volvo B10M-61	Plaxton Supreme VI	C57F	1987	Billinghurst Coaches, 2000
D718CLC	Volvo B10M-61	Plaxton Paramount 3200 III	C53F	1987	Amport & District, Thruxton, 1990
F141PHM	Volvo Citybus B10M-50	Alexander RH	B46/29D	1988	Arriva London, 2003
F143PHM	Volvo Citybus B10M-50	Alexander RH	B46/29D	1988	Arriva London, 2003
ASV440	Volvo B10M-61	Duple 340	C55F	1988	Viking Coaches, 2004
YOI8115	Volvo B10M-61	Plaxton Paramount 3200 III	C57F	1988	Reliance, Gravesend, 1993
52CLC	Volvo B10M-61	Plaxton Paramount 3200 III	C57F	1988	
UNJ408	Volvo B10M-61	Plaxton Paramount 3200 III	C53F	1988	Skills, Nottingham, 1990
CLC145	Volvo B10M-61	Plaxton Paramount 3200 III	C57F	1988	Skills, Nottingham, 1990
LUO391	Volvo B10M-61	Plaxton Paramount 3500 III	C57F	1988	Truronian, Truro, 2000
1725LJ	Volvo B10M-61	Plaxton Paramount 3500 III	C51FT	1989	Don Smiths, Murton, 1997
F894SMU	Volvo B10M-60	Plaxton Paramount 3200 III	C53F	1989	Venture, Harrow, 2003
685CLC	Volvo B10M-60	Plaxton Paramount 3500 III	C53F	1990	Harker, Sudden, 1993
784CLC	Volvo B10M-60	Plaxton Paramount 3200 III	C57F	1990	Excelsior, Bournemouth, 1990
978VYD	Volvo B10M-60	Plaxton Expressliner	C57F	1991	Selwyns, Runcorn, 2001
H952DRJ	Volvo B10M-60	Plaxton Paramount 3500 III	C51FT	1991	The Kings Ferry, Gillingham, 2005
J10CLC	Volvo B10M-60	Plaxton Paramount 3200 III	C57F	1992	Capital, West Drayton, 1998
K2CLC	Volvo B10M-60	Plaxton Paramount 3200 III	C53F	1992	Dunn-Line, Nottingham, 1995
K3CLC	Volvo B10M-60	Plaxton Paramount 3200 III	C51FT	1992	Dunn-Line, Nottingham, 1995
K11CLC	Volvo B10M-60	Plaxton Paramount 3200 III	C57F	1992	Dunn-Line, Nottingham, 1994
VIL4766	Volvo B10M-60	Plaxton Première 350	C53F	1993	Stagecoach Red & White, 2002
K5CLC	Volvo B10M-60	Plaxton Première 350	C53F	1993	Edwards, Hailsham, 1996
789CLC	Volvo B10M-60	Plaxton Première 350	C48FT	1993	Ambassador, Gt Yarmouth, 1997
L6CLC	Volvo B10M-60	Plaxton Première 320	C57F	1993	Bebb, Llantwit Fardre, 1996
L9CLC	Volvo B10M-60	Plaxton Première 350	C53F	1994	Harry Shaw, Coventry, 1999
N7CLC	Volvo B10M-62	Plaxton Première 350	C53F	1995	Bus Eireann, 1999
CL5561	Volvo B10M-62	Plaxton Première 350	C51FT	1995	Bebb, Llantwit Fardre, 1999
M144KPA	Ford Transit VE6	Ford	M8	1995	Bristow Helicopters, Redhill, 2003
N12CLC	Volvo B10M-62	Plaxton Première 350	C53F	1996	Bradford Communities, 2004
687CLC	Volvo B10M-62	Plaxton Première 350	C55F	1996	Paul Winson, Loughborough, '01
171CLC	Volvo B10M-62	Plaxton Première 350	C51FT	1997	Wallace Arnold, 2002

Now after more than fifty years of operation Crawley Luxury operates a fleet comprising mostly Volvo coaches with Plaxton bodywork. Illustrating the Première is W82JBN which has now been re-registered W30CLC.
Dave Heath

Now one of the older coaches, 978VYD started as an Expressliner and differs from the similar-looking Plaxton Paramount 3500 in several ways, including a partition behind the driver. It is seen resplendent in its current colours.
Dave Heath

P14CLC	Volvo B10M-62	Plaxton Première 350	C55F	1997	Heyfordian, Bicester, 2002
P15CLC	Volvo B10M-62	Plaxton Première 350	C55F	1997	Wallace Arnold, 2002
R20CLC	Volvo B10M-62	Plaxton Première 350	C51F	1998	Wallace Arnold, 2004
T16CLC	Volvo B10M-62	Plaxton Première 350	C48FT	1999	Wallace Arnold, 2003
T538EUB	Volvo B10M-62	Plaxton Première 350	C48FT	1999	Brian Isaac, Morriston, 2005
V22CLC	Volvo B7R	Plaxton Prima	C55F	1999	Renton, Kirknewton, 2004
W30CLC	Volvo B7R	Plaxton Prima	C55F	2000	Mayne, Manchester, 2004
W656FUM	Volvo B10M-62	Plaxton Première 350	C50FT	2000	Wallace Arnold, 2005
W40CLC	Volvo B10M-62	Plaxton Première 350	C51FT	2000	Wallace Arnold, 2005
X50CLC	Volvo B10M-62	Plaxton Première 350	C51F	2000	Wallace Arnold, 2005

Previous registrations:

52CLC	E269KRT	K3CLC	K1WED, K830KAU
171CLC	P337VWR	K5CLC	K321BTM
685CLC	G81RGG	K11CLC	K3RAD
687CLC	N227HWX	L6CLC	L45CNY
784CLC	G511EFX	L9CLC	L654XVV
789CLC	K69BKG	LBZ2577	D877EEH, BVA300, BIW3496, D778NYG
978VYD	H113OON	LUO391	F185UGL, 260ERY, F874YAF
1725LJ	F247OFP, HIL5834, F515NBR	N7CLC	95D41606(EI), N761AHP
A4FPK	E966NMK	N12CLC	N246HWX
ASV440	E152XHS, KSK291	P14CLC	P335VWR
B8JHN	B911FAM, 6750BP, B278AWV, A20GPS, B913MWV	P15CLC	P349VWR
CL5561	M37KAX	R20CLC	R416FWT
CLC145	F449HNN	T16CLC	T545EUB
D32CLC	D635WNU	UNJ408	F45GTO
D176CLC	-	V22CLC	V440EAL
D718CLC	D257HFX, 687CLC	W30CLC	W82JBN
DJI654	B190XJD	W40CLC	W612FUM
F894SMU	F894SMU, HIL5952	X50CLC	X661NWY
J10CLC	J432LLK	YDL435	-
K2CLC	K5RAD, K778KAU	YOI8115	E976NMK

Depots: Stephenson Way, Crawley and Chartwell Road, Lancing.

CROSSKEYS

A Johnson, Crosskeys Business Park, Caesar's Way, Folkestone, CT19 4AL

Reg	Chassis	Body	Config	Year	History
MJG416R	Bedford YMT	Plaxton Supreme III	C49F	1976	Ayers, Dover, 1995
UPB331S	Leyland National 10351A/1R (Volvo)		B41F	1977	Arriva Southern Counties, 2000
Q255GRW	Leyland National 2 NL116AL11/2R		B30D	1981	P&O Stena Line, Dover, 2000
G788URY	Bova FHD12.290	Bova Futura	C51FT	1989	
G792URY	Bova FHD12.290	Bova Futura	C51FT	1989	
G793URY	Bova FHD12.290	Bova Futura	C51FT	1989	
G794URY	Bova FHD12.290	Bova Futura	C51FT	1989	
G865KKY	Mercedes-Benz 609D	Whittaker	C24F	1989	
N195DYB	Bova FHD12.340	Bova Futura	C49FT	1996	Garratt, Newton Abbot, 1999
P2RDJ	Bova FHD12.340	Bova Futura	C49FT	1998	Silverline, Torbay, 2000
P3RDJ	Bova FHD12.340	Bova Futura	C49FT	1998	Silverline, Torbay, 2000
S747XYA	Bova FHD12.340	Bova Futura	C49FT	1998	
WJ51BOU	Bova FHD12.340	Bova Futura	C49FT	2002	
GK53ETZ	TransBus Javelin 12m	TransBus Profile	BC70F	2004	

Previous registrations:
Q255GRW   ?

Depot: Caesar's Way, Cheriton

Typical of the Crosskeys fleet is Bova Futura G788URY, seen here leading a sister vehicle through London traffic. The Futura first appeared in 1983 and in 2005 is still being marketed with little change. Bova is now part of the VDL Groep and the new 2006 model continues the styling. *Colin Lloyd*

CRUISERS

Cruisers Ltd, Unit M Kingsfield Business Park, Redhill, RH1 4DP

	F649PLW	Mercedes-Benz 609D	Reeve Burgess Beaver	B23F	1989	Advance, Hemel Hempstead, 91
2	M770MKO	Renault Trafic		M8L	1994	
6	M104MVR	Renault Master	Oughtred & Harrison	M8L	1994	SE Sussex Dial-a-Ride, 2003
9	L119YFH	Citroën C25D		B5L	1993	Gloucester NHS Trust, 2003
11	CHZ5934	Mercedes-Benz 711D	Autobus Classique	BC24F	1997	
13	L126YFH	Citroën C25D		B5L	1993	Southampton Care, 2003
14	CHZ5981	Mercedes-Benz Sprinter 412D		M16	1997	
16	CHZ5938	Mercedes-Benz Sprinter 614D	Autobus Nouvelle	C24F	2000	
17	CHZ5942	Mercedes-Benz Vario 0814	Plaxton Beaver 2	BC33F	2001	
18	N102BMM	LDV Convoy	LDV	M8L	1994	
19	P451FVV	LDV Convoy	LDV	M16	1996	Smith, Buntingford, 2002
20	L531BDH	Iveco Daily 49.10	Mellor	B16FL	1994	MB Coventry, 2002
21	M67UKL	Renault Trafic		M8L	1994	
22	M539PKR	Renault Trafic		M8L	1994	
23	L639HKL	Renault Trafic		M8L	1993	
24	K873GOO	Ford Transit VE6	Dormobile	B8FL	1991	Southend BC, 2003
25	M463KFJ	LDV 400	G&M	M8L	1995	private owner, 2003
26	J26YHJ	Ford Transit VE6	Dormobile	B8FL	1991	Essex CC, 2003
27	M95DLN	LDV 400	LDV	M8L	1995	LB Redbridge, 2003
28	J412AOO	Ford Transit VE6	Dormobile	B8FL	1991	Essex CC, 2003
29	J34YHJ	Ford Transit VE6	Dormobile	B8FL	1991	Essex CC, 2003
31	CHZ2948	Dennis Dart 9.8m	Wadham Stringer Portsdown	BC33FL	1994	LB Redbridge, 2003
30	T984RJE	LDV Convoy	LDV	M16	1999	Brown, Royston, 2003
32	R218DNT	LDV Convoy	LDV	M8L	1998	
33	R716KHN	Iveco Daily 49.10		M8L	1998	
34	S340NVP	LDV Convoy	LDV	M8L	1999	
35	S345NVP	LDV Convoy	LDV	M4L	1999	?, 2003
36	SF53KUP	Mercedes-Benz Vario 0814	Plaxton Beaver 2	B33F	2003	
37	CHZ2889	Mercedes-Benz 811D	Wadham Stringer Wessex	B25F	19	
38	CHZ5937	Dennis Javelin 10m	Wadham Stringer Vanguard	B40DL	1993	MoD (74KK68), 2004
39	CHZ1784	Dennis Javelin 10m	Wadham Stringer Vanguard	B48F	1993	MoD (74KK41), 2004
41	CHZ2815	Dennis Dart 9.8m	Wadham Stringer Portsdown	B37F	1995	MoD (ES05AA), 2004
42	M165NJW	Ford Transit	Ford	M8L	1995	
43	CHZ5936	Dennis Javelin 12m	Plaxton Première 320	C53F	1993	
44		Mercedes-Benz Vario 0814	Plaxton Cheetah	C33F	2005	

Previous registrations:

CHZ1784	74KK41, K807CSC		CHZ5936	N101HMC
CHZ2889	?		CHZ5938	W601KFE
CHZ2948	L297VRV		CHZ5942	Y962GYJ
CHZ5934	P911YCD		CHZ5981	R488GWV

Latterly with the MoD, CHZ2815 is a Dennis Dart with Wadham Stringer Portsdown bodywork. *Dave Heath*

EASTBOURNE BUSES

Eastbourne Buses Ltd, Birch Road, Eastbourne, BN23 6PD

35	S835DPN		Dennis Dart SLF		Plaxton Pointer 2		N36F	1998		
36	T936WWV		Dennis Dart SLF		Caetano Compass		N38F	1999		
37	T937AYJ		DAF SB220		Ikarus Citibus		N43F	1999		
38-47			Optare Excel L1150		Optare		N42F	1997	Reading Bus, 2001-02	
38	R206DKG	40	R208DKG	42	R210DKG	44	R212DKG		46	R214DKG
39	R207DKG	41	R209DKG	43	R211DKG	45	R213DKG		47	R215DKG
48	T467EGT		Dennis Dart SLF		Plaxton Pointer 2		N33F	1999	Epsom Buses, 2002	
49	T468EGT		Dennis Dart SLF		Plaxton Pointer 2		N33F	1999	Epsom Buses, 2002	
50-55			DAF SB120		Wrightbus Cadet		N34F	2002		
50	GX02WXS	52	GX02WXU	53	GX02WXV	54	GX02WXW		55	GX02WXY
51	GX02WXT									
56-61			VDL Bus SB120		Wrightbus Merit		N39F	2004		
56	GX04LWR	58	GX04LWT	59	GX04LWU	60	GX04LWV		61	GX04LWW
57	GX04LWS									

117	L417UUF	DAF SB220	Ikarus CitiBus	B48F	1994	
118	N518LUF	DAF SB220	Ikarus CitiBus	B49F	1995	
119	P719FDY	DAF SB220	Ikarus CitiBus	B49F	1997	
120	R720LDY	DAF SB220	Ikarus CitiBus	B49F	1997	
121	J221FUF	Dennis Dart 9.8m	Wadham Stringer Portsdown	B43F	1992	
122	J122FUF	Dennis Dart 9.8m	Wadham Stringer Portsdown	B43F	1992	
125	P905PWW	DAF SB220	Northern Counties Paladin	B49F	1996	Airlinks, West Drayton, 2002
126	P906PWW	DAF SB220	Northern Counties Paladin	B49F	1996	Airlinks, West Drayton, 2002
127	P910PWW	DAF SB220	Northern Counties Paladin	B49F	1996	Airlinks, West Drayton, 2002
128	M528DPN	DAF SB220	Ikarus CitiBus	B49F	1995	
129	M529DPN	DAF SB220	Ikarus CitiBus	B49F	1995	
130	M530DPN	DAF SB220	Ikarus CitiBus	B49F	1995	
131	N631CDY	DAF SB220	Ikarus CitiBus	B49F	1996	
132	N26FWU	DAF SB220	Northern Counties Paladin	B49F	1995	Southampton, 1996
134	N27FWU	DAF SB220	Northern Counties Paladin	B49F	1995	Southampton, 1996
257	E857DPN	Leyland Olympian ONCL10/1RZ	Northern Counties	B47/30F	1988	
258	E858DPN	Leyland Olympian ONCL10/1RZ	Northern Counties	B47/30F	1988	
269	M441CCD	DAF DB250	Northern Counties Palatine II	B47/30F	1994	

Eastbourne is one of just seventeen municipally-owned bus fleets remaining in the country. The bus fleet is currently dominated by DAF products with the latest being VDL Bus SB120s. Bodywork is by Wrightbus which when badged as the Merit is the Cadet supplied through Volvo. Shown is 57, GX04LWS.
Richard Godfrey

Six Optare Spectra double-decks are operated by Eastbourne which were latterly with Reading. Based on the DAF DB250, 272, R872MDY, is seen in the town centre. *Dave Heath*

270-275			DAF DB250		Optare Spectra		B48/29F	1998	Reading Buses
270	R870MDY	272	R872MDY	273	R873MDY	274	R874MDY	275	R875MDY
271	R871MDY								

276	G362YUR	Leyland Olympian ONCL10/1RZ	Alexander RL	B47/30F	1989	Blue Bus, Bolton, 2004		
277	G363YUR	Leyland Olympian ONCL10/1RZ	Alexander RL	B47/30F	1989	Blue Bus, Bolton, 2004		
302	YE52FGZ	Optare Solo M850	Optare	N29F	2002	Zak's, Birmingham, 2005		
325	L325YDU	Mercedes-Benz 709D	Alexander Sprint	B23F	1994	Stagecoach, 2004		
330	L330YKV	Mercedes-Benz 709D	Alexander Sprint	B23F	1994	Stagecoach, 2004		
900	V200RAD	Scania L94IB	Irizar InterCentury	C53F	2000	Radley, Brigg, 2004		
905	R115GNW	DAF SB3000	Ikarus Blue Danube	C53F	1998			
906	X498AHE	Scania L94IB4	Irizar InterCentury	C53F	2000	Bus Eireann, 2005		
931	AHZ1253	Scania K113CRB	Van Hool Alizée	C55F	1988	Calne Coaches, 2005		
950	P144GHE	Scania K113CRB	Irizar Century 12.35	C49FT	1999	Blue Iris, Nailsea, 2003		
951	S51KNW	Scania L94IB4	Irizar Century 12.35	C49FT	1999	Eddie Brown, Harrogate, 2003		
952	S551KNW	Scania L94IB4	Irizar Century 12.35	C49FT	1999	Eddie Brown, Harrogate, 2003		
953	W343MKY	Scania L124IB4	Irizar Century	C49FT	2000	Buddens, Romsey, 2005		
954	GB04EBL	Scania K114EB4	Irizar Century	C49FT	2004			

Heritage vehicles:
11	AHC411	AEC Regal III 6821A	East Lancashire	BC30R	1950	
282	DHC782E	Leyland Titan PD2A/30	East Lancashire	H32/28R	1967	

Ancillary vehicles:
116	L416UNJ	DAF SB220	Ikarus CitiBus	TV	1994	
990	Q424CHH	Dennis Javelin	WS Coachbuilders Vanguard 2	TV	1995	MoD, 2005

Previous registration:
AHZ1253   E442JAR, 160EBK, E663YDT   Q424CHH   N152OJD

Named buses: 57, The Marshmallow; 95 Westham Flyer; 60, Anderida; 61, Pevensey Leveller.
Web: www.eastbournebuses.co.uk

EASTONWAYS

Eastonways Ltd, Manston Road, Ramsgate, CT12 6HJ

	Reg	Chassis	Body	Type	Year	History
	SIB6713	Leyland National 1051/1R (6LXB)	East Lancs Greenway(1992)	B41F	1974	Arriva Southern Counties, 2004
	BYX247V	MCW Metrobus DR101/12	MCW	B43/29F	1980	Go-Ahead Northern, 2003
	BYX290V	MCW Metrobus DR101/12	MCW	B43/28F	1980	Arriva The Shires, 2003
w	VCA461W	Bristol VRT/SL3/6LXB	Eastern Coach Works	B43/31F	1980	Arriva Southern Counties, 1999
	JIL8213	MCW MetroBus DR102/29	Alexander RH	B45/31F	1982	Kingstons, Hockley, 2002
	A640BCN	MCW Metrobus DR102/45	MCW	B46/31F	1984	Go-Ahead Northern, 2004
	B240XHM	Volkswagen Caravelle	Volkswagen	M8	1985	private owner, 2003
w	BAZ7296	Leyland Tiger TRCTL11/3RH	Berkhof Everest 370	C49FT	1986	Horsham Buses, 1998
	H670ATN	Toyota Coaster HB31R	Caetano Optimo	C21F	1990	Luker, Crondall, 1999
	H120THE	Dennis Dart 8.5m	Plaxton Pointer	B28F	1991	Arriva London, 2002
	H127THE	Dennis Dart 8.5m	Plaxton Pointer	B28F	1991	Arriva London, 2002
w	H169WWT	Optare MetroRider MR03	Optare	B26F	1991	Lancaster Bus, 2001
	J974JNL	Optare MetroRider MR03	Optare	B25F	1991	Arriva Southern Counties, 2000
	J975JNL	Optare MetroRider MR03	Optare	B25F	1991	Arriva Southern Counties, 2000
	KDZ5803	Dennis Dart 9m	Wright Handybus	B34F	1991	Stagecoach Manchester, 2003
	K871ANT	Dennis Dart 9.8m	Marshall C37	B40F	1992	Coastal, Newick, 2005
	K576MGT	Dennis Dart 9m	Plaxton Pointer	B32F	1993	London Central, 2003
	K990CBO	Dennis Dart 8.5m	Wright Handybus	B29F	1993	Stagecoach Red & White, 2004
	K987SCU	Dennis Dart 9.8m	Wright Handybus	B40F	1993	Go-Ahead Northern, 2003
	L838MWT	Optare MetroRider MR07	Optare	B31F	1993	Arriva Southern Counties, 2001
	L835CDG	Volvo B6 9.9m	Alexander Dash	B40F	1994	Stagecoach Red & White, 2004
	L933ABJ	LDV 400	LDV	M16	1994	Caldwell, Largs, 2003
	P290MLD	Dennis Dart 9.8m	Plaxton Pointer	B39F	1996	Metroline, 2004
	Y203JPM	LDV Convoy	LDV	M16	2001	private owner, 2004
	AK52LWF	LDV Convoy	LDV	M16L	2002	private owner, 2005
	YX03OUL	LDV Convoy	LDV	M16	2003	private owner, 2005

Previous registrations:

BAZ7296	C128PPE	K990CBO	NDZ3145
JIL8213	DEM761Y	SIB6713	UPE215M
K871ANT	K871ANT, 210WVK		

Web: www.eastonways.demon.co.uk

Eastonways operates on the Isle of Thanet and is represented here by Wright-bodied Dart K987SCU which was pictured while operating one of the Island Hoppa routes. This network of ten routes covers the whole of Thanet linking the various villages. *Martin Smith*

EDWARD THOMAS & SONS

IE Thomas, 442 Chessington Road, West Ewell, KT19 9EJ

Reg	Chassis	Body	Seats	Year	History
NUW672Y	Leyland Titan TNLXB2RR	Leyland	B44/32F	1982	Stagecoach London, 2003
HIL4017	Leyland Tiger TRCTL11/2R	Plaxton Supreme V	C53F	1982	
H312HPF	Leyland Tiger TRCTL11/3R	Van Hool Alizée H(1990)	C53F	1983	MoD (chassis only), 1989
HIL3207	Leyland Tiger TRCTL11/3R	Plaxton Paramount 3200	C53F	1983	
ETO585	Leyland Tiger TRCTL11/3R	Plaxton Paramount 3500	C50FT	1983	A & D, Worcester Park, 1997
435UPD	Leyland Tiger TRCTL11/3R	Plaxton Paramount 3500	C49FT	1983	Langham, Wellingborough, 1998
576DXC	Leyland Tiger TRCTL11/3R	Plaxton Paramount 3200	C53F	1983	Frames Rickards, Brentford, 1989
TJI8780	Leyland Tiger TRCTL11/2R	Plaxton Paramount 3200	C49F	1983	Fowler, Holbeach Drove, 2004
EBF806Y	Leyland Tiger TRCTL11/3R	Plaxton Paramount 3200	C57F	1983	Bassetts, Tittensow, 2003
AEZ1360	Leyland Tiger TRCTL11/3R	Plaxton Paramount 3200	C53F	1984	Beckenham Coaches, 2005
A777RBV	Leyland Tiger TRCTL11/3R	Duple Caribbean	C53F	1984	Abbots, Blackpool, 2001
TIL8272	Leyland Tiger TRCTL11/3R	Plaxton Paramount 3200	C53F	1984	
XJI5691	Leyland Tiger TRCTL11/3R	Plaxton Paramount 3500	C53F	1984	George Young, Newent, 2001
SJI8094	Leyland Tiger TRCTL11/3RH	Plaxton Paramount 3500	C55F	1984	Lacey, East Ham, 1999
B288KPF	Leyland Tiger TRCTL11/3RH	Plaxton Paramount 3200 IIE	C53F	1985	Country Liner, Guildford, 2002
C377PCD	Leyland Tiger TRCTL11/3RH	Plaxton Paramount 3500 II	C51F	1986	Nostagiabus, Mitcham, 2002
267PPH	Leyland Tiger TRCTL11/3R	Plaxton Paramount 3200 II	C53F	1986	
D982JJD	Leyland Tiger TRCTL11/3LZ	Plaxton Derwent 2	B70F	1986	MoD (82KF34), 2001
TVS986	Volvo B10M-61	Van Hool Alizée	C53F	1986	Bookham Coaches, 2003
S757CKO	Volvo B10M-62	Plaxton Première 350	C53F	1998	Sunray, Worcester Park, 2005
160CLT	Volvo B10M-62	Plaxton Première 350	C46FT	1995	Guilchrist, Quarrington Hill, 2002
N955DWJ	Volvo B10M-62	Plaxton Première 350	C53F	1996	Lakeland, Hurst Green, 2003
P350VWR	Volvo B10M-62	Plaxton Première 350	C50F	1997	Wallace Arnold, 2002
R403FWT	Volvo B10M-62	Plaxton Première 350	C48FT	1998	Wallace Arnold, 2004
R413FWT	Volvo B10M-62	Plaxton Première 350	C46FT	1998	Wallace Arnold, 2003
R414FWT	Volvo B10M-62	Plaxton Première 350	C46FT	1998	Wallace Arnold, 2004

Previous registrations:

160CLT	M43KAX		H312HPF	20KB76, FSU183
267PPH	C913UPB		HIL3207	APJ445Y
435UPD	FNM857Y, JEF61, WWE96Y, HIL8405...,		HIL4017	UPE755X
	...WWE283Y, WCT502, ODO837Y		R403FWT	R403FWT, 4WA
576DXC	A518LPP		SJI8094	82LUP, A828MRW, MJI7861, A170NAC
AEZ1360	B253AMG, 524DXH		TIL8272	A51GPG
C377PCD	C377PCD, PCN762, VLT71		TVS986	D238MKX
ETO585	WWA303Y, 3063VC, GAC97Y		XJI5691	A586WNY, LIB7134

Edward Thomas's Titan, NUW672Y, is principally used on school duties. It is seen in Ewell. *Dave Heath*

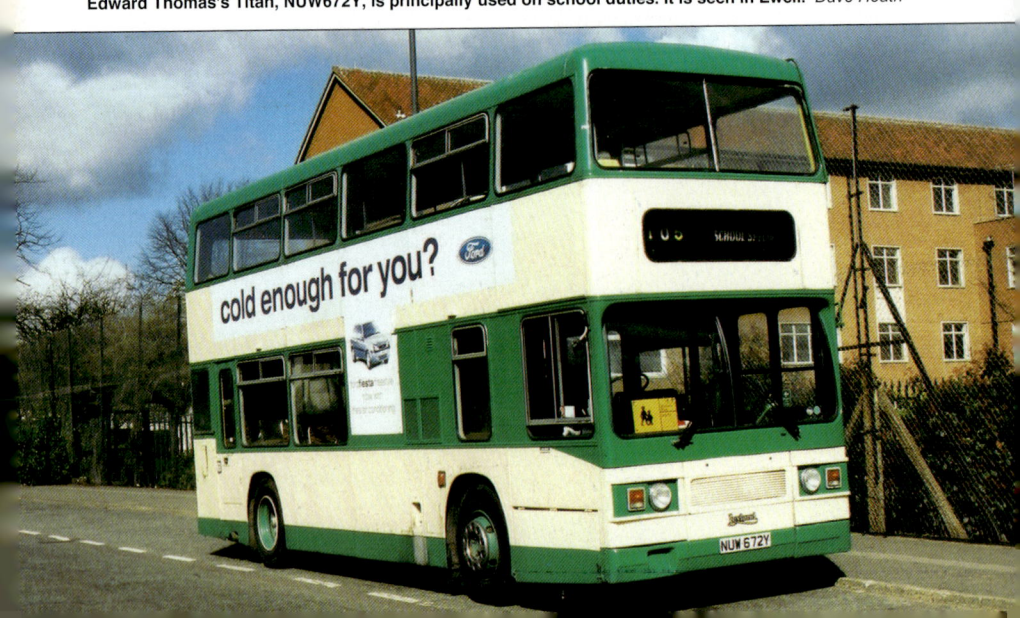

EMPRESS OF HASTINGS

Empress Coaches Ltd, 10/11 St Margaret's Road, St Leonards on-Sea, TN37 6EH

36	H389KPY	CVE Omni	CVE	BC21F	1990	Patten, Hastings, 1998
37	H390KPY	CVE Omni	CVE	BC21F	1990	Patten, Hastings, 1998
57	LIB1066	Ford Transit VE6	Devon Conversions	BC16FL	1995	Lewes Community, 2001
58	KIW1066	Mercedes-Benz 709D	Plaxton Beaver	BC25F	1992	First Potteries, 2002
60	WIL1066	Mercedes-Benz 814D	Autobus Classique	BC33F	1994	Dawson, Heywood, 2003
63	UG1066	Ford Transit VE6	Ford	M8	1996	Parkhurst Taxis, 2004
64	JIL1066	Ford Transit	Dormobile	BC16FL	1998	MB Wakefield, 2004
65	FAZ1066	Ford Transit	Chassis Developments	BC16F	1998	Bexhill Community, 2004
66	JAZ1066	Mercedes-Benz 709D	Alexander Sprint	BC25F	1994	Stagecoach, 2004
67	PAZ1066	Iveco TurboDaily 59.12	Bedwas	BC24F	1996	LB Wandsworth, 2005
68	CAZ1066	Mercedes-Benz 614	Mellor	BC16F	1998	Mike Halford, Bridport, 2005
69	GAZ1066	Dennis Javelin 10m	Wadham Stringer Vanguard II	BC41F	19	MoD, 2005

Previous registrations:

CAZ1066	R128AWF		KIW1066	J430WFA
FAZ1066	T361AFG		KLZ1066	-
GAZ1066	?		LIB1066	M965RKJ
H389KPY	H389KPY, CAZ1066		PAZ1066	P639ROU
H390KPY	H390KPY, KLZ1066		UG1066	N183WMS
JAZ1066	L317YDU		WIL1066	M351TDO, BHZ1066
JIL1066	R46JUB			

Web: www.empressofhastings.co.uk

Empress of Hastings has now moved from coaches to an all-minibus operation based in St Leonards-on-Sea and specialising in vehicles with disabled and wheelchair access. Representing the fleet, which continues a tradition of using 1066 index marks, is LIB1066, a Devon Conversions-bodied Ford Transit. *Martin Smith*

EMSWORTH & DISTRICT

Emsworth & District Motor Services Ltd, Bus Garage, Clovelly Road, Emsworth, PO10 7NS

OUC45R	Leyland Fleetline FE30AGR	MCW	B44/32F	1976	West Kingsdown Coaches, 1999
TND409X	DAF MB200	Plaxton Supreme IV	C51DL	1982	Hatts, Foxham, 2002
NYH161Y	Bedford YNT	Plaxton Supreme V Express	C45DL	1983	Netley Waterside Home, 1996
A829SUL	Leyland Titan TNTL11/2RR	Leyland	B44/26D	1983	Stagecoach London, 2001
A883SUL	Leyland Titan TNTL11/2RR	Leyland	B44/32F	1983	Stagecoach London, 2001
TJI8792	Van Hool T815	Van Hool Alicron	C49FT	1983	Springall, Grimsby, 1997
UOI2679	Van Hool T815	Van Hool Alicron	C49FT	1984	Morgan, Bristol, 1999
A405BHL	Van Hool T815	Van Hool Alicron	C51FT	1984	McDermot, Barlestone, 1999
A889FPM	Bedford YMT	Plaxton Derwent 2	B55F	1984	Tillingbourne, Cranleigh, 1996
B999CUS	Bedford YMPS	Plaxton Paramount 3200	C35F	1985	Sussex Country Tours, 1998
C8LEA	Mercedes-Benz Vario O814	Autobus Classique	C29F	1986	Palmer, Southall, 2001
D602RGJ	Bedford YMT	Plaxton Derwent 2	B53F	1987	Metrobus, 1999
E459ANC	Mercedes-Benz 609D	Made-to-Measure	BC24F	1988	Blue Lake, Chichester, 2000
G505XLO	Leyland Swift LBM6T/2RA	Reeve Burgess Harrier	B41F	1989	Parfitts, Rhondda, 1998
G727RGA	Leyland Swift LBM6T/2RA	Reeve Burgess Harrier	B39F	1989	Arriva Cymru, 2001
G39TGW	Dennis Dart 8.5m	Carlyle Dartline	B34F	1990	Tilley, Wainhouse Corner, 2003
G767CDU	Leyland Swift LBM6T/2RA	Reeve Burgess Harrier	B39F	1990	Stagecoach Ribble, 1999
H36YCW	Leyland Swift ST2R44C97A4	Reeve Burgess Harrier	B39F	1990	Stagecoach Ribble, 1998
H37YCW	Leyland Swift ST2R44C97A4	Reeve Burgess Harrier	B39F	1990	Stagecoach Ribble, 1998
H226EDX	Optare MetroRider MR01	Optare	B31F	1990	Ipswich Buses, 2001
H421GPM	Mercedes-Benz 709D	Dormobile Routemaker	B27F	1990	Tillingbourne, Cranleigh
H201DVM	Van Hool T815	Van Hool Alizée	C53F	1991	Warners, Tewkesbuy, 2005
H204DVM	Van Hool T815	Van Hool Alizée	C49FTL	1991	Chambers, Bures, 2002
J504GCD	Dennis Dart 9.8m	Alexander Dash	B41F	1992	Stagecoach South, 2004
J539GCD	Dennis Dart 9.8m	Alexander Dash	B41F	1992	Stagecoach South, 2004
L452UEB	Dennis Dart 9.8m	Marshall C27	B40F	1993	Town & Around, Folkestone, 2003
M3KFC	MAN 11.190	Berkhof Excellence 1000L	C33FT	1994	AR, Hemel Hempstead, 2003

Previous registrations:
A405BHL   A991DJS, 4672NT
H201DVM   H201DVM, 315ASV

UOI2679   A102OYG, WPT43
TJI8792   VFT203Y, LIB5442

Named Vehicles: B999CUS *Maid Marian,* OLJ192W *Lord of the Ems,* TJI8792 *Manfred;* ODL525X *Earl Mountbatten of Burma.*
Web: www.emsworth&district.co.uk

The Emsworth fleet contains Reeve Burgess Harrier H37YCW. New to Hyndburn, it was one of five Leyland Swifts to be taken into the Stagecoach group with that operation. *Martin Smith*

FARLEIGH COACHES

Carosa Ltd, St Peters Works, Hall Road, Wouldham, Rochester, ME1 3XL

HUD479S	Bristol VRT/SL3/6LXB	Eastern Coach Works	B43/27D	1977	Stagecoach Midland Red, 1999
YBO16T	Leyland Leopard PSU3E/4R	East Lancashire	B51F	1979	Stagecoach Midland Red, 2001
LFR873X	Leyland National NL106L11/1R		B44F	1982	Stagecoach Cheltenham, 2001
NUW595Y	Leyland Titan TNLXB2RR	Leyland	B44/27F	1982	West Kent Buses, 2005
G102NGN	Volvo Citybus B10M-50	Northern Counties	BC45/35D	1989	Go-Ahead London, 2005
H435GVL	Setra S215HR	Setra Rational	C53F	1991	Boon's, Boreham, 2000

Recent changes at Farleigh Coaches have seen the fleet reduce to just six vehicles. Pictured at its base in Wouldham, YBO16T is an East Lancs-bodied Leopard.
Richard Godfrey

Now the oldest vehicle with Emsworth & District, OUC45R was one of the DMS-class of buses with London Transport. The Leyland Fleetline has since been converted to single-entrance.
Dave Heath

FLEETWING

Fleetwing Travel, 36 Martlands Ind Est, Smarts Heath Lane, Woking, GU22 0RQ

LIL2180	Leyland National 11351/1R	East Lancs Greenway (1995)	B49F	1975	Countryliner, Guildford, 2005
NIW6509	Leyland National 11351A/1R	East Lancs Greenway ('93)	B49F	1977	Frimley, Aldershot, 2004
NIW6510	Leyland National 2 NL116AL11/2R	East Lancs Greenway ('93)	B49F	1982	Frimley, Aldershot, 2004
NIW6512	Leyland National 2 NL116AL11/2R	East Lancs Greenway ('93)	B49F	1982	Frimley, Aldershot, 2004
J739CWT	Volvo B10M-60	Plaxton Première 350	C48FT	1992	Frimley, Aldershot, 2004
J742CWT	Volvo B10M-60	Plaxton Première 350	C48FT	1992	Frimley, Aldershot, 2004
J743CWT	Volvo B10M-60	Plaxton Première 350	C48FT	1992	Shearer, Mayford, 2004
J744CWT	Volvo B10M-60	Plaxton Première 350	C48FT	1992	Shearer, Mayford, 2004
J745CWT	Volvo B10M-60	Plaxton Première 350	C48FT	1992	Shearer, Mayford, 2004
M775XHW	Dennis Javelin 12m	Wadham Stringer Vanguard III	BC70F	1995	Frimley, Aldershot, 2004
M778XHW	Dennis Javelin 12m	Wadham Stringer Vanguard III	BC70F	1995	Frimley, Aldershot, 2004
M780XHW	Dennis Javelin 12m	Wadham Stringer Vanguard III	BC70F	1995	Frimley, Aldershot, 2004
M251XWS	Dennis Javelin 12m	Wadham Stringer Vanguard III	BC70F	1995	Frimley, Aldershot, 2004
N359WHH	Volvo B10M-62	Plaxton Première 350	C49FT	1995	Shearer, Mayford, 2004
P423HNT	Volvo B10M-62	Plaxton Première 350	C49FT	1997	Shearer, Mayford, 2004
P943EBB	Volvo B10M-62	Plaxton Première 350	C49FT	1997	Shearer, Mayford, 2004
P943YSB	Mercedes-Benz 814D	Mellor	BC33F	1997	Shearer, Mayford, 2004
W485ASB	Volvo B10M-62	Plaxton Panther	C53F	2000	Shearer, Mayford, 2004
W487ASB	Volvo B10M-62	Plaxton Panther	C53F	2000	Shearer, Mayford, 2004
W488ASB	Volvo B10M-62	Plaxton Panther	C53F	2000	Shearer, Mayford, 2004
W492ASB	Volvo B10M-62	Plaxton Panther	C53F	2000	Shearer, Mayford, 2004
BU51AYC	Mercedes-Benz Sprinter 614	Excel	C24F	2001	Shearer, Mayford, 2004

Previous registrations:

M251XWS	16RN63, M514LWN		NIW6512	FCA6X
M775XHW	16RN64, M374NJW		P423HNT	7025RU
M778XHW	00RN39, M180ATR		P943EBB	P9CLA
M780XHW	64RN28, M604GGD		W485ASB	HSK654
NIL2180	KPA375P		W487ASB	HSK655
NIW6509	TEL491R		W492ASB	HSK659
NIW6510	FCA8X			

Depots: Smarts Heath Lane, Woking and Hollybush Lane, Aldershot.

One of four Plaxton Panthers acquired with the Shearer operation in 2004, W488ASB, is seen with its new names.
Dave Heath

GRAYLINE

Grayline Coaches (Hartwool) Ltd, Station Approach, Bicester, OX26 6HU

Reg	Chassis	Body	Seats	Year	History
YPB834T	Bedford YMT	Plaxton Supreme IV	C53F	1979	Sidhu, Bicester, 1996
SPV860	Bova FHD12.290	Bova Futura	C55F	1990	
H536XGK	Dennis Dart 8.5m	Plaxton Pointer	B28F	1991	London General, 2004
K623PGO	Dennis Dart 9m	Plaxton Pointer	B35F	1992	Metrobus, Crawley, 2004
947CBK	Dennis Javelin 12m	Caetano Algarve II	C53F	1994	Supreme, Coventry, 1997
MJI1679	Mercedes-Benz 811D	Plaxton Beaver	B31F	1994	Glyn Williams, Crosskeys, 2001
MJI1678	Mercedes-Benz 811D	Plaxton Beaver	B31F	1995	Glyn Williams, Crosskeys, 2001
98CLJ	Scania K113CRB	Van Hool Alizée	C53FT	1997	
R524EUD	MAN 11.220	Berkhof Excellence 1000 Midi	C35F	1998	
940HFJ	MAN 24.400	Noge Catalan 370	C53FT	1998	
T285CGU	Iveco EuroRider 391E.12.35	Beulas Stergo ε	C53F	1999	Woottens, Henlow, 2003
W358EOL	Mercedes-Benz O404-15R	Hispano Vita	C53F	2000	
Y141HWE	MAN 18.350	Neoplan Transliner	C49FT	2001	Hancock, Saltney Green, 2004
OV51OOA	Optare Solo M920	Optare	N29	2001	
OV51OOB	Optare Solo M920	Optare	N29	2001	
OV51OOC	Optare Solo M920	Optare	N29	2001	
LV02LLA	Irisbus EuroRider 391E.12.35	Beulas Stergo ε	C53F	2002	Redwing, Herne Hill, 2005

Previous registrations:

98CLJ	P159FJO		MJI1678	M528KTG, M1GWT, M528KTG
940HFJ	R621VNN		MJI1679	M242JHB
947CBK	L195YDU		SPV860	G441WFC
K623PGO	CMN108L		Y141HWE	Y141HWE, M2WMT

Web: www.grayline.co.uk

Three MAN coaches are currently operated by Grayline including R524EUD which carries the shorter Berkhof Excellence 1000 body. Berkhof is now also part of Dutch VDL Groep. *Dave Heath*

HAM'S TRAVEL

DW PP & J Ham, The White House, London Road, Flimwell, Wadhurst, TN5 7PL

Reg	Chassis	Body	Seating	Year	History
WYV64T	Leyland Titan TNLXB2RRSp	Park Royal	B44/32F	1979	Eastonways, Ramsgate, 1998
CUL162V	Leyland Titan TNLXB2RRSp	Park Royal	B44/32F	1980	Eastonways, Ramsgate, 1998
KYV312X	Leyland Titan TNLXB2RR	Leyland	B44/32F	1981	London Central, 1998
NHM465X	Leyland Titan TNLXB2RR	Leyland	B44/32F	1981	Driver Express, Horsham, 1999
KYV432X	Leyland Titan TNLXB2RR	Leyland	B44/32F	1982	Metroline, 1999
KYV481X	Leyland Titan TNLXB2RR	Leyland	B44/32F	1982	Metroline, 1999
A305MKJ	Leyland Tiger TRCTL11/3R	Plaxton Paramount 3200	C57F	1983	
A933SYE	Leyland Titan TNLXB2RR	Leyland	B44/32F	1984	London Central, 1998
HAM496N	Volvo B10M-61	Van Hool Astral	C47/11FT	1984	Ferris, Senghenydd, 1988
B522HAM	Volvo B10M-61	Plaxton Paramount 3200 III	C57F	1985	Crawley Luxury, 2002
B542HAM	Volvo B10M-61	Plaxton Paramount 3200 II	C53F	1986	Davis Coaches, Hawkhurst, 1997
C521DND	Volvo B10M-61	Plaxton Paramount 3200 II	C53F	1986	Davis Coaches, Hawkhurst, 1997
E274HRY	Volvo B10M-61	Plaxton Paramount 3500 III	C51FT	1988	Bowens, Birmingham, 1998
F865LCU	MCW MetroRider MF158	MCW	B31F	1988	Guide Friday, Stratford, 2002
F254HAM	Volvo B10M-60	Van Hool Alizée	C51FT	1989	Amport & District, Thruxton, 1993
MIB5354	Leyland Tiger TRCLT10/3ARZA	Plaxton Paramount 3500 III	C53F	1989	Wimco, Mitcham, 2005
B518HAM	Volvo B10M-60	Plaxton Paramount 3200 III	C53F	1989	Williams, Witney, 2002
LOI8643	Volvo B10M-60	Plaxton Paramount 3500 III	C49FT	1990	Leon, Stafford, 2000
H124THE	Dennis Dart 8.5m	Plaxton Pointer	B28F	1991	Arriva London, 2003
J229HGY	Dennis Dart 9m	Plaxton Pointer	B35F	1992	Metrobus, Crawley, 2004
B44HAM	Volvo B10M-60	Plaxton Première 350	C49FT	1992	Stagecoach Midland Red, 2000
L6HAM	Volvo B10M-62	Jonckheere Deauville 50	C49FT	1994	Redwing, Camberwell, 1997
M84MY	Volvo Olympian YN2RC16Z4	Alexander Royale	B45/29F	1995	National Express, 2004
M91MY	Volvo Olympian YN2RC16Z4	Alexander Royale	B45/29F	1995	National Express, 2004
N50HAM	Volvo B10M-62	Van Hool Alizée HE	C49FT	1995	Inland Travel, Flimwell, 2001
N1HAM	Volvo B10M-62	Van Hool Alizée HE	C51FT	1996	
N11HAM	DAF SB3000	Berkhof Excellence 1000LD	C51FT	1996	
R16HAM	Volvo B10M-62	Berkhof Axial 50	C51FT	1998	Limebourne, Battersea, 1999
S3HAM	Volvo B10M-62	Van Hool Alizée II	C51FT	1998	
S4HAM	Volvo B10M-62	Berkhof Axial 50	C51FT	1999	

Hams Travel's attractive colours scheme is seen here on recent arrival DW54HAM, a Mercedes-Benz Vario with Italian-built Sitcar Beluga bodywork. It is seen passing through Parliament Square in London. *Colin Lloyd*

The East Lancs Vyking double-deck has started to appear with several small independent operators who require low-floor access double-decks to meet contract needs. Hams Travel now operates three 7-litre Volvo B7TL, a model which will be augmented by the more powerful 9-litre B9TL in 2006. MC52HAM is seen in Margate bus station. *Martin Smith*

T70HAM	Volvo B10M-62	Plaxton Excalibur	C53F	1999	Bus Eireann, 2003
T80HAM	Volvo B10M-62	Plaxton Excalibur	C53F	1999	Bus Eireann, 2003
T90HAM	Volvo B10M-62	Plaxton Excalibur	C53F	1999	Bus Eireann, 2003
W5HAM	Volvo B10M-62	Berkhof Axial 50	C49FT	2000	
R17HAM	LDV Convoy	LDV	M16	2000	private owner, 2002
X8HAM	Scania N113DRB	East Lancs Cityzen	B47/31F	2000	
X7HAM	Volvo B12M	Berkhof Axial 50	C49FT	2001	
X9HAM	Volvo B10M-62	Berkhof Axial 50	C51FT	2001	
Y10HAM	LDV Convoy	LDV	M16	2001	
DW52HAM	Volvo B7TL	East Lancs Vyking	NC46/32F	2003	
MC52HAM	Volvo B7TL	East Lancs Vyking	NC46/32F	2003	
PA52HAM	Scania K114IB4	Irizar InterCentury	C57F	2003	
EU03XOJ	LDV Convoy	LDV	M16	2003	
WR53VYW	Ford Transit	Ford	M8	2004	
DW54HAM	Mercedes-Benz Vario O815	Sitcar Beluga	C33F	2004	
DW05HAM	Volvo B7TL	East Lancs Vyking	NC49/31F	2005	

Previous registrations:

B44HAM	J446HDS	MIB5454	F634UBL
B142AKN	B420CMC, B20FUG, B44HAM	N50HAM	N750CYA
B518HAM	F424DUG	N60HAM	N54MDW, A10WHF
B522HAM	B270TLJ, 171CLC	NHM465X	KYV377X, 361CLT
B542HAM	C515DND	R16HAM	R927ULA
B552HAM	-	R17HAM	W187TNG
F254HAM	F263NUT	T70HAM	99D41332, T266UCH
HAM496N	A548XUH	T80HAM	99D41317, T425UCH
L6HAM	L757YGE	T90HAM	99D41329, T308UCH
LOI8643	H330JVT	WYV64T	WYV64T, LIL2515

Depots: London Road, Flimwell and Cranbrook Road, Benenden.

HELLYERS

Hellyers of Fareham Ltd, Fort Fareham Business Park, Newgate Lane, Fareham, P014 1AH8

Reg	Chassis	Body	Type	Year	History
LVS441V	Leyland Leopard PSU3E/4R	Plaxton Supreme IV	C53F	1980	
LVS442V	Leyland Leopard PSU3E/4R	Plaxton Supreme IV	C53F	1980	
IAZ4816	Leyland Tiger TRCTL11/3R	Plaxton Supreme V	C51F	1981	
TJI4926	Leyland Tiger TRCTL11/3R	Van Hool Alizée	C50FT	1986	
A16HOF	Volvo B10M-60	Plaxton Expressliner	C46FT	1990	Dorset Travel, 1999
A20HOF	Scania K93CRB	Plaxton Première 320	C53F	1992	Shearings, 1999
A12 HOF	Volvo B10M-60	Plaxton Excalibur	C49FT	1993	Dodsworth, Boroughbridge, 1999
M477UYA	Bova FLD12.270	Bova Futura	C53F	1994	Cowdrey, Gosport, 2001
M214UYD	Bova FLD12.270	Bova Futura	C57F	1995	Cowdrey, Gosport, 2001
A8HOF	Volvo B10M-62	Jonckheere Deauville 45	C49FT	1995	Whitelaw's, Stonehouse, 1999
M664KVU	Volvo B10M-62	Van Hool Alizée	C46FT	1995	Shearings, 2002
B10HOF	Volvo B10M-62	Van Hool Alizée	C46FT	1995	Shearings, 2002
A18HOF	Scania K113CRB	Van Hool Alizée HE	C49FT	1996	Harry Shaw, Coventry, 1999
A19HOF	Scania K113TRB	Irizar Century 12.35	C49FT	1996	Harry Shaw, Coventry, 1999
A13HOF	Volvo B10M-62	Plaxton Première 350	C F	1996	Whitelaw's, Stonehouse, 1999
P49JJU	Volvo B10M-62	Plaxton Première 350	C49FT	1997	Bus Eireann, 2002
A17HOF	Scania K113CRB	Van Hool Alizée	C49F	1997	
P953DNR	Toyota Coaster BB50R	Caetano Optimo IV	C21F	1997	
P933KYC	Bova FLD12.300	Bova Futura	C53F	1997	Cowdrey, Gosport, 2001
A4HFY	Bova FLD10.340	Bova Futura	C36F	1997	Cowdrey, Gosport, 2001
A6HFN	Bova FLD12.340	Bova Futura	C49FT	1998	Cowdrey, Gosport, 2001
R146COR	Dennis Dart SLF	Plaxton Pointer 2	N39F	1998	

Recent arrivals with Hellyers have been two models of Setra coaches. The expanding range configured for right-hand drive has been increasing since the S250 Special, the last of which entered service in 2000. Pictured here is one of the latest Setra S415s, AF03HOF. *Dave Heath*

Over two hundred of the Setra S315 GT-HD have been built for the right-hand-drive market since its introduction in 1999. The model is powered by Mercedes engines, Mercedes-Benz is also a constituent of the Evobus company. Illustrating the 315 model is JF04HOF. *Dave Heath*

A3HFU	Bova FHD12.340	Bova Futura	C49FT	1999	Cowdrey, Gosport, 2001
T759JYB	Bova FLD10.340	Bova Futura	C36FT	1999	Cowdrey, Gosport, 2001
T763JYB	Bova FLD12.340	Bova Futura	C53F	1999	Cowdrey, Gosport, 2001
W2HOF	Volvo B10M-62	Jonckheere Mistral 50	C51FT	2000	
Y10HOF	Mercedes-Benz O404-15R	Hispano Vita	C49FT	2001	
Y14HOF	Mercedes-Benz O404-15R	Hispano Vita	C49FT	2001	
YN51MFZ	Scania K114IB4	Irizar Century 12.32	C53F	2002	Z Cars, Bristol, 2005
SA02UGN	Mercedes-Benz Vario O814	?	C24F	2002	
HF03HOF	Volvo B12B	Jonckheere Mistral 50	C49FT	2003	
BF03HOF	Setra S415 HD	Setra	C40FT	2004	
AF03HOF	Setra S415 HD	Setra	C40FT	2003	
UF03HOF	Setra S315 GT-HD	Setra	C40FT	2003	
PG04HOF	Setra S415 HD	Setra	C40FT	2004	
TG04HOF	Setra S415 HD	Setra	C40FT	2004	
JF04HOF	Setra S315 GT-HD	Setra	C40FT	2003	
SF05HOF	Setra S315 GT-HD	Setra	C40FT	2005	
KF05HOF	Volvo B12B 13.75m	Jonckheere Mistral 70	C49FT	2005	

Previous registrations:

A3HFU	S749XYA	A19HOF	N95WVC
A6HFN	R204VYD	A20HOF	J290NNC
A8HOF	M730KJU	B10HOF	M665KVU
A12HOF	K730JWX	IAZ4816	UUR345W
A13HOF	P228AUT	P49JJU	97D7829
A16HOF	H338KPR	R409EOS	LSK499
A17HOF	P102GHE	TJI4926	C262EME
A18HOF	N92WVC, 3KOV, N605CVC		

Depots: Fort Fareham Ind Est, Newgate Lane, Fareham; Quarry Lane Ind Est, Gosport and New Lane, Havant.
Web: www.hellyers-coaches.co.uk

HERITAGE TRAVEL

Coach Hire Coaches Ltd; Round and About Ltd, Heritage House, Sussex Wharf, Shoreham-by-Sea, Brighton, BN43 5BQ

PJI1861	Leyland Fleetline FE33ALR	Northern Counties	B49/31D	1979	First Western National, 2000
PIB5891	Leyland Fleetline FE33ALR	Northern Counties	B49/31D	1981	First Western National, 2000
CYJ375Y	Mercedes-Benz O303/15R	Mercedes-Benz	C53F	1983	Williams, Brecon, 2004
HIL3455	Leyland Olympian ONLXB/1R	Roe	B47/29F	1983	Stagecoach South, 2004
4754RU	Leyland Olympian ONLXB/2R	East Lancs	B51/37F	1984	Warrington Buses, 2004
CLV84X	Leyland Olympian ONLXB/2R	East Lancs	B51/37F	1984	Warrington Buses, 2004
1168BY	Neoplan Cityliner N116/2	Neoplan	C34FT	1984	Blueways, Battersea, 1999
1521YG	DAF SB2300	Jonckheere Jubilee	C49FT	1984	Redby, Sunderland, 1995
RJI6860	DAF SBR2300	Jonckheere Jubilee P95	C57/14CT	1984	Silver Knight, Malmesbury, 1998
8957FN	DAF SB2300	Berkhof Esprite 350	C57F	1985	Limebourne, Victoria, 1988
6300RU	DAF SB2305	Berkhof Esprite 350	C53F	1985	Limebourne, Victoria, 1988
PJI5627	DAF SB2300	Jonckheere Jubilee P	C57FT	1985	C&S Coaches, Heathfield, 1996
FIL7617	Scania K112TRS	Jonckheere Jubilee P90	C51/19CT	1985	Harvey, Harlow, 1995
1194PO	Scania K112TRS	Berkhof Emperor	C57/19CT	1986	Dashminster, Bromley, 1994
4885UR	MCW Metroliner DR130	MCW	C55/17DT	1986	First Western National, 1992
7855PU	Bedford YNV	Duple 320	C53FT	1986	Birkby, Abbey Wood, 1994
9022KV	DAF SB2300	Duple Caribbean 2	C53FT	1986	Byron's, Skewen, 1993
BJZ2804	DAF SBR3000	Berkhof Emperor	C57/16CT	1987	Snow, Great Wakering, 2001
JBZ5056	DAF SBR3000	Berkhof Esprite 350	C46/30CT	1987	Keir, Kenmay, 2003
SJI8128	Scania K92CRB	Van Hool Alizée H	C55F	1988	Buddens, Romsey, 2001
7572MW	Setra S210HD	Setra Optimal	C35FT	1989	Simmonds, Letchworth, 1999
XXI7357	DAF SB2305	Plaxton Paramount 3200 III	C53F	1990	Shaw, Maxey, 1998
BNZ3466	DAF SB2305	Jonckheere Deauville P599	C51FT	1990	Gatwick Flyer, Romford, 2001
4638UG	DAF SB2305	Jonckheere Deauville	C51FT	1990	Barry, Weymouth, 2001

Taking time out in London's Trafalgar Square is 3544FH, a Volvo B12 with a trailing third axle. Bodywork on this Heritage Travel coach is the Van Hool Astrobel. About forty of these models were built on Volvo B12 chassis for the British market.
Colin Lloyd

Another Van Hool coach with Heritage Travel is 2941VU. This time the coach is built on a Scania K113 chassis which also has a third axle. *Colin Lloyd*

1455MV	Scania K113TRB	Van Hool Alizée SH	C51FT	1992	Abbots of Leeming, 1999
6170PX	Scania K113TRB	Van Hool Alizée SH	C52FT	1992	Abbots of Leeming, 2000
2941VU	Scania K113TRB	Van Hool Alizée SH	C52FT	1992	Abbots of Leeming, 1999
8665UB	Neoplan Skyliner N122/3	Neoplan	C57/22CT	1993	Buzzlines, Hythe, 2003
9041PU	Neoplan Cityliner N116/2	Neoplan	C48FT	1993	Burgin, Darnall, 2002
2851NX	Neoplan Cityliner N116/3	Neoplan	C48FT	1995	Embling, Wisbech, 1994
SV9314	Volvo B12(T)	Van Hool Astrobel	C57/14CT	1995	First Midland Bluebird, 2002
3544FH	Volvo B12(T)	Van Hool Astrobel	C57/14CT	1995	First Western National, 2002
KV4644	Scania K113TRB	Irizar Century 12.37	C49F	1996	Durham Travel, 2003
8357KV	Scania K113TRB	Irizar Century 12.35	C49FT	1996	Durham Travel, 2003
2719DT	Scania K113TRS	Van Hool Alizée SH	C49FT	1996	Durham Travel, 2002
HSV989	Scania K113CRB	Van Hool Alizée	C44FT	2003	Aldershot Coaches, 2004

Previous registrations:

869UYB	?
1168BY	A344UFE, PIB5891
1194PO	C590KTW
1455MV	J240VVN
1521YG	B21LNR
2719DT	J15DTS
2851NX	M15HMC
2941VU	J238VVN
3544FH	M103ECV
4638UG	G408WPF, YHA320
4754RU	A487HKB
4885UR	C674GRL
6170PX	J239VVN
6300RU	B685BTW
7572MW	9466MW
7855PU	C655XSK
8357KV	N8DTS
8665UB	K921EWG
8957FN	B687BTW
9022KV	C306AHP, 7404BY
9041PU	K933EWG, 4672NT
BJZ2804	D401SHJ, A20APT, D215YHK
BNZ3466	G469JNH
CYJ375Y	PUL88Y, ALJ505A, 801WHT, PIJ79
FIL7617	B506GBD
HIL3455	CUB72Y, CAP270Y
JBZ5056	2513PP, 3036PP, D283DJU, 5049VC
KV4644	N9DTS
PIB5891	MRJ232W
PJI1861	XTE224V
PJI5627	5946PP, B998PJF
RJI6860	A47JLW, 625PP, A278KBC, 5515LJ
SJI8128	F162DET
SV9314	N319BYA
XXI7357	G959KJX

The South East Bus Handbook

HERTZ

Hertz (UK) Ltd, Northern Perimeter Road West, Heathrow Airport, Hounslow, TW6 2QD

6-24			Mercedes-Benz Sprinter 411 CDi	Koch		M13*	2001	*seating varies
6	Y991TOJ	10	Y984TOJ	14	Y988TOJ		22	BJ03JHU
7	Y981TOJ	11	Y985TOJ	15	Y989TOJ		23	DE52OLK
8	Y982TOJ	12	Y986TOJ	16	Y979TOJ		24	BJ03JHV
9	Y983TOJ	13	Y987TOJ	21	DE52OLJ			

HOTELINK

Hotelink Ltd, Southways Park, London Road, Lowfield Heath, Crawley, RH10 9TQ

M392EGF	Ford Transit VE6	Advanced Vehicle Bodies	M8	1995		
M906EGK	Ford Transit VE6	Advanced Vehicle Bodies	M8	1995		
M907EGK	Ford Transit VE6	Advanced Vehicle Bodies	M8	1995		
	Mercedes-Benz Sprinter 412D	Constable	M14	1999-2000		
T980WPN	T983WPN	W518NNJ	W522NNJ		W526NNJ	
T981WPN	T984WPN	W519NNJ	W523NNJ		W527NNJ	
T982WPN	T985WPN	W521NNJ	W524NNJ			
	Mercedes-Benz Sprinter 413 CDi	Constable	M14	2001		
Y951GFG	Y954GFG	Y958GFG	Y961GFG		Y963GFG	
Y952GFG	Y956GFG	Y959GFG	Y962GFG		Y964GFG	
Y953GFG	Y957GFG					
	Mercedes-Benz Sprinter 413 CDi	Traveliner	M14	2004		
BU04EYH	BU04EYK	BU04EYL	BU04EYM		BU04EYP	
BU04EYJ						
	Mercedes-Benz Sprinter 413 CDi	Eurospire	M14	2005		
RX05EOU	RX05EOW	RX05EOY	RX05EOZ			

Depots: Southways Park, Lowfield Heath and North Ramp coach park, Heathrow.

AIRPORT PARKING

Airport Parking & Hotels Ltd, Down Garage, Snow Hill, Copthorne, nnn xnn.

...02APH	Volvo B7R	Jonckheere Modulo	C55F	2002
...APH	Volvo B7R	TransBus Profile	C53F	2004
	Volvo B7R	TransBus Profile	C53F	2004
	Volvo B7R	Plaxton Profile	C53F	2004
...PH	Volvo B7R	Plaxton Profile	C53F	2004

HEYFORDIAN

Heyfordian Travel Ltd, Murdock Road, Bicester, OX26 4PP

FIL7662	Leyland Olympian ONLXB/1R	Eastern Coach Works	B45/32F	1981	Red Kite Services, Tilsworth, 2000
FIL8317	Leyland Olympian ONLXB/1R	Eastern Coach Works	B45/32F	1981	Red Kite Services, Tilsworth, 2000
FIL8441	Leyland Olympian ONLXB/1R	Eastern Coach Works	B45/32F	1981	Red Kite Services, Tilsworth, 2000
FIL7664	Leyland Olympian ONLXB/1R	Eastern Coach Works	B45/32F	1983	Arriva North East, 2001
4827WD	Scania K112CRS	Jonckheere Jubilee P599	C51FT	1984	BTS Borehamwood, 1991
ESU940	Scania K112CRS	Jonckheere Jubilee P599	C51FT	1984	Goodwin, Stockport, 1994
868AVO	Scania K112CRS	Jonckheere Jubilee P599	C49FT	1984	Hardings, Huyton, 1992
9682FH	Scania K112CRS	Jonckheere Jubilee P50	C53F	1985	
6595KV	Scania K112CRS	Jonckheere Jubilee P50	C53F	1985	
XCT550	Scania K112CRS	Jonckheere Jubilee P599	C51FT	1985	Cross Gates Coaches, 1992
9467MU	Scania K112CRS	Jonckheere Jubilee P599	C55F	1985	Cresswell, Moira, 1991
SJI4428	Scania K112CRS	Jonckheere Jubilee P599	C51FT	1985	Constable, Long Melford, 1995
B739GCN	Leyland Olympian ONLXB/1R	Eastern Coach Works	B45/32F	1985	Go-Ahead Northern, 2003
7958NU	Leyland Olympian ONLXB/1R	Eastern Coach Works	B45/32F	1985	Arriva North East, 2001
2185NU	Leyland Olympian ONLXB/1R	Eastern Coach Works	B45/32F	1985	Arriva North East, 2001
8216FN	Leyland Olympian ONLXB/1R	Eastern Coach Works	B45/32F	1985	Arriva North East, 2001
8548VF	Leyland Olympian ONLXB/1R	Eastern Coach Works	B45/32F	1985	Arriva North East, 2001
7209RU	Leyland Olympian ONLXB/1R	Eastern Coach Works	BC42/30F	1986	Arriva North East, 2001
7298RU	Leyland Olympian ONLXB/1R	Eastern Coach Works	BC42/30F	1986	Arriva North East, 2001
LDZ2502	Scania K112CRS	Jonckheere Jubilee P599	C51FT	1987	Gillespie, Kelty, 1992
LDZ2503	Scania K112CRS	Jonckheere Jubilee P599	C51FT	1987	Buddens, Romsey, 1992
YAY537	Volvo B10M-60	Van Hool Alizée	C49FT	1989	Durham City Coaches, 1996
2482NX	Volvo B10M-60	Van Hool Alizée	C49F	1989	Lewis Meridian, Greenwich, 2001
2622NU	Toyota Coaster HB31R	Caetano Optimo	C21F	1990	
8779XV	Volvo B10M-60	Van Hool Alizée	C51FT	1990	Heather, Ruckinge, 2005
4078NU	Neoplan Skyliner N122/3	Neoplan	C57/22CT	1991	Oak Hall, Caterham, 1995
481HYE	Optare MetroRider MR03	Optare	B28F	1993	London General, 1999
943YKN	Optare MetroRider MR03	Optare	B28F	1993	London General, 1999

One of two Optare MetroRiders operating the Heyfordian bus service in Oxford, 943YKN is seen on Magdalen Bridge.
Richard Godfrey

Shearings of Wigan and Park's of Hamilton have a large, frequent turnover of coaches and they are quickly acquired by other coach operators who do not require new products. Heyfordian has examples from each, including M634KVU, one of three Volvo B10M coaches with Van Hool Alizée bodies originating with Shearings. It is seen here in its new colours.
Dave Heath

7396LJ	Volvo B10M-60	Jonckheere Deauville P599	C53FT	1993	Turner, Bristol, 1999
L26CAY	MAN 10-190	Caetano Algarve II	C33FT	1994	
VSF438	Toyota Coaster HDB30R	Caetano Optimo II	C14FT	1992	Blenheim Palace, Kidlington, 1998
L579JSA	Volvo B10M-60	Plaxton Première Interurban	BC51F	1993	Stagecoach, 2005
L584JSA	Volvo B10M-60	Plaxton Première Interurban	BC51F	1993	Stagecoach, 2005
L585JSA	Volvo B10M-60	Plaxton Première Interurban	BC51F	1993	Stagecoach, 2005
L587JSA	Volvo B10M-60	Plaxton Première Interurban	BC51F	1993	Stagecoach, 2005
1435VZ	Toyota Coaster HZB50R	Caetano Optimo II	C18F	1994	
L409GPY	Volvo B6 9.9m	Plaxton Pointer	B40F	1994	Go-Ahead Northern, 2005
L740YGE	Volvo B10M-62	Jonckheere Deauville 45	C49FT	1994	Park's of Hamilton, 1995
L743YGE	Volvo B10M-62	Jonckheere Deauville 45	C49FT	1994	Park's of Hamilton, 1995
L745YGE	Volvo B10M-62	Jonckheere Deauville 45	C49FT	1994	Park's of Hamilton, 1996
L752YGE	Volvo B10M-62	Jonckheere Deauville 45	C49FT	1994	Durham City Coaches, 2002
M993HHS	Volvo B10M-62	Jonckheere Mistral 50	C49FT	1995	Compass Royston, Stockton, 02
M833HNS	Volvo B10M-62	Van Hool Alizée HE	C49FT	1995	Wickson, Walsall Wood, 2002
M634KVU	Volvo B10M-62	Van Hool Alizée HE	C46FT	1995	Shearings, 2003
M639KVU	Volvo B10M-62	Van Hool Alizée HE	C46FT	1995	Shearings, 2003
N605JGP	Mercedes-Benz 811D	Crystals	B29F	1995	Crystals, Dartford, 2002
N802NHS	Volvo B10M-62	Jonckheere Mistral 50	C53F	1996	Jeffs, Helmdon, 2002
N803NHS	Volvo B10M-62	Jonckheere Mistral 50	C53F	1996	Jeffs, Helmdon, 2002
N808NHS	Volvo B10M-62	Jonckheere Mistral 50	C53F	1996	Jeffs, Helmdon, 2002
N809NHS	Volvo B10M-62	Jonckheere Mistral 50	C53FT	1996	Johnson's, Hodthorpe, 1998
N722UVR	Volvo B10M-62	Jonckheere Mistral 50	C46FT	1996	Shearings, 2004
N724UVR	Volvo B10M-62	Jonckheere Mistral 50	C46FT	1996	Shearings, 2004
N726UVR	Volvo B10M-62	Jonckheere Mistral 50	C46FT	1996	Shearings, 2004
N727UVR	Volvo B10M-62	Jonckheere Mistral 50	C46FT	1996	Shearings, 2004
N728UVR	Volvo B10M-62	Jonckheere Mistral 50	C46FT	1996	Shearings, 2004
N731UVR	Volvo B10M-62	Jonckheere Mistral 50	C46FT	1996	Shearings, 2004
N732UVR	Volvo B10M-62	Jonckheere Mistral 50	C46FT	1996	Shearings, 2004
N733UVR	Volvo B10M-62	Jonckheere Mistral 50	C46FT	1996	Shearings, 2004
N734UVR	Volvo B10M-62	Jonckheere Mistral 50	C46FT	1996	Shearings, 2004
N735UVR	Volvo B10M-62	Jonckheere Mistral 50	C46FT	1996	Shearings, 2004
R998KKO	Neoplan Skyliner N122/3	Neoplan	C57/20DT	1998	Holmeswood Coaches, 2004

R415EOS	Volvo B10M-62		Van Hool Alizée HE	C53F	1998	Park's of Hamilton, 2002
T723UOS	Volvo B10M-62		Jonckheere Mistral 50	C53F	1999	Paul S Winson, Loughborough, 03
T725UOS	Volvo B10M-62		Jonckheere Mistral 50	C53F	1999	Park's of Hamilton, 2003
YN53YGZ	Optare Solo M850		Optare	N29F	2003	

Previous registrations:

481HYE	K428HWY	ESU940	A60JLW
868AVO	A52JLW	FIL7662	JTY373X
943YKN	K434HWY	FIL7664	AEF227Y, 1430PP
1435VZ	L535XUT, 2462FD	FIL8317	JTY375X
2185NU	B246NVN	FIL8441	JTY398X
2482NX	E743TCS, 439BUS, E418JKS, 90RYD	L26CAY	L26CAY, 9467MU
2622NU	G152ELJ	L579JSA	L579JSA, GSU950
4078NU	H297GKN	L584JSA	L584JSA, WLT526
4128AP	F139LJO	L585JSA	L585JSA, NSU132
4827WD	A59JLW, ESU930, A545TMJ	L587JSA	L587JSA, ESU435
6595KV	B156YBW, 5089LG	LDZ2502	D313VVV
7209RU	C266XEF	LDZ2503	D312VVV
7298RU	C265XEF	M833HNS	LSK504, WT3667
7396LJ	K906RGE	M993HNS	KSK986
7958NU	B245NVN	R415EOS	LSK502
8216FN	B253PHN	SJI4428	B505CBD, RDU4, B989MAB
8548VF	B255RAJ	T723UOS	LSK830
8779KV	H48VNH, H10JHC	T725UOS	LSK832
9467MU	B71MLT, C47CKR, 6960TU	VSF438	J27OPC, 1636VB
9682FH	B157YBW, 1246LG	XCT550	B504CBD, HYY3, B984MAB
		YAY537	F483OFT

Web: www.heyfordian.co.uk
Depots: Murdock Road, Bicester; West Wycombe Road, High Wycombe; Woodstock Road, Yarnton, Oxford and Downs Road, Witney.

One of four Jonckheere Deauville 45s originating with Park's of Hamilton is L752YGE. These vehicles were joined by sixteen of the later Mistral styling between 2002 and 2004. *Dave Heath*

HODGE'S

Hodge's Coaches (Sandhurst) Ltd, 100 Yorktown Road, Sandhurst, GU47 9AD

8466PH	Bedford YMT	Duple Dominant II	C53F	1981	Suffolk CC, 2001
SJI2586	Bedford YNV	Plaxton Paramount 3200 III	C53F	1988	Rambler, Hastings, 2001
7107PH	Toyota Coaster HZB50R	Caetano Optimo III	C21F	1995	
9489PH	MAN 11.190	Berkhof Excellence 1000 Midi	C35F	1995	
3900PH	DAF SB3000	Berkhof Excellence 1000 LD	C53F	1996	
4402PH	DAF SB3000	Berkhof Excellence 1000 LD	C53F	1996	
4631PH	Toyota Coaster HZB50R	Caetano Optimo III	C21F	1996	
2568PH	Volvo B10M-62	Berkhof Axial 50	C51FT	1998	
8874PH	Volvo B10M-62	Berkhof Axial 50	C51FT	1998	
5226PH	Volvo B10M-62	Berkhof Axial 50	C51FT	1998	
6967PH	Volvo B10M-62	Berkhof Axial 50	C51FT	1999	
8896PH	Volvo B10M-62	Berkhof Axial 50	C51FT	1999	
2480PH	Volvo B10M-62	Caetano Enigma	C49FT	2001	
5134PH	Volvo B10M-62	Caetano Enigma	C49FT	2001	
9649PH	Volvo B10M-62	Caetano Enigma	C49FT	2001	
3556PH	Volvo B10M-62	Caetano Enigma	C53F	2001	
8990PH	Volvo B10M-62	Caetano Enigma	C41FT	2001	
1598PH	Volvo B12M	Berkhof Axial 50	C51FT	2003	

Previous registrations:

1598PH	From new	6967PH	From new
2480PH	From new	7107PH	From new
2568PH	R984PMO	8466PH	RGV690W
3556PH	FN52MZJ	8874PH	R986PMO
3900PH	N460VPH	8896PH	From new
4402PH	N461VPH	8990PH	From new
4631PH	From new	9489PH	From new
5134PH	From new	9649PH	From new
5226PH	R986PMO	SJI2586	E571TYG, SJI2586, JDY673

Livery: Dark blue and champagne
Depot: St John's Road, Sandhurst.

Hodge's fleet contains five Volvo B10Ms with Caetano Enigma bodywork. Built in Portugal the Enigma was introduced into Britain in 1997. 5134PH is seen in leaving Bracknell bus station.
Colin Lloyd

HORSEMAN

Horseman Coaches Ltd, Whitley Wood Road, Reading, RG2 8GG

Reg	Chassis	Body	Seating	Year	History
L901NWW	Volvo B10M-62	Jonckheere Deauville 45	C57F	1994	Wallace Arnold, 1999
L902NWW	Volvo B10M-62	Jonckheere Deauville 45	C57F	1994	Wallace Arnold, 1999
L903NWW	Volvo B10M-62	Jonckheere Deauville 45	C57F	1994	Wallace Arnold, 1999
L904NWW	Volvo B10M-62	Jonckheere Deauville 45	C57F	1994	Wallace Arnold, 1999
L905NWW	Volvo B10M-62	Jonckheere Deauville 45	C57F	1994	Wallace Arnold, 1999
L948NWW	Volvo B10M-62	Jonckheere Deauville 45	C57F	1994	Wallace Arnold, 1999
L951NWW	Volvo B10M-62	Jonckheere Deauville 45	C57F	1994	Wallace Arnold, 1999
L952NWW	Volvo B10M-62	Jonckheere Deauville 45	C57F	1994	Wallace Arnold, 1999
L954NWW	Volvo B10M-62	Jonckheere Deauville 45	C57F	1994	Wallace Arnold, 1999
L955NWW	Volvo B10M-62	Jonckheere Deauville 45	C57F	1994	Wallace Arnold, 1999
L957NWW	Volvo B10M-62	Jonckheere Deauville 45	C57F	1994	Wallace Arnold, 1999
L958NWW	Volvo B10M-62	Jonckheere Deauville 45	C57F	1994	Wallace Arnold, 1999
L959NWW	Volvo B10M-62	Jonckheere Deauville 45	C53F	1994	Wallace Arnold, 1999
L960NWW	Volvo B10M-62	Jonckheere Deauville 45	C53F	1994	Wallace Arnold, 1999
L961NWW	Volvo B10M-62	Jonckheere Deauville 45	C53F	1994	Wallace Arnold, 1999
M659SBL	Volvo B10M-62	Plaxton Excalibur	C49FT	1995	
N660VJB	Volvo B10M-62	Plaxton Excalibur	C49FT	1995	
N661VJB	Volvo B10M-62	Plaxton Excalibur	C49FT	1995	
N662VJB	Volvo B10M-62	Plaxton Excalibur	C49FT	1995	
N663VJB	Volvo B10M-62	Plaxton Excalibur	C49FT	1996	
N664VJB	Volvo B10M-62	Plaxton Excalibur	C39FT	1996	
N665VJB	Volvo B10M-62	Plaxton Excalibur	C37FT	1996	
N669VJB	Toyota Coaster HZB50R	Caetano Optimo III	C21F	1995	
N670VJB	Toyota Coaster HZB50R	Caetano Optimo III	C21F	1995	
N672VJB	Toyota Coaster HZB50R	Caetano Optimo III	C21F	1995	
N673VJB	Toyota Coaster HZB50R	Caetano Optimo III	C21F	1995	
R204STF	Dennis Javelin	UVG S320	C69F	1997	
S192WAN	Volvo B10M-60	Berkhof Axial 50	C53F	1998	
S193WAN	Volvo B10M-60	Berkhof Axial 50	C53F	1998	
S484KJT	Volvo B10M-60	Berkhof Axial 50	C51F	1998	Chiltern Queens, Woodcote, 2002
T10DMB	Volvo B10M-60	Berkhof Axial 50	C51F	1999	Chiltern Queens, Woodcote, 2002
T20DMB	Volvo B10M-60	Berkhof Axial 50	C51F	1999	AWRE, Aldermaston, 2002
W56SJH	Toyota Coaster BB50R	Caetano Optimo IV	C24F	2000	
W57SJH	Toyota Coaster BB50R	Caetano Optimo IV	C24F	2000	
W59SJH	Toyota Coaster BB50R	Caetano Optimo IV	C24FL	2000	
RX51EXM	Volvo B10M-62	Plaxton Première 350	C49F	2001	
RX51EXN	Volvo B10M-62	Plaxton Première 350	C49F	2001	
RX51EXO	Volvo B10M-62	Plaxton Première 350	C55F	2001	
RX51EXP	Volvo B10M-62	Plaxton Première 350	C55F	2001	

Depots: Whitley Wood Road, Reading and The Green, Theale

Representing the Horseman fleet is Berkhof Axial T20DMB. The Axial is assembled in Holland and was first produced in 1995. Three heights are available, the 50, at 3.55 metres, the 70 at 3.7 metres and 100 4-metre double-deck model. For the British market these are all supplied on Volvo or Scania chassis while a wider range of chassis options are available for the left-hand drive variant.
Dave Heath

JOHN PIKE

J S Pike, 77 Scott Close, Walwash Ind Est, Andover, SP10 6JW

	Reg	Chassis	Body	Type	Year	Notes
	IUI5036	Bristol VRT/SL3/6LXB	Eastern Coach Works	B43/31F	1980	Stagecoach South, 1997
	XJJ663V	Bristol VRT/SL3/6LXB	Eastern Coach Works	B43/31F	1980	Stagecoach South, 2001
	XJJ669V	Bristol VRT/SL3/6LXB	Eastern Coach Works	B43/31F	1980	Stagecoach South, 2000
	JWV265W	Bristol VRT/SL3/6LXB	Eastern Coach Works	B43/31F	1981	Ward, Alresford, 2004
	SKL680X	Bristol VRT/SL3/6LXB	Eastern Coach Works	B43/31F	1981	Stagecoach South, 2000
	IUI5035	Bristol VRT/SL3/6LXB	Eastern Coach Works	B43/31F	1981	Stagecoach South, 1997
w	5300RU	Ford Transit	Pike	M6L	1986	McLardy, Andover, 1990
w	IUI5045	Mercedes-Benz 609D	Pike	BC25FL	1988	van, 1997
	K341RBB	Mercedes-Benz 609D	Pike	BC25F	1993	van, 1999
w	M771BHU	Ford Transit VE6	Ford	M14	1994	Nash, Southampton, 2000
	P237AUT	Volvo B10M-62	Plaxton Première 350	C51FT	1996	Watson, Newcastle, 2000
	P132YEL	Mercedes-Benz 711D	Pike	BC-F	1996	van, 2004
	A11UFB	Ford Transit	Pike	M9L	1998	van, 2001
	T532EUB	Volvo B10M-62	Plaxton Première 350	C48FT	1999	Wallace Arnold, 2002
	T801FRU	Volvo B10M-62	Plaxton Première 350	C49FT	1999	Excelsior, Bournemouth, 2001
	T39APO	Ford Transit VE6	Ford	M11	1999	Freydern College, 2003
	V687MDA	Ford Transit VE6	Pike	M8L	2000	van, 2002
	W626FUM	Volvo B10M-62	Plaxton Première 350	C48FT	2000	Wallace Arnold, 2003
	NJ51TXH	Ford Transit	Ford	M14	2001	Northflex, 2003

Previous registrations:

5300RU	P708VRX	IUI5037	EAP978V
A11UFB	R341EDM	IUI5045	E367GHD
HIL3670	XJJ657V	P550CLJ	A9XEXC
IUI5035	JWV266W	T801FRU	A17XEL
IUI5036	JWV256W		

Bristol VRs meet John Pike's double-deck needs his school transport commitments of six are currently employed in the fleet. Carrying the all-white livery is SKL680X, an example new to East Kent. *Phillip Stephenson*

KENT COACH TOURS

Kent Coach Tours Ltd, The Coach Station, Malcolm Sargent Road, Ashford, TN23 6JW

M804PRA	MAN 11.190	Optare Vecta	B40F	1994	TrentBarton, 2004
KCT638	Volvo B10M-62	Plaxton Première 350	C49FT	1996	Wallace Arnold, 2001
KCT986	Volvo B10M-62	Plaxton Excalibur	C53F	1997	Excelsior, Bournemouth, 2000
KCT353	Volvo B10M-62	Plaxton Excalibur	C53F	1998	Wallace Arnold, 2002
KCT415	Volvo B10M-62	Plaxton Première 350	C53F	1998	North Kent Express, 2003
KCT255	Volvo B10M-62	Plaxton Première 350	C53F	1999	Owen's, Yateley, 2005
W84XKP	Mercedes-Benz Vario 0814	Plaxton Beaver 2	BC33F	2000	
Y353CKR	Mercedes-Benz Vario 0814	Plaxton Beaver 2	B33F	2001	
GJ52GYD	Mercedes-Benz Vario 0814	Plaxton Beaver 2	B31F	2002	
GK04CWP	Mercedes-Benz Vario 0814	Plaxton Beaver 2	B33F	2004	
GN54SBX	Mercedes-Benz Vario 0814	Plaxton Beaver 2	B33F	2004	
GN05DZU	Mercedes-Benz Vario 0814	Plaxton Beaver 2	B33F	2005	

Previous registrations:

J3KCT	-		KCT415	S758CKO
KCT255	T526EUB		KCT638	N216HWX
KCT353	R428FWT		KCT986	A8XEL, P783AAA

Web: www.kentcoachtours.co.uk

Entering service with Kent Coach Tours in 2004, K804PRA has one of Optare's Vecta bodies, a model supplied only on the MAN 11.190 chassis. In the six years of production just 130 of the type were built, before low-floor midibuses from other suppliers took over the market. It is seen in Ashford's Beaver Road. *Martin Smith*

KENT COUNTY COUNCIL

Kent County Council, Passenger Services, Forstal Road, Aylesford, ME20 7HB

Code	Reg	Chassis	Body	Layout	Year	Notes
PS001	GN02XCU	Peugeot 106	Peugeot	M5	2002	
PS002	R487YKM	Ford Fiesta	Ford	M5	1997	
PS003	S729SKE	Ford Courier	Constable	M4	1998	
PS004	GK53AFU	Mercedes-Benz Sprinter 313	Transport Engineering	M8	2003	
PS005	GK53AFV	Mercedes-Benz Sprinter 313	Transport Engineering	M8	2003	
PS006	GK53CUA	Mercedes-Benz Sprinter 313	Stanford	M8	2003	
PS007	GK53CUC	Mercedes-Benz Sprinter 313	Stanford	M8	2003	
PS008	GK53CUG	Mercedes-Benz Sprinter 313	Stanford	M8	2003	
PS009	GK53CUH	Mercedes-Benz Sprinter 313	Stanford	M8	2003	
PS010	GK53CUJ	Mercedes-Benz Sprinter 313	Stanford	M8	2003	
PS011	GK53DLD	Mercedes-Benz Sprinter 313	Stanford	M8	2003	
PS012	GK53DLE	Mercedes-Benz Sprinter 313	Stanford	M8	2003	
PS103	GK51FHL	Iveco Daily 45C11	Euromotive	B16FL	2001	
PS104	GK51FHN	Iveco Daily 45C11	Euromotive	B16FL	2001	
PS105	GK51FHO	Iveco Daily 45C11	Euromotive	B16FL	2001	
PS106	GK51FHP	Iveco Daily 45C11	Euromotive	B16FL	2001	
PS107	GN03EHP	Iveco Daily 45C11	Euromotive	B16FL	2003	
PS108	GN03EHR	Iveco Daily 45C11	Euromotive	B16FL	2003	
PS109	GN04PKC	Irisbus Daily 50C13	Transport Engineering	B16FL	2004	
PS110	GN04PKD	Irisbus Daily 50C13	Transport Engineering	B16FL	2004	
PS111	GN04PLX	Irisbus Daily 50C13	Transport Engineering	B16FL	2004	
PS112	GN04PLZ	Irisbus Daily 50C13	Transport Engineering	B16FL	2004	
PS113	GN51DFU	Iveco Daily 45C11	Euromotive	B16FL	2001	
PS115	GN51DGU	Iveco Daily 45C11	Euromotive	B16FL	2001	
PS119	S190VKM	Iveco Daily 52-10	Euromotive	B16FL		
PS121	Y331UKN	Iveco Daily 40-10	Iveco	B14F		
PS122	Y918UKR	Iveco Daily 45C11	Euromotive	B16FL	2001	
PS123	MX03YDC	Optare Alero AL1	Optare	N16C	2003	Huyton Travel, Liverpool, 2004
PS124	GK02WDJ	Renault Master	Rohill Harrier	B15F	2002	
PS125	GK02YKY	Renault Master	Rohill Harrier	B15F	2002	
PS126	GK02YKZ	Renault Master	Rohill Harrier	B15F	2002	
PS127	GK02OLA	Renault Master	Rohill Harrier	B15F	2002	
PS200	T606LKL	Iveco Daily 59.12	Mellor	B22FL	1999	
PS201	T607LKL	Iveco Daily 59.12	Mellor	B22FL	1999	
PS202	V386MKJ	Iveco Daily 59.12	Mellor	B22FL	1999	
PS203	V387MKJ	Iveco Daily 59.12	Mellor	B22FL	1999	
PS300	GK53FHR	Mercedes-Benz Vario O814	TransBus Beaver	BC33F	2004	
PS301	R931AMB	Mercedes-Benz Vario O810	Plaxton Beaver 2	B31F	1997	Careline, Birmingham, 2003
PS302	S101KNR	Mercedes-Benz Vario O810	Leicester Carriage	B33F	1998	
PS303	S507KJU	Mercedes-Benz Vario O810	Leicester Carriage	B33F	1998	
PS304	S766SKK	Mercedes-Benz Vario O814	Plaxton Beaver 2	BC33F	1998	Kent Coach Tours, 2001

The composition of the Kent County Council fleet has changed significantly in recent months with the entry into service on new high-capacity single-deck coaches primarily intended for school services. However, commercial services are also undertaken and Optare Solo PS307, Y332HWT, is seen in fleet colours.
Phillip Stephenson

Two Lynx latterly used within the Blazefield Group are operated by Kent County Council. First of the pair is F167SMT which was new to Millers of Foxton. *Dave Heath*

PS305	Y32HBT	Optare Solo M850	Optare	N29F	2001	
PS306	Y52HBT	Optare Solo M920	Optare	N33F	2001	
PS307	Y332HWT	Optare Solo M850	Optare	N29F	2001	
PS308	YJ51JWX	Optare Solo M920	Optare	N33F	2001	
PS309	S540RKL	Dennis Dart SLF	Plaxton Pointer 2	N39F	1998	Kent Coach Tours, 2001
PS310	S775RNE	Dennis Dart SLF	Plaxton Pointer 2	N41F	1998	
PS311	S776RNE	Dennis Dart SLF	Plaxton Pointer 2	N41F	1998	Ludlows, Halesowen, 2001
PS312	S778RNE	Dennis Dart SLF	Plaxton Pointer 2	N41F	1998	Munro's of Jedburgh, 2001
PS600	F167SMT	Leyland Lynx LX112L10ZR1	Leyland	B49F	1989	Burnley & Pendle, 2002
PS601	F168SMT	Leyland Lynx LX112L10ZR1	Leyland	B49F	1989	Lancashire United, 2002
PS503	KIW5196	Volvo B10M-61	Plaxton Paramount 3200 III	C53F	1988	Reliant, Heather, 2002
PS511	TJI6313	Volvo B10M-61	Plaxton Paramount 3200 II	C53F	1986	Waterson, Hemsworth, 2002
PS513	YN05XZP	Volvo B7R	Plaxton Profile	BC70FL	2005	
PS514	YN05XZR	Volvo B7R	Plaxton Profile	BC70F	2005	
PS515	YN05XZS	Volvo B7R	Plaxton Profile	BC70F	2005	
PS516	YN05XZT	Volvo B7R	Plaxton Profile	BC70F	2005	
PS517		Volvo B7R	Plaxton Profile	BC70F	On order	
PS518		Volvo B7R	Plaxton Profile	BC70FL	On order	
PS519		Volvo B7R	Plaxton Profile	BC70FL	On order	
PS520		Volvo B7R	Plaxton Profile	BC70FL	On order	
PS521		Volvo B7R	Plaxton Profile	BC70FL	On order	
PS600	E109JYV	Scania N112DRB	East Lancs	B46/29F	1988	Travelspeed, Burnley, 2002
PS601	M794VJO	Dennis Javelin 12m	Wadham Stringer	BC70F	?	

Previous registrations:

HBZ2459	D705RAK, MIW5795, D384ENV	N445PYS	HSK644
KIW5196	E658UNE, YBP692, E658UNE	TJI6313	C103LUS
KIW6419	A379ROU	X312RBD	?
M794VJO	M794VJO, L18LUE	YXI2748	E568UHS

The South East Bus Handbook

THE KINGS FERRY

The Kings Ferry - The Travel Link - V.I.P.

The Kings Ferry Ltd, The Travel Centre, 199 Eastcourt Lane, Gillingham, ME8 6HW

1.1	N511YHN	Mercedes-Benz 412D	Autobus Classique	M15	1996	Collins, Roch, 2000
1.3	GN51UNY	Mercedes-Benz Sprinter 413 Cdi	Optare-Ferqui Soroco	C16F	2001	
1.4	YX05AVN	Mercedes-Benz Sprinter 413 Cdi	Optare-Ferqui Soroco	C16F	2005	
1.5	YX05AVO	Mercedes-Benz Sprinter 413 Cdi	Optare-Ferqui Soroco	C16F	2005	
1.6	YX05AVP	Mercedes-Benz Sprinter 413 Cdi	Optare-Ferqui Soroco	C16F	2005	
2.1	FN02VBD	Irisbus EuroMidi CC80.E.18	Indcar Maxim	C29F	2002	
2.2	FN02VBE	Irisbus EuroMidi CC80.E.18	Indcar Maxim	C29F	2002	
3.1	W558RYC	Bova FHD10.370	Bova Futura	C37FT	2000	Stones, Bath, 2002
3.2	A18TKF	Scania L94IB4	Irizar Century 12.35	C38FT	1998	Holmeswood Coaches, 2003
4.4	Y10TTL	Volvo B10M-62	Berkhof Axial 50	C51FT	2001	Tim's Travel, Sheerness, 2002
4.5	Y11TTL	Volvo B10M-62	Berkhof Axial 50	C51FT	2001	Tim's Travel, Sheerness, 2002
4.7	A4TKF	Setra S315 GT-HD	Setra	C44FT	1999	Coventry University, 2003
4.8	GN51WCA	Scania K124IB4	Van Hool T9 Alizée	C49FT	2001	
4.9	ECZ9142	Setra S250	Setra Special	C44FT	1998	Memories for Tomorrow, 2003
4.10	A6TKF	Setra S315 GT-HD	Setra	C44FT	1999	MacArthur, Strathpeffer, 2003
4.13	V899LOH	Mercedes-Benz O404-15R	Hispano Vita	C49FT	2000	
4.14	T556UOX	Mercedes-Benz O404-15R	Hispano Vita	C49FT	1999	
4.15	V762MKK	Scania L94IB	Van Hool T9 Alizée	C49FT	1999	
4.16	V585MKK	Scania L94IB	Van Hool T9 Alizée	C49FT	1999	
4.17	V998JKK	Scania L94IB	Van Hool T9 Alizée	C49FT	1999	
4.19	W904XKR	Scania L94IB	Van Hool T9 Alizée	C49FT	2000	
4.20	W903XKR	Scania L94IB	Van Hool T9 Alizée	C49FT	2000	
4.21	R625GKO	Setra 250	Setra Special	C48FT	1998	
4.22	R626GKO	Setra 250	Setra Special	C48FT	1998	
4.23	W533YKN	Scania L94IB	Irizar Century 12.35	C49FT	2000	
4.24	A8TKF	Scania L94IB	Van Hool T9 Alizée	C49FT	1998	
4.25	T570LKM	Scania L94IB	Van Hool T9 Alizée	C49FT	1999	
4.26	Y875TKO	Scania L94IB	Irizar Century 12.35	C49FT	2001	
4.30	W359EOL	Mercedes-Benz O404-15R	Hispano Vita	C49FT	2000	
4.31	W869VGY	Volvo B10M-62	Berkhof Axial 50	C49FT	2000	
4.72	H956DRJ	Volvo B10M-60	Plaxton Paramount 3500 III	C49FT	1991	Ensign, Purfleet, 1998
4.73	H281NRF	Volvo B10M-60	Plaxton Paramount 3500 III	C51F	1991	Tim's Travel, Sheerness, 2000

The Kings Ferry provides commuter services from the Kent area through to London in addition to specialist and premium coach hire and tours. Pictured passing through Parliament Square is Setra S250 4.9, ECZ9142. *Colin Lloyd*

The first digit of the fleet number represents the size and purpose of vehicle, the double-deck coaches starting 7. One of these is Scania K114, 7.1, GJ52OMZ, a Berkhof Axial 100. In addition to coaching activities The Kings Ferry operates a fleet of chauffeur-driven cars and a new Kings Ferry helicopter service which offers travel in executive comfort from Manston airport. *Colin Lloyd*

5.1	T401OWA	Scania L94IB4	Van Hool T9 Alizée	C53F	1999	Dunn-Line, Nottingham, 2003
5.2	A14TKF	Scania K113CRB	Van Hool Alizée HE	C53F	1997	
5.3	A15TKF	Scania K113CRB	Van Hool Alizée HE	C53F	1997	
5.4	A17TKF	Scania K113CRB	Van Hool Alizée HE	C53F	1997	
5.5	A19TKF	Scania K113CRB	Van Hool Alizée HE	C53F	1997	
5.6	W452AKN	Volvo B10M-62	Berkhof Axial 50	C53F	2000	
5.7	W453AKN	Volvo B10M-62	Berkhof Axial 50	C53F	2000	
5.8	S373SET	Scania L94IB	Irizar Century 12.35	C53F	1998	Ludlows, Halesowen, 2001
5.9	WJI3814	Setra 250	Setra Special	C53F	1997	Setra demonstrator, 1998
5.10	Y449TKN	Volvo B10M-62	Berkhof Axial 50	C53F	2001	
5.11	Y448TKN	Volvo B10M-62	Berkhof Axial 50	C53F	2001	
5.12	Y447TKN	Volvo B10M-62	Berkhof Axial 50	C53F	2001	
5.13	Y451TKN	Volvo B10M-62	Berkhof Axial 50	C53F	2001	
5.14	R871SDT	Scania L94IB4	Irizar Century 12.35	C53F	1998	Gilchrist, Quarrington, 2003
5.15	R882SDT	Scania L94IB4	Irizar Century 12.35	C53F	1998	Gilchrist, Quarrington, 2003
5.16	FJ53KZF	Volvo B7R	Sunsundegui Sideral	C53F	2004	
5.17	FD54DHL	Volvo B7R	Sunsundegui Sideral	C53F	2005	
5.18	FD54DHM	Volvo B7R	Sunsundegui Sideral	C53F	2005	
5.19	FJ05ANV	Volvo B7R	Sunsundegui Sideral	C53F	2005	
5.20	FJ05AOD	Volvo B7R	Sunsundegui Sideral	C53F	2005	
5.51	P168RWR	DAF SB3000	Plaxton Première 350	C53F	1997	North Kent Express, 2003
5.53	A16TKF	Scania K113CRB	Van Hool Alizée HE	C53F	1997	
5.71	P118RSF	Volvo B10M-62	Plaxton Première 350	C53F	1997	Tim's Travel, Sheerness, 2003
5.72	P119RSF	Volvo B10M-62	Plaxton Première 350	C53F	1997	Tim's Travel, Sheerness, 2003
5.74	S151JUA	DAF SB3000	Plaxton Première 320	C53F	1998	Airport Parking, Copthorne, 2004
5.75	S152JUA	DAF SB3000	Plaxton Première 320	C53F	1998	Airport Parking, Copthorne, 2004
7.1	GJ52OMZ	Scania K114EB6	Berkhof Axial 100	C55/19DT	2003	
7.2	YR52VFE	Scania K114EB6	Berkhof Axial 100	C55/19DT	2003	
7.3	GN03TYB	Scania K114EB6	Berkhof Axial 100	C55/19DT	2003	
7.4	GJ52MUV	Scania K114EB6	Berkhof Axial 100	C55/19DT	2003	
7.5	GJ02JJL	Scania K114EB6	Berkhof Axial 100	C55/19DT	2002	
7.6	GJ02LUZ	Scania K114EB6	Berkhof Axial 100	C55/19DT	2002	
7.7	X77CCH	Ayats Bravo A3E/BRI	Ayats	C57/16DT	2001	Chambers, Moneymore, 2004
7.10	K14KFC	Scania K113TRA	Berkhof Excellence 2000HD	C57/19DT	1993	Luckett's, Foreham, 2002
7.20	L8KFC	Scania K113TRA	Berkhof Excellence 2000HD	C57/21DT	1994	Luckett's, Foreham, 2002

The South East Bus Handbook

The Kings Ferry operates three buses two of which are double-deck Scania N113s with East Lancs Cityzen bodywork. Pictured on a rail replacement service is B10, V4BLU. The operator has recently secured a major contract to provide vehicles and drivers for the short-notice evacuation of the City of London in event of a major incident. *Martin Smith*

B.8	YP52CUU	Scania N94UB	Castrosua	N34F	2003	Scania demonstrator, 2004
B.9	V3BLU	Scania N113DRB	East Lancs Cityzen	BC45/31F	1999	Bluebird, Middleton, 2004
B.10	V4BLU	Scania N113DRB	East Lancs Cityzen	BC45/31F	1999	Bluebird, Middleton, 2004
S.1	H2KFC	Scania K124IB6	Irizar Century 12.37	C34FT	1998	
S.2	YN53GFK	Scania K124EB6	Irizar PB	C38FT	1998	Holmeswood Coaches, 2003
S.3	V1PKF	Neoplan Starliner N516/2	Neoplan	C32FT	1990	Reeve, Scarning, 2002
S.5	YN54AKF	Scania K124EB6	Irizar PB	C34FT	2004	
S.6	YN05HAE	Scania K124EB6	Irizar PB	C52FT	2004	

Ancillary vehicles:

.	AFY184X	Leyland Atlantean AN68/1R	Willowbrook	O45/33F	1981	Pringle, Glasgow, 2002
.	YFJ639X	Bova EL26-581	Bova Europa	TV	1982	Streets, Chivenor, 2003
.	SIB3057	DAF SB2300	Caetano Algarve	TV	1989	Farleigh Coaches, Rochester

Previous registrations:

A4TKF	V32HAX	K6KFC	-
A6TKF	V35HAX	K8KFC	-
A8TKF	R998MKN	K14KFC	K14KFC, 666VMX
A14TKF	-	L8KFC	L338DTG, 8686DN, L338DTG
A15TKF	-	M2KFC	-
A16TKF	-	P118RSF	P118RSF, K5KFC
A17TKF	-	P119RSF	P119RSF, K6KFC
A18TKF	S4HWD	R871SDT	98D10279
A19TKF	-	R887SDT	98D10336
CNZ3817	H411CJF	S151JUA	S151JUA, M2KFC
ECZ9142	R42EDW	S152JUA	S152JUA, K8KFC
GIL8490	E989KJF	WJI3814	P49YTL
K5KFC		YFJ639X	VDX893X, BOV415, VFJ639X, WOI3814

Depots: Eastcourt Lane, Gillingham; Cullet Drive, Queensborough, Isle of Sheppey.
Web: www.thekingsferry.co.uk

KINGSMAN

Kingsman - Terry's Travel

J A Mancini, 57 Bramley Avenue, Faversham, ME13 8LP

FKX279T	Bristol LHL6L	Plaxton Supreme III	C53F	1979	Provence, St Albans, 1997
WTL921	Neoplan Cityliner N116/2	Neoplan	C49FT	1983	Brylaine, Boston, 1994
UOI2609	Neoplan Cityliner N116/2	Neoplan	C53FT	1984	Skelton, Chilton Polden, 1996
F267OFJ	Neoplan Cityliner N116/2	Neoplan	C48FT	1989	Travelrich, Clacton, 1998
D785GCD	Mercedes-Benz O303/15RHS	Mercedes-Benz	C53F	1987	Empress, St Leonards, 2004
R955TLD	Mercedes-Benz 412D	Autobus Classique	M16	1998	Cosh, Peasedown, 2003
GJ02JJF	Mercedes-Benz Vario O814	Plaxton Beaver 2	BC31F	2002	
KM02HGG	Mercedes-Benz Vario O814	Plaxton Beaver 2	BC31F	2002	
KT03BUS	Mercedes-Benz Citaro O530	Mercedes-Benz	N42F	2004	
KT04BUS	Mercedes-Benz Citaro O530	Mercedes-Benz	N42F	2004	

Previous registrations:

D785GCD	D352CBC, GIL1684, D410OSJ, HBZ4673, JAZ1066			
F267OFJ	F622CWJ, USV330, F267OFJ, UGV847	UOI2609	A91KLK	

Depot: The Old Lime Works, Canterbury Road, Faversham

Pride of the Kingsman fleet are two integral Mercedes-Benz Citaro buses. Only recently new to the British market the Citaro was introduced to the continental market as far back as 1997, displacing the O407 model. KT03BUS was photographed in Faversham while working route 666 to Ashford. *Martin Smith*

LUCKETTS

H Luckett & Co Ltd, Broad Cut, Wallington, Fareham, PO16 8TB

2108	W2HLC	Toyota Coaster BB50R	Caetano Optimo IV	C21F	2000	
2109	HX03BYT	Toyota Coaster BB50R	Caetano Optimo V	C21F	2003	
3603	A13HLC	Bova FHD10.370	Bova Futura	C36FT	2000	Mayne's, Buckie, 2003
3801	A19LTG	Dennis Javelin (10m)	Berkhof Axial 50	C38FT	1997	
4201	YR02ZZA	Scania K114IB4	Irizar Century 12.35	C42FT	2002	
4202	YR02ZZC	Scania K114IB4	Irizar Century 12.35	C42FT	2002	
4801	YN05HFK	Scania K124EB6	Irizar PB	C48FT	2005	
4802	YN05HFL	Scania K124EB6	Irizar PB	C48FT	2005	
4910	A12HLC	Scania K113CRB	Irizar Century 12.35	C49FT	1996	
4915	A7HLC	Scania K113CRB	Irizar Century 12.35	C49FT	1997	
4916	A16HLC	Scania K113CRB	Irizar Century 12.35	C49FT	1997	
4920	R4HLC	Dennis Javelin GX 12m	Berkhof Axial	C49FT	1998	
4921	T3HLC	Scania K124IB4	Irizar Century 12.35	C49FT	1999	
4923	W3HLC	Mercedes-Benz 0404-15R	Hispano Vita	C49FT	2000	
4924	W5HLC	Mercedes-Benz 0404-15R	Hispano Vita	C49FT	2000	
4925	Y2HLC	Volvo B10M-62	Berkhof Axial 50	C49FT	2001	
4926	Y3HLC	Volvo B10M-62	Berkhof Axial 50	C49FT	2001	
4927	YN04GOH	Scania K114IB4	Irizar Century 12.35	C49FT	2004	
4928	YN04GOJ	Scania K114IB4	Irizar Century 12.35	C49FT	2004	
4929	YN04GOC	Scania K114IB4	Irizar Century 12.35	C49FT	2004	
4930	YN04GOK	Scania K114IB4	Irizar Century 12.35	C49FT	2004	
5338	A20HLC	Dennis Javelin GX 12m	Berkhof Axial	C53F	1997	
5339	R10HLC	Dennis Javelin GX 12m	Berkhof Excellence 1000L	C53F	1997	
5343	YR02ZZB	Scania K124IB4	Irizar Century 12.35	C53F	2002	
5344	YR02ZZD	Scania K124IB4	Irizar Century 12.35	C53F	2002	
5345	YS03ZLK	Scania K124IB4	Irizar Century 12.35	C53F	2003	
5506	R5HLC	Scania L94IB4	Irizar InterCentury 12.32	C55F	1998	
5702	A17HLC	Dennis Javelin 12m	Plaxton Première 320	C57F	1996	Marbill, Beith, 2000
7001	T7HLC	Dennis Javelin 12m	Plaxton Première 320	C70F	1999	
7002	Y4HLC	Dennis Javelin 12m	Plaxton Première 320	C70F	2001	
7003	YR52MDV	Dennis Javelin 12m	Plaxton Première 320	C70F	2002	
7701	666VMX	Neoplan Skyliner N122/3	Neoplan	C57/20DT	1998	The Kings Ferry, Gillingham, 2002
8301	YN04AVL	Neoplan Skyliner N122/3	Neoplan	C57/26DT	2004	

Previous registrations:

666VMX	R330YKK		A17HLC	P554KSU, BJI6853
A7HLC	P130GHE		A18HLC	P881MTR
A12HLC	N855DKU, 8589EL		A19LTG	P483GTF
A13HLC	W500GSM		A20HLC	P668GJB
A16HLC	P140GHE			

Web: www.lucketts.co.uk

Delivered during 2005 was a pair of Scania PB coaches. One of these tri-axle models is 4802, YN05HFL. Evolving from a haulage business, David Luckett purchased the company's first coach in 1976. By the mid-80's the coach fleet had outnumbered the haulage fleet.
Dave Heath

MK METRO

M K Metro Ltd; Green Travel Ltd, 3 Arden Park, Old Wolverton Road, Milton Keynes, MK12 5RN

1-4		Optare Solo M920		Optare	N35F	1999	
1	S401ERP	2	S402ERP	3	S403ERP	4	S404ERP

5-10		Optare Solo M850		Optare	N31F	1999	
5	T405ENV	7	T407ENV	9	T409ENV	10	T410ENV
6	T406ENV	8	T408ENV				

11	S903DUB	Optare Solo M920		Optare	N33F	1998	Optare demonstrator, 1999

12-16		Optare Solo M850		Optare	N31F	1999-2000	12/3 Classic, Annfield Plain, 2005
12	V412UNH	14	W414KNH	15	W415KNH	16	W416KNH
13	V413UNH						

17	X417BBD	Optare Solo M920	Optare	N35F	2000	
18	X418BBD	Optare Solo M920	Optare	N35F	2000	
19	X419BBD	Optare Solo M920	Optare	N35F	2000	
20	V82EVU	Optare Solo M920	Optare	N37F	1999	J P Travel, Middleton, 2002
21	MK02BUS	Optare Solo M920	Optare	N33F	2002	
22	KJ02JXT	Optare Solo M920	Optare	N33F	2002	
23	W681DDN	Optare Solo M920	Optare	N33F	2000	Henderson, Hamilton, 2003
24	YN53SVG	Optare Solo M920	Optare	N33F	2003	
25	YN04LXM	Optare Solo M920	Optare	N33F	2004	
26	YJ05JXU	Optare Solo M1020	Optare	N37F	2005	
27	YJ05JXV	Optare Solo M1020	Optare	N37F	2005	
28	YN03NEF	Optare Solo M920	Optare	N31F	2003	Courtney, Bracknell, 2005
29	YN03NCF	Optare Solo M920	Optare	N31F	2003	Courtney, Bracknell, 2005
30	T45KAW	Optare Solo M850	Optare	N31F	1999	Choice, Wolverhampton, 2005
31	X351AUX	Optare Solo M850	Optare	N31F	2000	Choice, Wolverhampton, 2005

45-48		Dennis Dart SLF		Plaxton Pointer	N43F	1998	Tellings-Golden Miller, 2003
45	HDZ2611	46	HDZ2607	47	HDZ2605	48	HDZ2604

MK Metro was established in 1997 and provides the bus services for Milton Keynes, a city designed, like some other new towns, for the car. The fleet is dominated by minibuses and midibuses. Early Mercedes-Benz van conversions are now being replaced by Optare Solo buses, like 25, YN04LXM, seen here. *Dave Heath*

Joining the fleet in 2001, 51, HX51LSO, illustrates the Caetano Compass body, as this Dart heads for Stoney Stratford on route 5. *Dave Heath*

49	W986WDS	Dennis Dart SLF 10.7m		Caetano Compass	N43F	2000	Dart Buses, Paisley, 2002
50	HDZ2606	Dennis Dart SLF		UVG	N44F	1997	Scotsways, Glasgow, 2002
51	HX51LSO	Dennis Dart SLF 10.7m		Caetano Compass	N45F	2001	
52	W3CTS	Dennis Dart SLF 10.7m		Caetano	N44F	2000	Cheney Cs, Banbury, 2003
53-58		Dennis Dart SLF		Caetano Compass	N42F	1999	Connex Bus, 2003-04
53	NDZ7935	55	NDZ7919	57	NDZ4521	58	NDZ7918
54	NDZ7933	56	NDZ7926				
59	KX54AVE	VDL Bus SB120		Wrightbus Cadet 2	N39F	2004	
60	KX54AVD	VDL Bus SB120		Wrightbus Cadet 2	N39F	2004	
61	YG52CMU	DAF SB120		Wrightbus Cadet 2	N39F	2002	Wright, Millport, 2005
106	M70TGM	Mercedes-Benz 709D		Plaxton Beaver	B23F	1995	Tellings-Golden Miller, 2003
107-115		Mercedes-Benz Vario O810		Plaxton Beaver 2	B27F	1997-98	*115 is B31F
107	R107DNV	109	R109DNV	112	R112DNV	115	R949AMB
108	R108DNV	110	R110DNV	113	R113DNV		
111	R825MJU	Mercedes-Benz Vario O810		Plaxton Beaver 2	B31F	1997	Trent, 2004
114	R826MJU	Mercedes-Benz Vario O810		Plaxton Beaver 2	B31F	1997	Trent, 2004
116	R116DNV	Mercedes-Benz Vario O814		Plaxton Beaver 2	B27F	1998	
117	R117DNV	Mercedes-Benz Vario O810		Plaxton Beaver 2	B31F	1998	
118	R118DNV	Mercedes-Benz Vario O810		Plaxton Beaver 2	B31F	1998	

The only Scania operated by MK Metro is Wright Axcess-ultralow 140, S340SET, seen here showing its destination as Lakes Estate, the terminus of route 13. *Steve Maskell*

119-122		Mercedes-Benz Vario 0814	Plaxton Beaver 2	B31F	1998-99	
119	R119DNV	**120**	R120DNV	**121**	R121DNV	**122**	S122KBD
123	T93JBA	Mercedes-Benz Vario 0814	Plaxton Beaver 2	B31F	1999	Henderson, Hamilton, 2003

125-128		Mercedes-Benz Vario 0814	Plaxton Beaver 2	B31F	1999	
125	T125LRP	**126**	T126LRP	**127**	T127LRP	**128**	V128UNH

129	T587KGB	Mercedes-Benz Vario 0814	Plaxton Beaver 2	B31F	1999	Holgate, Chinley, 2003
130	R824MJU	Mercedes-Benz Vario 0810	Plaxton Beaver 2	B31F	1997	Trent, 2004
131	R827WBC	Mercedes-Benz Vario 0814	Plaxton Beaver 2	B31F	1998	Trent, 2004
140	S340SET	Scania L94UB	Wright Axcess-ultralow	N43F	1998	Coach Services, Thetford, 2004
141	M53PRA	Volvo B10M-60	Alexander Q	BC51F	1994	Green Triangle, Atherton, 2004
202	K302FYG	DAF DB250	Optare Spectra	B44/26F	1992	Bennett's, Gloucester, 2001
216	F116PHM	Volvo Citybus B10M-50	Alexander RV	B46/30D	1988	Arriva London, 2004
224	F124PHM	Volvo Citybus B10M-50	Alexander RV	B46/30F	1988	Arriva London, 2004
236	F136PHM	Volvo Citybus B10M-50	Alexander RV	B46/30F	1988	Arriva London, 2003
266	PAX466F	Leyland Titan PD3/4	Massey	L35/33R	1968	Green Bus, Great Wyrley, 1999

300-309		Mercedes-Benz Sprinter 411Cdi	Traveliner	N16F	2004	
300	KE04WBD	**303**	KE04WBJ	**306**	KE04WBM	**308**	KE04WBP
301	KE04WBF	**304**	KE04WBK	**307**	KE04WBN	**309**	KE04WBT
302	KE04WBG	**305**	KE04WBL				

416	L711JUD	Dennis Dart 9.8m	Plaxton Pointer	B37D	1994	Stagecoach South, 2003
418	L713JUD	Dennis Dart 9.8m	Plaxton Pointer	B37D	1994	Stagecoach South, 2003
419	L709JUD	Dennis Dart 9.8m	Plaxton Pointer	B37D	1994	Stagecoach South, 2003
420	M10CLA	Dennis Dart 9.8m	Plaxton Pointer	B40F	1994	Classic, Annfield Plain, 2000
421	J941MFT	Dennis Dart 9.8m	Wright Handybus	B37F	1992	Go-Ahead Northern, 2000
423	N133XND	Dennis Dart 9.8m	Plaxton Pointer	B40F	1995	Stuart's, Dukinfield, 1997
424	N134XND	Dennis Dart 9.8m	Plaxton Pointer	B40F	1995	Stuart's, Dukinfield, 1997
426	K379RTY	Dennis Dart 9.8m	Wright Handybus	B40F	1993	Go-Ahead Northern, 2000
427	H858NOC	Dennis Dart 9.8m	Carlyle Dartline	B37F	1991	
428	M801OJW	Dennis Dart 9.8m	Plaxton Pointer	B40F	1995	Burton's, Haverhill, 2000

The South East Bus Handbook

MK Metro's Solo fleet contains a mix of the various lengths thus far manufactured. Illustrating the M920 variant is 3, S403ERP. *Dave Heath*

601-605				Renault Trafic		Cymric		M3	1999
601	-	T701RBX	**603**	-	T703RBX	**604**	-	T704RBX	**605**	-	T705RBX
602	-	T702RBX							

606	H	K426FAV	Mercedes-Benz 709D	Marshall C19	BC16FL	1993	Milton Keynes Citybus, 1995
607	H	T622RBX	Renault Trafic	Cymric	M3	1999	
608	H	K428FAV	Mercedes-Benz 709D	Marshall C19	BC16FL	1993	Milton Keynes Citybus, 1995
609	H	K419FAV	Mercedes-Benz 709D	Marshall C19	BC16FL	1993	Milton Keynes Citybus, 1995
610	M	T692LNV	Mercedes-Benz Vario O814	Plaxton Beaver 2	B16FL	1999	
611	M	F393DHL	Mercedes-Benz 709D	Reeve Burgess Beaver	B16FL	1988	London General, 1997
612	M	K616HVV	Mercedes-Benz 709D	Alexander Sprint	B14FL	1993	D&G, Longton, 2004
614	H	T214BBR	Renault Master	Oughtred & Harrison	M6L	1999	Classic, Anfield Plain, 2004
617	H	R517NTF	Ford Escort	Ford	Car 3	1997	private owner, 2001
653	H	RX53RYW	Renault Master	Rohil	B16F	2003	

Previous registrations:

HDZ2606	R808WJA, MSU445, R808WJA	K510FYN	NDZ7936
HDZ2611	R511SJM	K616HVV	K3FET
HDZ2612	R512SJM	NDZ7918	T404LGP
HDZ2613	R513SJM	NDZ7919	T409LGP
HDZ2614	R514SJM	NDZ7933	T406LGP
HDZ7935	T410LGP	V897DNB	V897DNB, 99D72544

Special liveries: White and green (Community Transport 600>) ; orange and white (Easybus 300-9)
Web: www.mkmetro.co.uk

McLEANS

McLeans Coaches Ltd, 5 Two Rivers Ind Est, Station Lane, Witney, OX28 6BH

L672OHL	Volvo B10M-62	Plaxton Première 320	C53F	1994	Fleet Coaches, Fleet, 2001
L673OHL	Volvo B10M-62	Plaxton Première 320	C53F	1994	Fleet Coaches, Fleet, 2001
P297MLD	Dennis Dart 9.8m	Plaxton Pointer	B39F	1996	Metroline, 2005
S497UAK	Mercedes-Benz Vario O814	Plaxton Cheetah	C32F	1998	
W605FUM	Volvo B10M-62	Plaxton Première 350	C48FT	2000	Wallace Arnold, 2002
W638FUM	Volvo B10M-62	Plaxton Première 350	C48FT	2000	Wallace Arnold, 2002
Y752NAY	Volvo B10M-62	Caetano Enigma	C49FT	2001	
Y829NAY	Irisbus EuroMidi CC80E.18	Indcar Maxim	C29F	2001	
Y834NAY	Irisbus EuroMidi CC80E.18	Indcar Maxim	C29F	2001	
FE51RGZ	Irisbus EuroRider 391E.12.35	Beulas Stergo ε	C53F	2001	
FE51RGX	Irisbus EuroMidi CC80E.18	Indcar Maxim	C29F	2002	
FN02RXF	MAN 18.310	Caetano Enigma	C53F	2002	
FN02RXG	MAN 18.310	Caetano Enigma	C53F	2002	
FJ03VMT	Volvo B12M	Caetano Enigma	C49FT	2003	
FJ03VMU	Volvo B12M	Caetano Enigma	C49FT	2003	
FJ53VDE	Volvo B12M	Caetano Enigma	C49FT	2003	
FJ53VDF	Volvo B12M	Caetano Enigma	C49FT	2003	

web: www.mcleanscoaches.co.uk

Proudly carrying the Irisbus logo, McLeans' Y834NAY is a EuroMidi model with Indcar Maxim bodywork. This 8.4-metre mini-coach generally seats 29 and is manufactured in Spain. *Dave Heath*

MARCHWOOD MOTORWAYS

Marchwood Motorways (Southampton) Ltd, 200 Salisbury Road, Totton, Southampton, SO40 3PF

JUO983	Bristol LL6B	Eastern Coach Works	B39F	1948	Marchwood, Haverfordwest, '81
CEL105T	Bedford YMT	Plaxton Supreme IV	C53F	1979	Swallow, Bristol, 1986
C337VRY	Bova FLD12.250	Bova Futura	C57F	1986	
F247RJX	DAF SB2305	Duple 340	C57F	1989	
F248RJX	DAF SB2305	Duple 340	C57F	1989	
225ASV	Bova FLD12.270	Bova Futura	C57F	1994	
5184MM	DAF SB2700	Van Hool Alizée HE	C51FT	1994	?, 2003
1045MM	DAF SB3000	Van Hool Alizée HE	C51FT	1995	Galloway, Mendlesham, 2003
670DHO	Toyota Coaster HZB50R	Caetano Optimo III	C18F	1995	
M846LFP	MAN 11.190	Caetano Algarve II	C35F	1995	
M104BPX	Ford Transit VE6	Passenger Vehicle Bodies	M12	1995	
N593DOR	Ford Transit VE6	Passenger Vehicle Bodies	M14L	1995	
P190PBP	Iveco TurboDaily 59-12	Mellor	B27F	1997	
P191PBP	Iveco TurboDaily 59-12	Mellor	B27F	1997	
P591MTR	Ford Transit Tourneo	Ford	M6	1997	
8015MM	DAF SB3000	Ikarus Blue Danube	C53F	1997	North Kent Express, 2004
P124RWR	DAF SB3000	Ikarus Blue Danube	C55F	1997	
P125RWR	DAF SB3000	Ikarus Blue Danube	C55F	1997	
P126RWR	DAF SB3000	Ikarus Blue Danube	C55F	1997	
P886PWW	DAF SB3000	Ikarus Blue Danube	C49FT	1997	C&H, Fleetwood, 1999
P887PWW	DAF SB3000	Ikarus Blue Danube	C49FT	1997	Cropper, Leeds, 1999
R63GNW	DAF SB3000	Ikarus Blue Danube	C53F	1998	
S602KUT	Toyota Coaster BB50R	Caetano Optimo IV	C21F	1998	
S603KUT	Toyota Coaster BB50R	Caetano Optimo IV	C18F	1998	
V87SOT	Ford Transit	Ford	M14	2000	
W181CDN	DAF SB3000	Van Hool T9 Alizée	C51F	2000	
W182CDN	DAF SB3000	Van Hool T9 Alizée	C51F	2000	
W184CDN	DAF SB3000	Van Hool T9 Alizée	C51F	2000	
YJ03PPF	DAF SB4000	Van Hool T9 Alizée	C49FT	2003	
YJ03PPK	DAF SB4000	Van Hool T9 Alizée	C49FT	2003	
YJ03PPU	DAF SB4000	Van Hool T9 Alizée	C49FT	2003	
YJ03PPV	DAF SB4000	Van Hool T9 Alizée	C49FT	2003	
YJ03PPX	DAF SB4000	Van Hool T9 Alizée	C49FT	2003	

As well as its coaching business, Marchwood Motorways provide some vehicles under franchise for the Solent Blue Line network and these carry Blue Line livery. Representing the batch of fourteen DAF SB120s is 559, YG52CEK.
Phillip Stephenson

In addition to the many DAF coaches operated, Marchwood Motorways bus fleet is predominantly DAF too. A recent addition to the larger SB220 single-deck buses is Northern Counties Paladin 509, M846RCP, which carries the later Solent Blue Line colours. *Richard Godfrey*

Solent Blueline franchise vehicles:

231	W231CDN	DAF DB250	Optare Spectra	N47/28F	2000		
232	W232CDN	DAF DB250	Optare Spectra	N47/28F	2000		
263	N301FOR	Iveco TurboDaily 59-12	Mellor	B29F	1995		
266	N304FOR	Iveco TurboDaily 59-12	Mellor	B29F	1996		
502	F246RJX	DAF SB220	Optare Delta	B47F	1989		
503	J45GCX	DAF SB220	Optare Delta	B49F	1992		
504	L509EHD	DAF SB220	Ikarus Citibus	BC48F	1993		
505	L510EHD	DAF SB220	Ikarus Citibus	BC48F	1993		
506	T186AUA	DAF SB220	Ikarus Citibus	N43F	1999		
507	T187AUA	DAF SB220	Ikarus Citibus	N43F	1999		
509	M846RCP	DAF SB220	Northern Counties Paladin	B49F	1995	Arriva Bus & Coach, 2003	
	V710LWT	DAF SB220	Ikarus Citibus	N43F	1999		

551-565		DAF SB120		Wrightbus Cadet 2	N39F	2002	
551	YG52CME	554	YG52CEF	558	YG52CLV	561	YG52CLO	564	YG52CLX
552	YG52CEJ	556	YG52CEN	559	YG52CEK	562	YG52CLU	565	YG52CDZ
553	YG52CEA	557	YG52CLZ	560	YG52CLY	563	YG52CMF		

Previous registrations:

225ASV	L382RYC		8015MM	R171GNW	
670DHO	M845LFP		C337VRY	C337VRY, 225ASV	
1045MM	M826RCP, M600WCM, M826RCP		M846RCP	M846RCP, 8015MM	
5184MM	L526EHD				

The South East Bus Handbook

MENZIES

Menzies Aviation Group (UK) Ltd, 560 Shoreham Road West, Heathrow Airport, Hounslow, TW6 3NQ

H01-H25			Scania OmniCity CN94UB4		Scania		N42F	2003		
H01	-	YN03UVM	H08	-	YN03UVX	H14	-	YN03UWD	H20	-	YN03UWL
H02	-	YN03UVP	H09	-	YN03UVZ	H15	-	YN03UWG	H21	-	YN03UWM
H03	-	YN03UVT	H10	-	YN03UWB	H16	-	YN03UWF	H22	-	YN03UWP
H04	-	YN03UVR	H11	-	YN03UVY	H17	-	YN03UWH	H23	-	YN03UWT
H05	-	YN03UVU	H12	-	YN03UVW	H18	-	YN03UWJ	H24	-	YN03UWR
H06	-	YN03UVV	H13	-	YN03UWA	H19	-	YN03UWK	H25	-	YN03UWS
H07	-	YN03UVS									

B26-B35			Scania OmniCity CN94UA6		Scania		AN46T	2003		
B26	-	YN03WRR	B29	-	YN03GHK	B32	-	YN03GHO	B34	-	YN03GHB
B27	-	YN03WRU	B30	-	YN03GHU	B33	-	YN03GHA	B35	-	YN03GHD
B28	-	YN03WRV	B31	-	YN03GHV						

T36-T56			Scania OmniCity CN94UB4		Scania		N42F	2003		
T36	-	YS03ZKX	T42	-	YN53GFX	T47	-	YN53GGP	T52	-	YN53GFE
T37	-	YS03ZKW	T43	-	YN53GGK	T48	-	YN53GGA	T53	-	YN53GEU
T38	-	YS03ZKT	T44	-	YN53GFY	T49	-	YN53GFZ	T54	-	YN53GFG
T39	-	YS03ZKU	T45	-	YN53GGF	T50	-	YN53GGE	T55	-	YN53GGO
T40	-	YS03ZKV	T46	-	YN53GGJ	T51	-	YN53GFA	T56	-	YN53GEY
T41	-	YS03ZKR									

G316YHJ	DAF SB220		Optare Delta	B49F	1989	Claribel, Birmingham, 2002
R527YRP	Dennis Dart SLF		Wrightbus Crusader	N38F	1997	Truronian, Truro, 2002
R530YRP	Dennis Dart SLF		Wrightbus Crusader	N41F	1997	Truronian, Truro, 2002
R813WJA	Mercedes-Benz Vario O814D		Plaxton Beaver 2	B31F	1998	Go West, King's Lynn, 2003
R816WJA	Mercedes-Benz Vario O814D		Plaxton Beaver 2	B31F	1998	Go West, King's Lynn, 2003
S556BNV	Mercedes-Benz Vario O814D		Plaxton Beaver 2	B31F	1999	Smith, Ashington, 2003

Menzies is one of the principal operators to serve London Heathrow. With a high volume of movements, especially between terminals, car parks and hotels, Heathrow has one of the largest concentrations of PCVs in the country. During 2003 Menzies took delivery of three batches of Scania OmniCity integral buses, including the articulated version. The first batch of 12-metre buses is represented by H23, YN03UWT. *Gerry Mead*

A silver livery is used for the main Menzies fleet as shown on articulated Scania OmniCity B32,YN03GHG. These ten 18-metre vehicles are generally found linking the central area with staff and public car parks, N1 and N2 being the names of such facilities. Menzies also operate the services for staff working on the new Terminal 5. *Dave Heath*

S551BNV	Dennis Dart SLF	East Lancs Spryte	N40F	1998	Durham Travel, New Cross, 2003
S721KNV	Dennis Dart SLF	Marshall Capital	N43F	1999	London Buses, 2003
S723KNV	Dennis Dart SLF	Plaxton Pointer 2	N39F	1999	Central Parking, Heathrow, 2002
S793RRL	Dennis Dart SLF	Plaxton Pointer 2	N41F	1998	Martin, Dublin, 2002
T443CBC	Dennis Dart SLF	Wrightbus Crusader	N33F	1999	Whittle, Kidderminster, 2002
T781KNW	Optare Excel L1150	Optare	N17D	1999	Concorde Express, Heathrow, 02
T782KNW	Optare Excel L1150	Optare	N17D	1999	Concorde Express, Heathrow, 02
T783KNW	Optare Excel L1150	Optare	N17D	1999	Concorde Express, Heathrow, 02
T784KNW	Optare Excel L1150	Optare	N17D	1999	Concorde Express, Heathrow, 02
T785KNW	Optare Excel L1150	Optare	N17D	1999	Concorde Express, Heathrow, 02
T787KNW	Optare Excel L1150	Optare	N17D	1999	Concorde Express, Heathrow, 02
T788KNW	Optare Excel L1150	Optare	N17D	1999	Concorde Express, Heathrow, 02
T454HNH	Mercedes-Benz Vario O814	Alexander ALX100	B27F	1999	?, 2003
T455HNH	Mercedes-Benz Vario O814	Alexander ALX100	B27F	1999	?, 2003
T456HNH	Mercedes-Benz Vario O814	Alexander ALX100	B27F	1999	Anglian, Ellough, 2003
V252BNV	Mercedes-Benz Vario O814	Plaxton Beaver 2	B31F	1999	First Potteries, 2003
V385SVV	Mercedes-Benz Vario O814	Plaxton Beaver 2	B27F	1999	Dunn-Line, Nottingham, 2003
V386SVV	Mercedes-Benz Vario O814	Plaxton Beaver 2	B27F	1999	Dunn-Line, Nottingham, 2003
V392SVV	Dennis Dart SLF	Plaxton Pointer 2	N39F	1999	Pete's Travel, West Bromwich, 02
W367EOL	Mercedes-Benz O404	Hispano Vita	C49FT	2000	Mitcham Belle, Mitcham, 2003
W368EOL	Mercedes-Benz O404	Hispano Vita	C49FT	2000	Mitcham Belle, Mitcham, 2003
X167BNH	Dennis Dart SLF	Marshall Capital	N37F	2000	Daybird Roadliner, Luton, 2003
KF02ZWY	Mercedes-Benz Vario O814	Plaxton Beaver 2	BC28FL	2002	Central Parking, Luton, 2003
KF52UAG	Mercedes-Benz Vario O814	Plaxton Beaver 2	B28FL	2002	
KF52UAN	Mercedes-Benz Vario O814	Plaxton Beaver 2	B28FL	2002	
RY03DDU	Mercedes-Benz Sprinter 313CDi	Crest	M15	2003	
RY03DDV	Mercedes-Benz Sprinter 313CDi	Crest	M15	2003	
YN03ZWV	Optare Alero	Optare	N16	2003	

Previous registrations:

R530YRP	R530YRP, 94D64217	T454HNH	T454HNH, J101745
S551BNV	S551BNV, 98D70817	T455HNH	T455HNH, J101750
S793RRL	S793RRL, 98D70898	V387SVV	V387SVV, 99D80587

Depots: buses are parked at various locations around Heathrow airport.

The South East Bus Handbook

MERVYNS COACHES

M CL & J Annetts and L Porter, The New Coach House, Innersdown, Micheldever, Winchester, SO21 3BW

AJB635	Bedford WS	Churchill	B11F	1937	Classic Coach, Jersey, 2002
HOD75	Bedford OB	Duple Vista	C29F	1949	Porter, Dummer, 1982
KYW335	Bedford OB	Whitson	B28F	1950	preservation, 2000
741UKL	Bedford YMP	Plaxton Paramount 3200	C45F	1984	Olivine, Hounslow, 1989
LUI8402	Bedford YMP	Plaxton Paramount 3200 III	C33F	1987	Reading & Wokingham Cs, 2002
E389FLD	Bedford YNV Venturer	Plaxton Paramount 3200 E	C53F	1988	Smith's, Pylle, 2000
E232GPH	Bedford YNV Venturer	Plaxton Paramount 3200 I	C57F	1988	Rambler, Hastings, 2001

Previous registrations:

741UKL	B566HRM	E232GPH	E232GPH, PYD42
AJB635	AJB635, J8588	HOD75	From new
E389FLD	E389FLD, 217NYA	LUI8402	D134VJK, TYW50, RDY155

Web: http://www.mervynscoaches.com

Probably the only operator to feature in this series with a fleet comprising entirely Bedford coaches, Mervyns Coaches' operations include nostalgia transport for such events as weddings. Bedford OB number HOD75 is quite a familiar sight, and this coach has also appeared in films such as *84 Charing Cross Road*, *The Last of the Blonde Bombshells* and *The End of the Affair*. Most recently it has been used in an episode of *Poirot* and also *Foyle's War*.

MOTTS TRAVEL

Motts Coaches (Aylesbury) Ltd, Garside Way, Stocklake, Aylesbury, HP20 1BH

CUB539Y	MCW Metrobus DR102/32	MCW	B46/30F	1983	London Buses, 1994
LIL7230	Leyland Olympian ONTL11/2R	Eastern Coach Works	C45/28F	1985	Brentwood Coaches, 1999
E153OMD	Leyland Olympian ONLXB/1R	Optare	B47/29F	1988	Arriva Southern Counties, 2002
E25UNE	Leyland Tiger TRBTL11/3ARZA	Alexander N	BC70F	1988	Arriva North Midlands, 2003
E26UNE	Leyland Tiger TRBTL11/3ARZA	Alexander N	BC70F	1988	Arriva North Midlands, 2003
E27UNE	Leyland Tiger TRBTL11/3ARZA	Alexander N	BC70F	1988	Arriva North Midlands, 2003
E28UNE	Leyland Tiger TRBTL11/3ARZA	Alexander N	BC70F	1988	Arriva North Midlands, 2003
E29UNE	Leyland Tiger TRBTL11/3ARZA	Alexander N	B53F	1988	Arriva North Midlands, 2003
E30UNE	Leyland Tiger TRBTL11/3ARZA	Alexander N	B53F	1988	Arriva North Midlands, 2003
F763EKM	MCW Metrobus DR132/15	MCW	BC43/27F	1989	Stagecoach South, 2000
F766EKM	MCW Metrobus DR132/15	MCW	BC43/27F	1989	Stagecoach South, 2000
5874MT	Volvo B10M-60	Jonckheere Deauville P599	C53F	1990	
1746MT	Volvo B10M-60	Jonckheere Deauville P599	C51FT	1991	
9920MT	Volvo B10M-60	Jonckheere Deauville P599	C53FT	1992	Henry Crawford, Neilston, 1995
5812MT	Volvo B10M-60	Jonckheere Deauville P599	C49FT	1993	Stagecoach Oxford, 1998
B10MMT	Volvo B10M-62	Jonckheere Deauville 45	C49FT	1993	Clarke's of London, 1997
6787MT	Volvo B10M-62	Jonckheere Deauville 45	C49FT	1994	Park's of Hamilton, 1997
4442MT	Volvo B10M-62	Jonckheere Deauville 45	C53F	1995	Park's of Hamilton, 1997
6601MT	Volvo B10M-62	Jonckheere Deauville 45	C53F	1995	Shearings, 1999
6247MT	Volvo B10M-62	Jonckheere Deauville 45	C53F	1995	Shearings, 1999
5705MT	Volvo B12T	Jonckheere Monaco	C57/14CT	1995	Stort Valley Travellers, 2000
B12RMT	Volvo B12T	Jonckheere Monaco	C57/14CT	1995	Dunn-Line, Nottingham, 2001
M971CVG	Mercedes-Benz 711D	Plaxton Beaver	BC25F	1995	Sanders, Holt, 1999
5723MT	Volvo B9M	Van Hool Alizée HE	C38FT	1996	Clyde Coast Coaches, 2001
P373XGG	Mercedes-Benz 709D	Mellor	BC29F	1997	Clyde Coast Coaches, 2001
6957MT	Volvo B10M-62	Jonckheere Mistral 50	C49FT	1998	
R50MTT	Volvo B10M-62	Jonckheere Mistral 50	C49FT	1998	Cedrics, Wivenhoe, 2001
9775MT	Neoplan Skyliner N122/3	Neoplan	C57/20DT	1999	Peter Carol, Bristol, 2005
S490UAK	Mercedes-Benz Vario 0814	Plaxton Cheetah	C29F	1998	
90WFC	Volvo B10M-62	Jonckheere Mistral 50	C49FT	1998	Bebb, Llantwit Fardre, 2000
S5MTT	Volvo B10M-62	Jonckheere Mistral 50	C49FT	1998	Lochs & Glens, Aberfoyle, 2002

One of two Jonckheere Monaco double-deck coaches operated by Motts, B12RMT is based on a Volvo B12T chassis.
Dave Heath

Pictured crossing Lambeth Bridge is Motts Travel's 6957MT, a Jonckheere Mistral 50. Motts Travel is one of the largest operators of Buckinghamshire. Based in Aylesbury, it was established in the 1960s, in addition to the coaching programme it also operates school transport in the Aylesbury area. Motts have recently relocated ther entire operation to new premises at Stocklake. *Colin Lloyd*

S300MTT	Volvo B9M	Jonckheere Mistral	C38FT	1998	B Kavanagh, Urlingford, 2002
S20MTT	Volvo B7	Plaxton Prima	C55F	1998	Alec Head, Lutton, 2002
T7MTT	Volvo B7	Plaxton Prima	C51DL	1999	
T9MTT	Volvo B7	Plaxton Prima	C53F	1999	Harding, Betchworth, 2002
T100MTT	Volvo B10M-62	Jonckheere Mistral 50	C49FT	1999	
T59MLL	Volkswagen Caravelle	Volkswagen	M8	1999	Berkeley, Hemel Hempstead, 2001
X400MTT	Volvo B10M-62	Plaxton Première 3	C51FT	2000	Logan, Dunloy, 2004
W200MTT	Volvo B10M-62	Jonckheere Mistral 50	C49FT	2000	
MT51MTT	Volvo B10M-62	Jonckheere Mistral 50	C49FT	2001	
MT02MTT	Mercedes-Benz Vario 0815	Sitcar Beluga	C29F	2002	
MT03MTT	Mercedes-Benz Vario 0815	Sitcar Beluga	C29F	2003	
GB03MTT	Volvo B12B	TransBus Panther	C49FT	2003	
GT03MTT	Volvo B12B	TransBus Panther	C49FT	2003	
MT04MTT	Volvo B12B	TransBus Panther	C51FT	2004	
MT05MTT	Volvo B12B	Plaxton Panther	C53F	2005	
GT05MTT	Mercedes-Benz Vario 0815	Sitcar Beluga	C29F	2005	

Previous registrations:

90WFC	S68UBO	9775MT	S150SET, ROI7435
1746MT	H65XBD,	9920MT	K266OGA
4442MT	LSK874, M573DSJ	B10MMT	K914RGE, 90WFC
5705MT	M20TCC	B12MTT	XFV257, M724VAO, L6BOB
5723MT	N364HSD, N4GLP	E209GNV	E209GNV, 6957MT
5812MT	L214GJO	LIL7230	B688BPU
5814MT	D108BNV	R50MTT	R16CED
5874MT	G380RNH, 90WFC	S5MTT	S575KJF
6247MT	M617ORJ	S20MTT	S333SJH
6601MT	M616ORJ	S300MTT	99KK469
6787MT	R968RCH	T9MTT	T9HCT
6957MT	E209GNV	X400MTT	X628AKW

Web: www.mottstravel.com

NEWNHAM COACHES

AS Bone & Sons Ltd, Hillside Service Station, London Road, Hook, RG27 9EQ

YDL674T	Bristol VRT/SL3/6LXB	Eastern Coach Works	B43/31F	1979	Southern Vectis, 1995
TRN468V	Leyland Atlantean AN68A/1R	Eastern Coach Works	B43/31F	1979	RoadCar, Lincoln, 2003
KPJ271W	Leyland Atlantean AN68B/1R	Roe	B43/30F	1980	Amos, Eydon, 2001
KPJ271W	Leyland Atlantean AN68B/1R	Roe	B43/30F	1980	Amos, Eydon, 2001
A70THX	Leyland Titan TNLXB2RR	Leyland	B44/30F	1984	Windmill, Great Bromley, 2003
B66GHR	Dennis Dominator DDA909	Northern Counties	BC43/31F	1985	Thamesdown, 2004
B68GHR	Dennis Dominator DDA909	Northern Counties	BC43/31F	1985	Thamesdown, 2004
HXI3012	Leyland Lynx LX563TL11FR	Alexander N	B53F	1986	Arriva North Midlands, 2002
F605RPG	Dennis Dominator DDA1026	Northern Counties	B45/31F	1989	Thamesdown, 2004
H580VWB	Leyland Swift ST2R44C97T5	Reeve Burgess Harrier	B20FL	1991	?, 2001

OFJ (Page 100) is one of the larger operator to provide services at Heathrow Airport. Recent arrivals, many of which work air-side, include YN04AHO which is seen in October 2005 outside the Queens Building in the centre of the airport. Of interest is the additional central offside door. *Mark Lyons*

NU-VENTURE

Nu-Venture Coaches Ltd, 86 Mill Hall, Aylesford, Maidstone, ME20 7JN

w	PMY177W	Leyland National NL106AL11/2R	East Lancs Greenway (1994)	B44F	1981	London General, 2002
139	IUI2139	Leyland National NL106AL11/2R	East Lancs Greenway (1994)	B44F	1981	London General, 2002
6706	SIB6706	Leyland National NL106AL11/1R	East Lancs Greenway	B41F	1981	Northumbria Coaches, 2005
T341	IUI2142	Leyland Titan TNLXB2RR	Leyland	B44/32F	1981	Metroline, 1996
T415	IUI2140	Leyland Titan TNLXB2RR	Leyland	B44/32F	1982	Metroline, 1996
	TPD103X	Leyland Olympian ONTL11/1R	Roe	B43/29F	1982	County, Brentwood, 1998
T455	KYV455X	Leyland Titan TNLXB2RR	Leyland	B44/30F	1982	Stagecoach Fife Scottish, 1999
T614	NUW614Y	Leyland Titan TNLXB2RR	Leyland	B44/32F	1982	Stagecoach London, 2001
T652	NUW652Y	Leyland Titan TNLXB2RR	Leyland	B44/32F	1982	Stagecoach London, 2001
2563	BXI2563	Bristol RELL6G	Alexander	B52F	1983	Ulsterbus, 2004
129w	XFG29Y	Leyland National 2 NL116HLXB/1R		B47F	1983	Bygone Tours, Smarden, 1998
T857	A857SUL	Leyland Titan TNLXB2RR	Leyland	B44/32F	1983	Kent CC, 2003
T867	A867SUL	Leyland Titan TNLXB2RR	Leyland	B44/29F	1983	Stagecoach, 2004
T873	A873SUL	Leyland Titan TNLXB2RR	Leyland	B44/32F	1983	Stagecoach, 2004
T975w	A975SYE	Leyland Titan TNLXB2RR	Leyland	B44/32F	1984	London Central, 1998
T1097	B97WUV	Leyland Titan TNLXB2RR	Leyland	B44/32F	1984	Stagecoach, 2004
V2w	A102SUU	Volvo B55-10	Alexander RV	B46/30F	1984	Bannister, Owston Ferry, 2004
	IUI2138	Leyland Olympian ONLXB/1RV	Alexander RL	BC43/27F	1986	Stagecoach, 2004
D101	D101NDW	Leyland Lynx LX112TL112R1	Leyland	B49F	1987	Metropolitan, North Acton, 2002
110	D110NDW	Leyland Lynx LX112TL112R1	Leyland	B51F	1987	Metrobus, Orpington, 2003
	8421RU	Scania K92CRB	Van Hool Alizée H	C53F	1988	Swallow, Rainham, 1996
166	F166SMT	Leyland Lynx LX112L10ZR1	Leyland	B51F	1989	Metrobus, Crawley, 2003
	G638REG	Ford Transit VE6	Ford	M8L	1990	private owner, 1999
2792	H792PTW	Leyland Olympian ON2R50C13Z4	Alexander RH	B47/33F	1990	Dublin Bus, 2003
2793	H793PTW	Leyland Olympian ON2R50C13Z4	Alexander RH	B47/33F	1990	Dublin Bus, 2003
2738	H838PTW	Leyland Olympian ON2R50C13Z4	Alexander RH	B47/33F	1990	Dublin Bus, 2003

A pair of Dennis Darts with Marshall Capital bodywork joined the Nu-Venture fleet in 2002. Pictured operating route 114 to Chatham is 718, R718BNF. *Phillip Stephenson*

Eleven Leyland Titans originally supplied to London Buses are now in service with Nu-Venture and all have been converted to single door. Seen at the Queen's Monument in Maidstone is T857, A857SUL. *Martin Smith*

698	J698CGK	Optare MetroRider MR03	Optare	BC27F	1991	London Central, 1998
705	J705CGK	Optare MetroRider MR03	Optare	BC27F	1991	London Central, 1998
	8447RU	Scania K113CRB	Van Hool Alizée HE	C49FT	1993	Cunningham, Corringham, 1996
	SIL2890	Scania K113CRB	Irizar Century 12.35	C49FT	1994	Isleworth Coaches, 1998
109	M109JHB	Optare MetroRider MR03	Optare	BC31F	1994	Southlands, Swanley, 2004
901	N901HWY	Optare MetroRider MR13	Optare	B26F	1996	Metrobus, Orpington, 2003
903	N903HWY	Optare MetroRider MR13	Optare	B26F	1996	Metrobus, Orpington, 2003
905	N905HWY	Optare MetroRider MR13	Optare	B26F	1996	Metrobus, Orpington, 2003
906	N906HWY	Optare MetroRider MR13	Optare	B26F	1996	Metrobus, Orpington, 2003
702	N2FPK	Dennis Dart 9.8m	UVG UrbanStar	B38F	1996	Flightparks, Horley, 2000
703	N3FPK	Dennis Dart 9.8m	UVG UrbanStar	B38F	1996	Flightparks, Horley, 2000
101	N101CKN	Mercedes-Benz 711D	UVG CitiStar	B25FL	1996	Wealden PSV, Tonbridge, 1997
102	N102CKN	Mercedes-Benz 711D	UVG CitiStar	B25FL	1996	Wealden PSV, Tonbridge, 1997
	MHS5P	Dennis Javelin GX 12m	Plaxton Première 320	C49FT	1997	Sullivan Bus, Potters Bar, 2005
311	LK55ABU	BMC Falcon 1100FE	BMC	BC55F	2005	
312	LK55ABV	BMC Falcon 1100FE	BMC	BC55F	2005	
313	LK55ABX	BMC Falcon 1100FE	BMC	BC55F	2005	
718	R718BNF	Dennis Dart SLF	Marshall Capital	N41F	1998	White Rose, Thorpe, 2002
720	R720BNF	Dennis Dart SLF	Marshall Capital	N41F	1998	White Rose, Thorpe, 2002
446	T446HRV	Dennis Dart SLF	Caetano Compass	N44F	1999	Alexcars, Cirencester, 2005
	3558RU	MAN 18.310	Marcopolo Continental 340	C51FT	2001	
719	GN53YUF	TransBus Dart 8.8m	TransBus Mini Pointer	N28F	2003	
721	SN53LWM	TransBus Dart 8.8m	TransBus Mini Pointer	N28F	2003	*Operated for Kent CC*
722	SN53LWO	TransBus Dart 8.8m	TransBus Mini Pointer	N28F	2003	*Operated for Kent CC*
723	SN53LWP	TransBus Dart 8.8m	TransBus Mini Pointer	N28F	2003	*Operated for Kent CC*

Previous registrations:

558RU	Y2NVC		IUI2140	KYV415X
3241RU	F100CWG		IUI2142	KYV341X
8447RU	K200CCC			
1792PTW	90D			
1793PTW	90D		MHS5P	P215TGP
1838PTW	90D1033		PMY177W	GUW448W, WLT648, IUI2138
JI2138	C465SSO, MHS5P		SIB6706	LFR855X
JI2139	GUW500W		SIL2890	L19UER, 3558RU

Web: www.nu-venture.co.uk
Depots: Mill Hall, Aylesford; Hoo Marina, St Werburgh and Tonbridge

OFJ CONNECTIONS

OFJ Connections Ltd, 1 Langley Road, Staines, TW18 2EH

104	-	YS02YXU	Mercedes-Benz Vario O814	Plaxton Cheetah	C25F	2002	
105	-	BX02UPW	Mercedes-Benz Sprinter 311	Mercedes-Benz	M12	2002	
107	-	YS02YXV	Mercedes-Benz Vario O814	Plaxton Cheetah	C29F	2002	
112	-	S297UBU	Ford Transit VE6	Mayflower	M16	1999	TLS, 2001
114	-	S706CMA	LDV Convoy	LDV	M16	1999	
115	-	V57KGT	Mercedes-Benz Sprinter 410	Mercedes-Benz	M	2000	
116	-	MK52UGP	Mercedes-Benz Sprinter 413cdi	Crest	M14	2002	
119	-	P535YEU	Dennis Javelin	Wadham Stringer Vanguard II	B41F	1996	Avalon, Glastonbury, 2002
125	-	T186RJD	Citroën Relay	Advanced	M8	1999	Airlinks, 2001
128	-	T189RJD	Citroën Relay	Advanced	M8	1999	Airlinks, 2001
129	-	T191RJD	Citroën Relay	Advanced	M8	1999	Airlinks, 2001
130	-	T192RJD	Citroën Relay	Advanced	M8	1999	Airlinks, 2001
131	-	T193RJD	Citroën Relay	Advanced	M8	1999	Airlinks, 2001
132	-	T194RJD	Citroën Relay	Advanced	M8	1999	Airlinks, 2001
133	-	T195RJD	Citroën Relay	Advanced	M8	1999	Airlinks, 2001
134	-	T196RJD	Citroën Relay	Advanced	M8	1999	Airlinks, 2001
135	-	T197RJD	Citroën Relay	Advanced	M8	1999	Airlinks, 2001
137	-	RE02NKU	Citroën Relay	Advanced	M8	2002	
140	-	WP02XYG	Ford Transit	Ford	M16	2002	van, 2003
141	-	LJ53LDG	LDV Convoy	LDV	M16	2003	
142	-	YN03WYJ	Mercedes-Benz Vario O814	TransBus Cheetah	C25F	2003	
143	-	LJ53LDF	LDV Convoy	LDV	M16	2003	
144	-	LJ53LDD	LDV Convoy	LDV	M16	2003	
145	-	LJ53LDV	LDV Convoy	LDV	M16	2003	
155	-	YN53CHH	Scania OmniTown N94UB	East Lancs	N--D	2003	
156	-	V673LWT	DAF SB220	Ikarus CitiBus	B26D	1999	BAA Glasgow, 2003
157	-	YN53CHG	Scania OmniTown N94UB	East Lancs	N--D	2003	
164	-	YN53VBX	Volvo B7R	TransBus Profile	C53F	2004	
165	-	CJ02XZK	Citroën Relay	Advanced	M8	2002	private owner, 2003
166	-	LT04CTV	Ford Transit	Ford	M8	2004	
168	-	YN04AHG	Scania OmniCity N94UB	Scania	N--D	2004	
173	-	YX04AXJ	Mercedes-Benz Sprinter 413cdi	Crest	M14	2004	

OFJ provide many of the services required at Heathrow Airport, including several vehicles retained air-side. One of three Cobus 2700 buses designed for such use is OFJ582. *Dave Heath*

In June 2001, Glebe Carriages was renamed 'OFJ Connections Ltd' and applied for an air-side licence to transport crews to and from Heathrow Airport. With the support of four major airlines, OFJ was awarded a licence in early 2002 and began operating services for Lufthansa, Austrian Airlines, Iberia and El-Al. Seen outside Terminal 2 is number 104, YS02YXU, a Mercedes-Benz Vario with Plaxton Cheetah coachwork. *Dave Heath*

	-	M683DGN	LDV Convoy	LDV	M16	1995	Airlinks, 2001
	-	M193UAN	Dennis Lance SLF 12m	Berkhof 2000	N37D	1995	Menzies, Heathrow, 2002
	-	M194UAN	Dennis Lance SLF 12m	Berkhof 2000	N37D	1995	Menzies, Heathrow, 2002
	-	M196UAN	Dennis Lance SLF 12m	Berkhof 2000	N37D	1995	Menzies, Heathrow, 2002
	-	P851JKK	LDV Convoy	Walsall Motor Bodies	M16	1996	Airlinks, 2001
	-	P971PNG	LDV Convoy	Walsall Motor Bodies	M16	1996	Airlinks, 2001
	-	P218VGN	LDV Convoy	LDV	M16	1997	
	-	S705CMA	LDV Convoy	LDV	M16	1999	, 2001
	-	S228LLT	Mercedes-Benz Vario 0814	Marshall Master	B23F	1998	MCH, Uxbridge, 2002
	-	S394LLT	Mercedes-Benz Vario 0814	Marshall Master	BC29F	1999	MCH, Uxbridge, 2002
	-	S303UBU	Ford Transit VE6	Mayflower	M16	1999	TLS, 2001
	-	T643NTW	Vauxhall Movano	Warnerbus	M8	1999	private owner, 2002
	-	V224LWU	Ford Transit	Mayflower	M16	2000	Halifax MBC, 2002
	-	V672LWT	DAF SB220	Ikarus CitiBus	B26D	1999	BAA, Glasgow Airport 2003
	-	RE02NKT	Citroën Relay	Advanced	M8	2002	private owner, 2002
	-	RX53LBJ	Mercedes-Benz Vario 0814	TransBus Beaver	B33F	2003	
	-	RA53BLK	Mercedes-Benz Sprinter 311cdi	Excel	M8	2003	
	-	YN53CHK	Scania OmniTown N94UB	East Lancs	N--D	2003	
	-	YN53CHL	Scania OmniTown N94UB	East Lancs	N--D	2003	
	-	YN04AHJ	Scania OmniCity N94UB	Scania	N--D	2004	
	-	YN04AHP	Scania OmniCity N94UB	Scania	N--D	2004	
	-	LT04CWL	Ford Transit	Ford	M7	2004	
	-	YN04WSY	Mercedes-Benz Vario 0814	TransBus Cheetah	C29F	2004	
	-	AE04PJY	MAN 14.220	MCV Evolution	N22D	2004	
	-	AE04PKA	MAN 14.220	MCV Evolution	N22D	2004	
	-	YN54WDE	Volvo B7R	Plaxton Profile	C53F	2004	
	-	YN05ZXJ	Mercedes-Benz Vario 0814	TransBus Cheetah	C29F	2005	
	-	AE05OVB	MAN 14.220	MCV Evolution	N22D	2005	
580		OFJ580	Cobus 2700 S	Cobus	B--D	20--	
581		OFJ581	Cobus 2700 S	Cobus	B--D	20--	
582		OFJ582	Cobus 2700 S	Cobus	B--D	20--	

Depots: Air-side, Heathrow Airport and Chippenham Road, Lyneham.

PARKING EXPRESS

Parking Express - Courtlands Parking - Europcar

APCOA Parking (UK) Ltd, 2 Windmill Business Village, Brooklands Close, Sunbury-on-Thames, TW16 7DY

	Reg	Chassis	Body	Seat	Year	
	N959UJT	Ford Transit VE6	Ford	M7	1996	
22	P912SUM	MAN 11.190	Optare Vecta	B39F	1996	
39	T739JHE	Scania L94UB	Wright Axcess Floline	NC33D	1999	
40	T743JHE	Scania L94UB	Wright Axcess Floline	NC33D	1999	
41	T746JHE	Scania L94UB	Wright Axcess Floline	NC33D	1999	
42	T354JWA	Scania L94UB	Wright Axcess Floline	NC33D	1999	
43	T356JWA	Scania L94UB	Wright Axcess Floline	NC33D	1999	
44	T357JWA	Scania L94UB	Wright Axcess Floline	NC33D	1999	
45	T362JWA	Scania L94UB	Wright Axcess Floline	NC33D	1999	
46	T364JWA	Scania L94UB	Wright Axcess Floline	NC33D	1999	
47	T365JWA	Scania L94UB	Wright Axcess Floline	NC33D	1999	
48	T367JWA	Scania L94UB	Wright Axcess Floline	NC33D	1999	
49	T368JWA	Scania L94UB	Wright Axcess Floline	NC33D	1999	
50	T374JWA	Scania L94UB	Wright Axcess Floline	NC33D	1999	
51	YN53CHD	Scania OmniCity CN94UB	Scania	N24D	2004	
52	YN53CHC	Scania OmniCity CN94UB	Scania	N24D	2004	
71	X471AHE	Scania L94UB	Wright Axcess Floline	NC28D	2001	
72	X472AHE	Scania L94UB	Wright Axcess Floline	NC28D	2001	
73	X473AHE	Scania L94UB	Wright Axcess Floline	NC28D	2001	
74	X474AHE	Scania L94UB	Wright Axcess Floline	NC28D	2001	
76	Y47HHE	Scania L94UB	Wright Axcess Floline	NC28D	2001	
77	Y48HHE	Scania L94UB	Wright Axcess Floline	NC28D	2001	
78	Y49HHE	Scania L94UB	Wright Axcess Floline	NC28D	2001	
83	V383SVV	Dennis Dart SLF 8.5m	Plaxton Mini Pointer	N29F	1999	Pink Elephant Parking, 2004
	T446EBD	Dennis Dart SLF 11m	Plaxton Pointer 2	N41F	1999	Dawson rentals, 2005
85	Y185HNH	Volvo B7L	Wrightbus Eclipse Urban	N26D	2001	NCP, Birmingham Airport, 2004

Livery: White (Courtlands Parking), green (Parking Express)
Depots: Long Term Car Park, Gatwick Airport (Parking Express)

With operations at Heathrow and Gatwick airports, Parking Express vehicles are kept busy linking their car parks with airport terminals. Pictured at Heathrow is 39, T739JHE, a Scania L94 with Wright Axcess Floline body. A batch of VW LT46s with VDL Kusters, low-floor bodywork is also used for the Europcar service. *Dave Heath*

PEARCES

Pearce Private Hire Ltd, Tower Road, Berinsfield, Wallingford, OX10 7LN

ODU856G	Bedford VAL 70	Duple Viceroy	C53F	1968	preservation, 2005
JUD597W	Ford R1014	Plaxton Supreme IV Express	C45F	1980	House, Watlington, 1987
G227YLU	Toyota Hiace	Toyota	M8	1990	private owner, 2004
J100OFC	Toyota Coaster HDB30R	Caetano Optimo II	C18F	1991	
L11VWL	Plaxton 425	Lorraine	C53F	1993	
M300MFC	Toyota Coaster HZB50R	Caetano Optimo III	C21F	1994	
M968RWL	Bova FLC12.280	Bova Futura Club	C53F	1995	
P1RWL	Toyota Coaster HZB50R	Caetano Optimo III	C21F	1997	
R329VJO	Dennis Javelin GX 12m	Neoplan Transliner	C53F	1998	
R902GJO	Dennis Javelin 10m	Plaxton Première 320	C39F	1998	
T403BFC	Dennis Javelin 10m	Plaxton Première 320	C43F	1999	
Y81LJO	Mercedes-Benz Vario O814	Plaxton Cheetah	C25F	2001	
Y82LJO	Mercedes-Benz Vario O814	Plaxton Cheetah	C25F	2001	
Y83LJO	Dennis Javelin GX 12m	Neoplan Transliner	C49F	2001	
OE02WAU	Dennis R345	Plaxton Panther	C53F	2002	
OU04KMX	TransBus R345	TransBus Panther	C49F	2004	

Previous registrations:
M300MFC   M489HBC   P1RWL   P677CUD

Based in Wallingford, Pearces Coaches are found far and wide. The latest arrival in the fleet came from the TransBus stable in 2004. On 1 January 2001 Henley's acquired a 30% shareholding in TransBus Holdings Limited, a company formed by the merger of the UK bus and coach operations of Henlys Group plc and The Mayflower Corporation plc. However, it was 2003 before the products were sold under the TransBus name. The R-series were conceived as Dennis (the R for rear-engined) and has been sold with bodywork from TransBus Scarborough (formerly and subsequently Plaxtons) and Caetano. Pearces' TransBus Panther OU04KMX is shown here.

POYNTER'S

Poynter's Coaches Ltd, Wye Coach Depot, Churchfield Way, Wye, TN25 5BX

	KYV488X	Leyland Titan TNLXB2RR	Leyland	B44/30F	1982	Stagecoach London, 2001
w	KYV529X	Leyland Titan TNLXB2RR	Leyland	B44/30F	1982	Stagecoach London, 2001
	NUW638Y	Leyland Titan TNLXB2RR	Leyland	B44/30F	1982	West Kent, W Kingsdown, 2005
	2448UE	DAF SB2300	Berkhof Esprit 340	C57F	1985	Travelfar, Henfield, 1991
	IIL3505	Volvo B10M-61	Van Hool Alizée	C49FT	1988	Stagecoach South East, 2000
	G73UYV	Leyland Lynx LX2R11C15Z4S	Leyland Lynx	B49F	1989	London United, 2000
	G74UYV	Leyland Lynx LX2R11C15Z4S	Leyland Lynx	B49F	1989	London United, 2000
	G75UYV	Leyland Lynx LX2R11C15Z4S	Leyland Lynx	B49F	1989	London United, 2000
	G77UYV	Leyland Lynx LX2R11C15Z4S	Leyland Lynx	B49F	1989	London United, 2000
	G252EHD	DAF SB220	Optare Delta	B49F	1989	Brylaine Travel, Boston, 2003
	G936MYG	DAF SB220	Optare Delta	B49F	1990	City Solutions, Walsall, 2004
	G937MYG	DAF SB220	Optare Delta	B49F	1990	Lynx Solutions, Smethwick, 2004
	G25YRY	Bova FHD 12.290	Bova Futura	C57F	1990	Paul S Winson, L'borough, 2001
	NIL4762	Bova FHD 12.290	Bova Futura	C51FT	1990	Elite, Stockport, 2001
	WIW4748	Neoplan Skyliner N112/3	Neoplan	C57/18CT	1990	TRS, Leicester, 2004
	M101ECV	Volvo B12T	Van Hool Astrobel	C57/14CT	1995	First Western National, 2003
	M903OVR	Dennis Javelin GX 12m	Neoplan Transliner	C49FT	1995	Palmer, Sothall, 2002
	M916OVR	Dennis Javelin GX 12m	Neoplan Transliner	C49FT	1995	Camden, West Kingsdown, 2002
	P293MLD	Dennis Dart 9.8m	Plaxton Pointer	B40F	1996	Metroline, 2005
	P524XBB	Dennis Dart 9.8m	Plaxton Pointer	B40F	1996	Coastal, Newick, 2005
	UIL9043	Volvo B10M-62	Berkhof Axial 50	C49FT	1998	Tim's Travel, Sheerness, 2003

Previous registrations:

2448UE	B688BTW	P524XBB	P524XBB, XS2210
G25YRY	G25YRY, 2968PW	UIL9043	R926ULA
IIL3505	E623UNE, XIA257, E942XSB	WIW4748	H203AOD
NIL4762	G330PRC		

Illustrating the Poynter's fleet is Leyland Lynx G74UYV, latterly used by London United. It is seen in Canterbury.
Richard Godfrey

R D H SERVICES

RDH Services Ltd, Ditchling Common, Ditchling, Hassocks, BN6 8SG

OIB3514	Leyland Tiger TRCTL11/2RP	Plaxton Paramount 3200 II	C51F	1984	Delta, Stockton, 1997
OIB3513	Leyland Tiger TRCTL11/2RP	Plaxton Paramount 3200 II	C51F	1984	Delta, Stockton, 1997
LIL9970	Leyland Tiger TRCTL11/3RZ	Plaxton Paramount 3200 III	C55F	1988	Evans, Tregaron, 1999
JUI4377	Volvo B10M-60	Jonckheere Deauville	C49FT	1989	Westbus, Hounslow, 1999
F43XPR	Mercedes-Benz 811D	Wadham Stringer Wessex	B31F	1989	Brighton & Hove, 1999
G54BEL	Mercedes-Benz 811D	Wadham Stringer Wessex	B31F	1989	Brighton & Hove, 2000
H848DNJ	Leyland Swift ST2R44C97T5	Reeve Burgess Harrier	BC32F	1991	MoD (01KK59), 1999
H550XGK	Dennis Dart 8.5m	Plaxton Pointer	B26F	1991	Camden, West Kingdown, 2003
H712LOL	Dennis Dart 9.8m	Carlyle Dartline	B40F	1991	Marchwood Motorways, 1997
TIB4922	Volvo B10M-60	Ikarus Blue Danube 358	C51FT	1991	WMT (Smiths), 1998
K479JHJ	Dennis Dart 9m	Plaxton Pointer	B34F	1992	Metroline, 2002
K480OKH	Dennis Dart 9m	Plaxton Pointer	B35F	1993	Isle of Man, 2000
K864LGN	Dennis Dart 9m	Plaxton Pointer	B34F	1993	Go-Ahead London, 2002
K376RTY	Dennis Dart 9.8m	Wright Handy-bus	B40F	1993	Go-Ahead Northern, 2001
K377RTY	Dennis Dart 9.8m	Wright Handy-bus	B40F	1993	Go-Ahead Northern, 2001
K860BOL	Dennis Javelin 8.5m	Wadham Stringer Vanguard 2	BC36F	1993	MoD, 2002
K861BOL	Dennis Javelin 8.5m	Wadham Stringer Vanguard 2	BC36F	1993	MoD, 2002
K867BOL	Dennis Javelin 8.5m	Wadham Stringer Vanguard 2	BC36F	1993	MoD, 2002
L103DNX	Dennis Javelin 10m	Wadham Stringer Vanguard 2	BC40F	1994	MoD, 2003
M509VJO	Dennis Dart 9m	Marshall C37	B36D	1995	Cityline, Oxford, 2002
M514VJO	Dennis Dart 9m	Marshall C37	B36D	1995	Cityline, Oxford, 2002
P975HWF	Dennis Javelin GX	Neoplan Transliner	C49FT	1997	Camden, West Kingsdown. 2001
P982HWF	Dennis Javelin GX	Neoplan Transliner	C49FT	1997	Camden, West Kingsdown. 2001
W558JVV	Dennis Dart SLF 10.1m	Plaxton Pointer 2	N39F	2000	Connex Bus, 2002
W689TNV	Dennis Dart SLF 10.1m	Plaxton Pointer 2	N39F	2000	Connex Bus, 2002
X601AHE	Dennis Dart SLF 10.1m	Plaxton Pointer 2	N39F	2000	Connex Bus, 2002
X602AHE	Dennis Dart SLF 10.1m	Plaxton Pointer 2	N39F	2000	Connex Bus, 2002
BU03LYG	Mercedes-Benz Sprinter 413cdi	Excel	M14	2003	

Previous registrations:

JUI4377	F906YNV, WIB8750	OIB3514	A453HPY
K479JHJ	CMN71P(IoM)		
LIL9970	E973NMK	TIB4922	H408LVC
OIB3513	A454HPY		

Note: This operator also provides services for County Rider using their vehicles.
Web: www.rdhservices.co.uk

RDH Services has now been running for over twenty years and with a staff of around eighty operates from purpose-built premises in Plumpton. The fleet comprises mainly Dennis products, with 9-metre Dart M509VJO shown here. Bodywork on this bus is the Marshall C37, a type that evolved from the Duple Dartline. *Phillip Stephenson*

RAMBLER

Rambler Coaches Ltd, Whitworth Road, St Leonards-on-Sea, TN37 7PZ

02	X500GDY	Mercedes-Benz O404-15R	Hispano Vita	C49FT	2000	
03	GX02AEE	Volvo B10M-62	Plaxton Paragon	C49FT	2003	
04	CR04RAM	Volvo B7R	Plaxton Profile	C53F	2004	
05	GX02AED	Volvo B10M-62	Plaxton Paragon	C49FT	2003	
06	Y222PDY	Volvo B10M-62	Berkhof Axial 50	C49FT	2001	
07	UDY512	Dennis Dart 9.8m	Marshall C37	B40F	1995	Fleetmaster, Horsham, 2002
08	NDY962	Volvo B10M-62	Plaxton Première 350	C53F	1996	Bus Eireann, 2001
10	V222PDY	Mercedes-Benz O1120L	Optare / Ferqui Solera	C35F	1999	
11	PDY42	Dennis Dart 9.8m	Alexander Dash	B41F	1992	Red Route, Northfleet, 2004
12	NDY820	Volvo B10M-61	Northen Counties Paladin	B51F	1992	Birmingham Omnibus, 2004
14	JG04RAM	Volvo B7R	Plaxton Profile	C53F	2004	
15	T222ADY	Mercedes-Benz 614D	Autobus	C24F	1999	
16	ODY395	Volvo B10M-62	Jonckheere Deauville 45	C53F	1995	Shearings, 2003
17	ODY607	Volvo B10M-62	Jonckheere Deauville 45	C53F	1995	Shearings, 2003
18	LDY173	Volvo B10M-61	Van Hool Alizée	C51FT	1988	
19	SDY788	Volvo B10M-61	Van Hool Alizée H	C53F	1987	Shearings, 1992
20	FDY83	Volvo B10M-60	Van Hool Alizée H	C57F	1991	Epsom Coaches, 1998
21	MDY397	Dennis Dart 9.8m	Alexander Dash	B41F	1992	Stagecoach South, 2004
22	BDY389	Volvo B10M-60	Van Hool Alizée H	C57F	1991	Epsom Coaches, 1998
23	JDY673	Volvo B10M-62	Van Hool Alizée HE	C51F	1995	Shearings, 2002
24	HDY565	Mercedes-Benz 709D	Alexander Sprint	BC25F	1990	Autocar, Five Oak Green, 2002
25	GDY493	Volvo B10M-62	Plaxton Première 350	C53F	1996	Bus Eireann, 2001
26	TDY946	Volvo B10M-55	Plaxton Derwent II	B55F	1993	St Buryan Garage, 2004
27	TDY388	Volvo B10M-62	Berkhof Axial 50	C49FT	1998	
28	DDY222	Scania K124IB4	Van Hool T9 Alizée	C49FT	2000	
30	E968KDP	Volvo B10M-61	Plaxton Paramount 3200 III	C57F	1988	Owen, Yateley, 1997
31	DDY557	Volvo B12M	Berkhof Axial 50	C49FT	2003	Bebb, Llantwit Fardre, 2005

The livery application of Rambler's 36, 1924RH, seen here at the British Coach Rally, disguises the body style of the Mark III Plaxton Paramount 3500 quite well. Rambler was originally formed in 1924 by R.G.Rowland, the father of one of the present owners, offering local sightseeing tours around Hastings, and thus in 2004 celebrated eighty years of service.
Dave Heath

In addition to extensive coaching activities, Rambler has also gained local services. Pictured heading for Pett on Sussex route 347 is Dart UDY512. This bus has Marshall C37 bodywork which, when new to City of Oxford, was dual-doored. *Dave Heath*

32	GDY500X	Bedford YNT	Plaxton Supreme V	C57F	1982	Craker, Maidstone, 1998
34	JG54RAM	Mercedes-Benz Vario 0814	Plaxton Cheetah	C33F	2004	
35	PDY272	Volvo B10M-62	Van Hool T9 Alizée	C49FT	1999	
36	1924RH	Volvo B10M-60	Plaxton Paramount 3500 III	C52F	1991	Wallace Arnold, 1994
37	HDY405	Volvo B10M-61	Plaxton Paramount 3500 III	C53F	1987	

Special event vehicles:

01	FCO314	Austin CXB	Plaxton	C29F	1950	Hickmott, Kingsnorth, 2004
	NG2414	Bedford WTB	Economy	B20F	1932	preservation, 1996
29	JDY888Y	Bedford VAS5	Plaxton Supreme IV	C29F	1983	Maye, Astley, 2000
33	UDY910	Bedford YMPS	Plaxton Paramount 3200 III	C33F	1987	

Previous registrations:

1924RH	H631UWR, KDY814, DDY557	NDY820	E364NEG, JIL5279
BDY389	H533WGH	NDY962	96D42485(EI), P427LJW
DDY222	W222KDY	ODY395	M605ORJ
DDY557	CA52LAO	ODY607	M613ORJ
E968KDP	E169OMD, OUJ317, ODY607	PDY42	J534GCD
FDY83	H532WGH	PDY272	T222GDY
GDY493	96D42478(EI), P428LJW	SDY788	D588MVR
HDY405	D137VJK	TDY388	R222VDY
HDY565	G200PAO	TDY946	K102XPA, TIL1185
JDY673	M649RVU	UDY512	M513VJO
KDY814	-	UDY910	D133VJK
LDY173	E184XJK	VDY468	-
MDY397	J505GCD		

Special livery: Grand UK Holidays (White); 03. Travelsphere (Blue & white): 02, 28.

READING BUSES

Reading Buses - Newbury Buses - Goldline

Reading Transport Ltd, Great Knollys Street, Reading, RG1 7HH

11-17			Leyland Olympian ONLXB/1RH*		Optare		B42/26F	1988		*11/2 are ONLXCT/1RH
11	RG	E911DRD	13	RG	E913DRD	15	RG	E915DRD	17	RG	E917DRD
12	RG	E912DRD	14	RG	E914DRD	16	RG	E916DRD			
75	RG	RMO75Y	Leyland Titan TNLXC1RF		Leyland		BC39/27F	1983		
77	RG	RMO77Y	Leyland Titan TNLXC1RF		Leyland		BC39/27F	1983		
78	RG	RMO78Y	Leyland Titan TNLXC1RF		Leyland		B42/31F	1983		
82	u	D82UTF	Leyland Olympian ONLXCT/1RH		Eastern Coach Works		B43/27F	1986		
101-108			Optare Solo M850		Optare		N30F	1999		
101	RG	S101LBL	103	RG	S103LBL	105	RG	S105LBL	107	NB	S107LBL
102	RG	S102LBL	104	RG	S104LBL	106	RG	S106LBL	108	NB	V108DCF
109	NB	V109DCF	Optare Solo M920		Optare		N34F	2000		
110	NB	V110DCF	Optare Solo M920		Optare		N34F	2000		
111	NB	V946DCF	Optare Solo M920		Optare		N34F	2000		
112	RG	V112DCF	Optare Solo M850		Optare		N30F	2000		
113	RG	V113DCF	Optare Solo M850		Optare		N30F	2000		
114	RG	V114DCF	Optare Solo M850		Optare		N30F	2000		
115	RG	V115DCF	Optare Solo M850		Optare		N30F	2000		
116	NB	W116SRX	Optare Solo M920		Optare		N34F	2000		
117	NB	W117SRX	Optare Solo M920		Optare		N34F	2000		
120	NB	Y594HPK	Optare Solo M920		Optare		N32F	2001		
121	NB	Y595HPK	Optare Solo M920		Optare		N32F	2001		
122	NB	YG02FVV	Optare Solo M850		Optare		N28F	2002		
123	NB	YG02FVW	Optare Solo M850		Optare		N28F	2002		
124	NB	YG02FVX	Optare Solo M850		Optare		N28F	2002		
125	NB	YG02FVY	Optare Solo M920		Optare		N32F	2002		
193	RG	LMO193X	MCW Metrobus DR102/30		MCW		B45/28F	1982		
201	RG	R901EDO	Mercedes-Benz Vario O814		Autobus Nouvelle		C29F	1998	Optare, 2001	

Reading was one of the few operators of Leyland's rear-engined Titan. Their intake including some of the twenty-six single-door examples with forward-located staircases. Three of these remain in the fleet, including 78, RMO78Y, which was re-seated with bus seats though it retains the Goldline lettering. *Colin Lloyd*

The last remaining first generation Metrobus at Reading is 193, LMO193X, which carries commemorative livery of the erstwhile municipal undertaking. It is seen in the town heading for Tilehurst. This will be replaced along with the former London versions when next years OnmiDekkas are delivered. *Colin Lloyd*

210-215			Scania K114EB4		Irizar Century 12.35		C49FT	2003-04	
210	RG	YN53OZK	212	RG	YN04AHC	214	RG	YN04AHE	215	RG	YN04AHF
211	RG	YN53OZL	213	RG	YN04AHD					

234	RG	J786KHD	DAF SB2700		Van Hool Alizée		C51F	1992	Chesterfield, 1994
235	RG	J788KHD	DAF SB2700		Van Hool Alizée		C55F	1992	Hallmark, Luton, 1996
237	RG	L529EHD	DAF SB2700		Van Hool Alizée		C51F	1994	RDJ International, Torquay, 98
239	RG	R37GNW	DAF SB3000		Van Hool Alizée		C49FT	1998	Landtourers, Farnham, 1999

455-469			MCW Metrobus DR102/63		MCW		B45/30F	1987-88	Metroline, 1991
455	NB	E454SON	459	RG	E459SON	463	RG	E463SON	467	RG	E467SON
456	NB	E456SON	460	RG	E460SON	464	RG	E464SON	468	RG	E468SON
457	NB	E457SON	461	RG	E247KCF	465	RG	E465SON	469	RG	E469SON
458	NB	E458SON	462	RG	E462SON	466	RG	E466SON		

471-476			Dennis Trident		Plaxton President		B47/29F	2001	Pete's Travel, West Bromwich, '03
471	RG	PO51WNF	473	RG	PO51WNJ	475	RG	PO51WNL	476	RG	PO51WNM
472	RG	PO51WNG	474	RG	PO51WNK					

501-510			DAF SB220		Optare Delta		B49F	1989	
501	NB	G501XBL	504	NB	G504XBL	507	NB	G507XBL	509	NB	G509XBL
502	NB	G502XBL	505	NB	G505XBL	508	NB	G508XBL	510	NB	G510XBL
503	NB	G503XBL	506	NB	G506XBL					

511-520			DAF SB220		Optare Delta		B47F	1995-96	
511	RG	M511PDP	514	RG	N514YTF	517	RG	N517YTF	519	RG	N519YTF
512	RG	M512PDP	515	RG	N515YTF	518	RG	N518YTF	520	RG	N520YTF
513	RG	M513PDP	516	RG	N516YTF					

The South East Bus Handbook

In addition to services in the town of Reading, this operator also serves parts of the Unitary Authorities of Wokingham and West Berkshire - of which Newbury is the centre. Buses allocated to the Newbury depot carry a different livery, shown here on Optare Delta 504, G504XBL. *Colin Lloyd*

624	w	N624ATF	Optare MetroRider MR17	Optare		B25F	1996	
626	NB	M930TYG	Optare MetroRider MR17	Optare		B27F	1995	Optare demonstrator, 1995
627	RG	R627SJM	Optare MetroRider MR17	Optare		B25F	1997	
628	NB	P914XUG	Optare MetroRider MR17	Optare		B29F	1997	Optare demonstrator, 1997
629	RG	R629SJM	Optare MetroRider MR17	Optare		B25F	1997	
630	NB	T553ADN	Optare MetroRider MR17	Optare		B31F	1999	
631	NB	T554ADN	Optare MetroRider MR17	Optare		B29F	1999	
632	NB	T556ADN	Optare MetroRider MR17	Optare		B29F	1999	
701	RG	MRD1	DAF DB250	Optare Spectra		B43/28F	1992	
702	RG	K702BBL	DAF DB250	Optare Spectra		B46/28F	1992	
704	RG	K170FYG	DAF DB250	Optare Spectra		B44/27F	1992	Optare demonstrator, 1993
705	RG	L705FRD	DAF DB250	Optare Spectra		B46/28F	1994	
706	RG	L706FRD	DAF DB250	Optare Spectra		B46/28F	1994	
707	RG	L707LJM	DAF DB250	Optare Spectra		B46/28F	1994	

708-713

708-713			DAF DB250			Optare Spectra		B48/29F	1998	Eastbourne Buses, 2001-02
708	RG	S876BYJ	710	RG	S878BYJ	712	RG	S880BYJ	713	RG	S881BYJ
709	RG	S877BYJ	711	RG	S879BYJ					

721-739

721-739			DAF DB250			Optare Spectra		N47/27F	2001-03	
721	RG	YJ51ZVE	726	RG	YE52FHF	731	RG	YJ51ZVH	736	RG	YJ51ZVO
722	RG	YJ51ZVF	727	RG	YE52FHG	732	RG	YJ51ZVK	737	RG	YG02FWA
723	RG	YJ51ZVG	728	RG	YJ03UMK	733	RG	YJ51ZVL	738	RG	YG02FWB
724	RG	YG02FWD	729	RG	YJ03UML	734	RG	YJ51ZVN	739	RG	YG02FWC
725	RG	YG02FWE				735	RG	YJ51ZVM			

Reading Buses made a significant change to its purchasing policy in 2003 when Scania buses were ordered, Seventeen OmniDekkas arrived in 2004, and a further vehicle to replace 703 is due shortly. These buses are route branded, and various colours are used. The cover picture shows one style, while here 804, YN54AEV, is seen on route 25. *Mark Lyons*

801-817   Scania OmniDekka N94UD   East Lancs   N51/39F   2004

801	RG	YN54AEP	806	RG	YN54AEX	810	RG	YN54AFE	814	RG	YN54AFO
802	RG	YN54AET	807	RG	YN54AEY	811	RG	YN54AFF	815	RG	YN54AFU
803	RG	YN54AEU	808	RG	YN54AEZ	812	RG	YN54AFJ	816	RG	YN54AFV
804	RG	YN54AEV	809	RG	YN54AFA	813	RG	YN54AFK	817	RG	YN54AFX
805	RG	YN54AEW									

818   -   -   Scania OmniDekka N94UD   East Lancs   N51/39F   On order for 2005

819-834   Scania OmniDekka N94UD   East Lancs   N51/39F   On order for spring 2006

819	-	-	823	-	-	827	-	-	831	-	-
820	-	-	824	-	-	828	-	-	832	-	-
821	-	-	825	-	-	829	-	-	833	-	-
822	-	-	826	-	-	830	-	-	834	-	-

901-916   Optare Excel L1150   Optare   N39F   1997

901	RG	P901EGM	905	RG	P905EGM	909	RG	P909EGM	913	RG	P913GJM
902	RG	P902EGM	906	RG	P906EGM	910	RG	P910EGM	914	RG	P914GJM
903	RG	P903EGM	907	RG	P907EGM	911	RG	P911GJM	915	RG	P915GJM
904	RG	P904EGM	908	RG	P908EGM	912	RG	P912GJM	916	RG	R916SJH

925-942   Optare Excel L1150   Optare   N39F   1998-99

925	RG	S925LBL	929	RG	S929LBL	933	RG	T933EAN	936	RG	T936EAN
926	RG	S926LBL	930	RG	S930LBL	934	RG	T934EAN	941	NB	V941DCF
927	RG	S927LBL	931	RG	S931LBL	935	RG	T935EAN	942	NB	V942DCF
928	RG	S928LBL	932	RG	T932EAN						

In addition to the OmniDekkas, twenty single-deck Scania N94UBs with Wrightbus Solar bodies have displaced Delta and Excel models. The first of the type, 1001, YN05GXA, is seen here with lettering for the 4, 5 and 6 group of routes. *Mark Lyons*

961	RG	X961BPA	Optare Excel L1180	Optare	N39F	2000	
962	RG	X962BPA	Optare Excel L1180	Optare	N39F	2000	
963	RG	X963BPA	Optare Excel L1180	Optare	N39F	2000	
964	RG	X964BPA	Optare Excel L1180	Optare	N39F	2000	

970-973			TransBus Enviro 300		TransBus	N44F	2003		
970	NB	KV03ZGK	971	NB	KV03ZGL	972	NB	KV03ZGM	973	NB	KV03ZGN

974	RG	SK52USS	TransBus Enviro 300	TransBus	N44F	2002	TransBus demonstrator, 2004

1001-1020			Scania N94UB		Wrightbus Solar		N42F	2005		
1001	RG	YN05GXA	1006	RG	YN05GXF	1011	RG	YN05GXO	1016	RG	YN05GXT
1002	RG	YN05GXB	1007	RG	YN05GXG	1012	RG	YN05GXL	1017	RG	YN05GXU
1003	RG	YN05GXD	1008	RG	YN05GXH	1013	RG	YN05GXP	1018	RG	YN05GXV
1004	RG	YN05GXC	1009	RG	YN05GXJ	1014	RG	YN05GXR	1019	RG	YN05GXW
1005	RG	YN05GXE	1010	RG	YN05GXM	1015	RG	YN05GXS	1020	RG	YN05GXX

Previous registrations:
E247KCF   E475SON, MRD1

Depots: Great Knollys Street, Reading and Mill Lane, Newbury.

The South East Bus Handbook

REBOUND

Carterton Coaches (Witney) Ltd, Supergas Ind Est, Downs Road, Minster Lovell, Witney, OX29 0SZ

	Reg	Model	Make	Body	Year	History
	UTC872	Neoplan Skyliner N122/3	Neoplan	C57/20CT	1983	Jordison, Murton, 2005
	A494JEC	Setra S215 H	Setra	C53F	1983	Stainton, Kendal, 1997
	IAZ6421	Setra S215 HD	Setra	C49FT	1983	Smith, Corby Glen, 2002
	RJI6611	Setra S215 HD	Setra	C49FT	1983	Palmer, Sothall, 2001
	A252TAG	Setra S215 HD	Setra	C49FT	1983	Palmer, Sothall, 2001
	B184BLG	Leyland Olympian ONLXB/1R	Eastern Coach Works	B45/32F	1984	Arriva The Shires, 2003
w	B182CBW	Setra S215 HD	Setra	C49FT	1985	?, 2004
	RJI7972	Setra S215 HD	Setra	C48FT	1985	Beeston, Hadleigh, 1999
	TIL6288	Setra S228 DT	Setra Imperial	C54/20CT	1986	Swan, Denham, 2005
	C724JTL	Neoplan Skyliner N122/3	Neoplan	C57/20CT	1986	Moroney, Ennis, 2004
	E470YWJ	Neoplan Skyliner N112/3	Neoplan	C57/18CT	1988	TRS, Leicester, 2004
	H310ECK	Setra S210H	Setra	C32FT	1991	Alec Head, Lutton, 2004
	N203PUL	Setra S250	Setra Special	C53F	1996	MacPhersons, Donnithorpe, '05
	P215RUU	Setra S250	Setra Special	C48FT	1997	Buzzlines, Hythe, 2005
	OE53LNZ	Ford Transit Torneo	Ford	M7	2004	
	CU04LTE	Ford Transit	Ford	M16	2004	

Previous registrations:

A252TAG	A33KBA, OXK373, A252TAG, ALZ7313	IAZ6421	OFB606Y, YOR456, URL149Y
A494JEC	A707DEC, LIB3768	RJI6611	515VTB, LAG706Y, LHJ736
B182CBW	-		
C724JTL	C724JTL, 86KK195	RJI7972	8760EL, B486OPJ, 8760EL
		TIL6288	D868FSX, APT42S, D782YEV, 841BMB, D941YHK
E470YWJ	E470YWJ, 163PBB, 2320DD	UTC872	C727JTL, 7878SC, C918CSL, 282GOT, C940CTP, TFX663
H310ECK	H479FLD, 466YMG, H310ECK, 6447PO		

Rebound's Setra B182CBW is a type S215HD and represents the only model available in right-hand drive when built in 1985. It has recently been been replaced in service by a later model Setra. *Dave Heath*

RED ROSE

Red Rose Travel Ltd, 110 Oxford Road, Aylesbury, HP21 8PB

185	N802GRV	Mercedes-Benz 709D	UVG CitiStar	B29F	1996	
186	N803GRV	Mercedes-Benz 709D	UVG CitiStar	B29F	1996	
187	N219HBK	Dennis Dart 9.8m	UVG UrbanStar	B40F	1996	
188	N784JBM	Mercedes-Benz 711D	UVG CitiStar	B29F	1996	
192	P507NWU	Optare MetroRider MR17	Optare	B25F	1996	Optare demonstrator, 1997
195	R796GSF	Mercedes-Benz Vario 0814	Plaxton Beaver 2	B29F	1997	
197	F49ENF	Leyland Tiger TRBL10/3ARZA	Alexander N	B53F	1987	Timeline, 1998
200	M260VEJ	Dennis Dart 9.8m	East Lancashire 2000	B43F	1995	Davies Bros, Pencader, 1998
204	T341FWR	Optare MetroRider MR17	Optare	B31F	1998	
206	D303PEV	Volvo B9M	Plaxton Bustler	B38F	1986	Rai, Birmingham, 1999
207	V108LVH	Optare MetroRider MR17	Optare	B31F	1999	
209	R843FWW	Optare MetroRider MR17	Optare	B31F	1997	
210	Y358LCK	Dennis Dart SLF	East Lancs Flyte	N41F	2001	
211	Y359LCK	Dennis Dart SLF	East Lancs Flyte	N41F	2001	
213	N902HWY	Optare MetroRider MR13	Optare	B26F	1996	Metrobus, Orpington, 2002
214	RR02BUS	Dennis Dart SLF 8.5m	Plaxton Pointer MPD	N29F	2002	
215	MX03EJY	Optare Solo M920	Optare	N33F	2003	
216	RR03BUS	Optare Solo M920	Optare	N33F	2003	
217	J124FUF	Dennis Javelin 11m	Wadham Stringer Portsdown	B55F	1991	Anglian, Beccles, 2001

Operating services around Aylesbury, Red Rose provides a network of services using mini and midibuses. Five Optare MetroRiders are in the current fleet, represented by 209, R843FWW, shown here. *Dave Heath*

REDROUTE BUSES

J & T Mee, Granby Coachworks, Grove Road, Northfleet, DA11 9AX

	Reg	Chassis	Body	Layout	Year	History
	CUV322C	AEC Routemaster R2RH1	Park Royal	B40/32R	1965	Arriva London, 2005
	JJD445D	AEC Routemaster R2RH	Park Royal	B40/32R	1966	Stagecoach London, 2003
	MLH304L	Daimler Fleetline CRG6LXB	MCW	O44/27F	1972	Guide Friday, Stratford, 2003
	MCY188M	Leyland Leopard PSU3B/4R	Plaxton Panorama Elite III	C53F	1974	Pearson, Old Whittington, 2004
	VIB8319	Leyland National 10351A/2R		B44F	1978	Imperial Bus, Rainham, 2004
	THX105S	MCW Metrobus DR101/3		B43/28D	1978	Metroline, 2002
w	BKE848T	Bristol VRT/SL3/6LXB	Eastern Coach Works	B43/31F	1979	preservation, 2000
	BHO442V	Leyland Leopard PSU5C/4R	Duple Dominant II	C57F	1980	Havercroft, Carlton, 2004
	LUA287V	Leyland Leopard PSU3F/4R	Plaxton Supreme IV	C53F	1979	Bluebird, Weymouth, 2005
	UPT680V	Leyland National NL116L11/1R (Volvo)		B49F	1980	Go-Ahead Northern, 2003
w	FKM304V	Dennis Dominator DD129	Willowbrook	B44/31F	1980	Liddell, Auchinleck, 2003
	EYE322V	MCW Metrobus DR101/12	MCW	B43/28D	1980	Imperial Bus, Rainham, 2002
	KYV771X	MCW Metrobus DR101/14	MCW	B43/28F	1982	Arriva The Shires, 2003
w	TJR715Y	Leyland National 2 NL116AHLXB/1R		B49F	1983	Go-Ahead Northern, 2004
	TJR719Y	Leyland National 2 NL116AHLXB/1R (Volvo)		B49F	1983	Ayrways, Ayr, 2004
	BPA66Y	Van Hool T813	Van Hool Acron	C36FT	1983	Duckworth, Gisburn, 2005
	A249SVW	Leyland Tiger TRCTL11/3RP	Duple Caribbean	C57F	1984	Village Coaches, Findon, 2005
	494WYA	Leyland Tiger TRCTL11/3R	Plaxton Paramount 3500	C57F	1984	Arriva Southern Counties, 2002
	B148EDP	MCW Metrobus DR102/44	MCW	BC39/27F	1984	John's School of Motoring, 2002
	B149EDP	MCW Metrobus DR102/44	MCW	BC39/27F	1984	Trimmer, Harold Park, 2004
	B229WUL	MCW Metrobus DR101/17	MCW	B43/28D	1985	Arriva London, 2001
	C347BUV	MCW Metrobus DR101/17	MCW	B43/28D	1985	London General, 2002
w	C652LJR	Leyland Olympian ONCL10/1RV	Eastern Coach Works	BC40/30F	1985	Go-Ahead Northern, 2002
	C670LJR	Leyland Olympian ONCL10/1RV	Eastern Coach Works	BC40/30F	1985	Go-Ahead Northern, 2002
	G905TYR	DAF MB230	Van Hool Alizée H	C53F	1990	Poynter's, Wye, 2005
	G78UYV	Leyland Lynx LX2R11C15Z4S	Leyland Lynx	B49F	1989	London United, 2000
	G778WFC	Optare MetroRider MR09	Optare	B25F	1990	Emsworth & District, 2005
	G779WFC	Optare MetroRider MR09	Optare	B25F	1990	Emsworth & District, 2005
	H613NJB	Optare MetroRider MR07	Optare	B25F	1991	Guide Friday, Stratford, 2003
	H172WWT	Optare MetroRider MR03	Optare	B26F	1991	Metrobus, Crawley, 2003
	J582CUB	Optare MetroRider MR07	Optare	BC25F	1992	White Rose, Thorpe, 2003
	L116HHV	Dennis Dart 9m	Northern Counties Paladin	B34F	1994	Metroline, 2003
	M425PVN	Volvo B6 9.9M	Alexander Dash	B40F	1994	Go-Ahead Northern, 2005

Previous registrations:

494WYA	A420HND, 507EXA, A268MEH	PKP550R	PKP550R, 9925AP
AAX465A	SDW916Y	VIB8319	THX130S
FKK942Y	FKK942Y, TSU642		
MCY188M	YWE506M, 440VT, GAW60M, YSV316, BTU447M, GAW112M, 467VT, WEY84M, OIL4473.		

Currently, the only Dart operated by Redroute Buses fleet is Northern Counties-bodied L116HHV, which joined the fleet in 2003 from Metroline.
Dave Heath

115

REGENT COACHES

PC, ID & KJ Regent, 16 St Augustine's Business Park, Swalecliffe, Whitstable, CT5 2QJ

1	FD03YOG	Irisbus EuroMidi CC80E18.MP	Indcar Maxim 2	C29F	2003	
2	FG03JCJ	Irisbus EuroMidi CC80E18.MP	Indcar Maxim 2	C29F	2003	
3	FE51RGO	Irisbus EuroMidi CC80E18.MP	Indcar Maxim	C29F	2001	
4	Y828NAY	Irisbus EuroMidi CC80E18.MP	Indcar Maxim	C29F	2001	
5	L933JFU	Mercedes-Benz 814D	Autobus Classique	BC33F	1994	Brown, South Kirkby, 1997
6	H672LCF	Mercedes-Benz 814D	Reeve Burgess Beaver	BC33F	1991	Coles, Eversley, 1995
7	MX05CZW	Mercedes-Benz Vario 0814			2005	
8	H510BND	Mercedes-Benz 609D	Made-to-Measure	BC24F	1990	
9	F655HVM	Mercedes-Benz 609D	Made-to-Measure	BC24F	1989	
10	M403MPD	Mercedes-Benz 609D	Olympus	BC21F	1995	
11	MX05CZY	Mercedes-Benz Sprinter 413CDi	Olympus	M16	2005	
12	MK02HAO	Mercedes-Benz Sprinter 413CDi	Olympus	M16	2002	
13	V480NKK	Mercedes-Benz Sprinter 410D	Olympus	M16	1995	
14	V490NKK	Mercedes-Benz Sprinter 410D	Olympus	M16	1995	
15	K797EPU	Mercedes-Benz 410D	Olympus	M14	1992	van, 1997
16	P984JKP	LDV Convoy	Euromotive	M12	1997	
17	P985JKP	LDV Convoy	Euromotive	M16	1997	
18	BX05DOA	Renault Master	VFS	M16	2005	
19	BX05DVA	Renault Master	VFS	M16	2005	
20	BX05DNU	Renault Master	VFS	M16	2005	
21	BX05AKK	Renault Master	VFS	M16	2005	
22	R334FVW	Mercedes-Benz Sprinter 312D	Olympus	M12	1998	
23	T414VVW	LDV Convoy	LDV	M8	1999	private owner, 2000
24	W207KNH	Mercedes-Benz Sprinter 311CDi	Mercedes-Benz	M16	2000	, 2005

Previous registration:
K2VMC   K795EPU

Depot: Pyramid Place, Swalecliffe.
Web: www.regentcoaches.co.uk

Regent Coaches displayed its Indcar with Maxim 2 minicoach bodywork at the 2003 British Coach Rally, though not as an entrant. The model is built on the Irisbus EuroMidi, the Irisbus dolphin motif affixed under the windscreen. *Dave Heath*

RENOWN TRAVEL

Renown Coaches Ltd, 13 Sea Road, Bexhill-on-Sea, TN40 1EE

12	W936JNF	Dennis Dart SLF 8.5m	Plaxton Pointer MPD	N29F	2002	Norbus, Kirkby, 2005
13	L881YVK	Dennis Dart SLF	Plaxton Pointer	B40F	1994	Boomerang Bus, Tewkesbury, '05
14	SN04EFL	TransBus Dart	TransBus Pointer	NC39F	2004	
15	H115THE	Dennis Dart 8.5m	Reeve Burgess Pointer	B28F	1991	Metroline, 2000
16	P690RUU	Dennis Dart SLF	Plaxton Pointer 2	N35F	1997	First Stop, Renfrew, 2004
17	P696RUU	Dennis Dart SLF	Plaxton Pointer 2	N35F	1997	Gibson Direct, Renfrew, 2004
18	P699RUU	Dennis Dart SLF	Plaxton Pointer 2	N35F	1997	Dickson, Erskin, 2004
19	FN54FLC	TransBus Dennis Dart	Caetano Nimbus	N28F	2004	
21	A616THV	Leyland Titan TNLXB2RR	Leyland	B44/26D	1984	London Central, 2000
26	G126NGN	Volvo B10M-50 Citybus	Northern Counties	B47/38F	1989	Pete's Travel, West Bromwich, 03
27	G127NGN	Volvo B10M-50 Citybus	Northern Counties	B47/38F	1989	Pete's Travel, West Bromwich, 03
29	J227HMY	Volvo B10M-50 Citybus	Northern Counties	B45/35F	1990	
33	G133PGK	Volvo B10M-50 Citybus	Northern Counties	B47/38F	1990	Pete's Travel, West Bromwich, 03
36	G866WGW	Volvo B10M-50 Citybus	Northern Counties	B45/35F	1990	
37	G867WGW	Volvo B10M-50 Citybus	Northern Counties	B45/35F	1990	
38	G138PGK	Volvo B10M-50 Citybus	Northern Counties	B47/38F	1990	Pete's Travel, West Bromwich, 03
41	C521LJR	Leyland Olympian ONLXB/1R	Eastern Coach Works	B40/32F	1985	Sterling European, Westcliff, 2005
42	D162FYM	Leyland Olympian ONLXB/1R	Eastern Coach Works	B42/26D	1986	Arriva London, 2005
44	D214FYM	Leyland Olympian ONLXB/1R	Eastern Coach Works	B42/26D	1986	Arriva London, 2005
45	C25CHM	Leyland Olympian ONLXB/1R	Eastern Coach Works	B42/26D	1986	Arriva London, 2005
47	C37CHM	Leyland Olympian ONLXB/1R	Eastern Coach Works	B42/26D	1986	Arriva London, 2005
50	D180FYM	Leyland Olympian ONLXB/1R	Eastern Coach Works	B42/26D	1986	Arriva London, 2005

In addition to the fleet listed here, Renown Travel operates many Optare Solo buses on behalf of East Sussex County Council. These are listed under County Rider. Number 29, J227HMY, is one of seven Volvo underfloor-engined Citybus double-decks pictured in Lewes. These all carry Northern Counties bodywork. *Dave Heath*

In 2004, Renown acquired TransBus Dart SN04EFL. The bus is seen in Lewes while heading for Peacehaven on route 123. Three Olympians were due to replace fleet numbers 21, 36 and 37 as we went to press. *Richard Godfrey*

100	K200SAS	Volvo B10M-62	Plaxton Première 350	C46FT	1993	National Express, 2005
	B637LJU	Volvo B10M-61	Duple 340	C51F	1984	2Travel, Swansea, 2005
105	N805NHS	Volvo B10M-62	Jonckheere Mistral 45	C53F	1996	Oakfield, Broxbourne, 2004
106	SJI7466	Volvo B10M-61	Van Hool Alizée SH	C49FT	1984	
107	HIL2279	Volvo B10M-61	Plaxton Paramount 3500 III	C50F	1988	J&H, Rye, 2005
108	TJI1688	Volvo B10M-60	Plaxton Paramount 3500 III	C53F	1990	J&H, Rye, 2005
109	N439XDV	Volvo B10M-62	Van Hool Alizée HE	C48FT	1996	Trathens, Plymouth, 2001
113	XIL1273	Volvo B10M-62	Van Hool Alizée HE	C46FT	1995	Shearings, 2002
114	XIL1274	Volvo B10M-62	Van Hool Alizée HE	C46FT	1995	Shearings, 2002
116	WJI7696	Volvo B10M-62	Van Hool Alizée HE	C46FT	1995	Shearings, 2002

Special event vehicles:

3989		Bedford SB3	Duple Super Vega	C41F	1964	Fowler, Holbeach Drove, 1998
5779		Bedford SB3	Duple Super Vega	C41F	1966	Fowler, Holbeach Drove, 1998

Previous registrations:

B637LJU	B637LJU, 716GRM	TJI1688	G88RGG
G866WGW	G106NGN, VLT60	WJI7696	M672KVU
G867WGW	G104NGN, WLT474	XIL1273	M637KVU
HIL2279	E300UUB	XIL1274	M644KVU
J227HMY	J139DGA, 839DYE		
N439XDV	N752CYA, LSK483	(3989)	610STT, J22095
SJI7466	A844UGB	(5779)	FNT231D, J9143

Depots: Beeching Road, Bexhill-on-Sea and New Harbour, Newhaven.

RICHARDSON TRAVEL

Richardson Travel Ltd, Russell House, Bepton Road, Midhurst, GU29 9NB

120	F120PHM	Volvo B10M-50 Citybus	Alexander RV	B47/28D	1988	
139	F139PHM	Volvo B10M-50 Citybus	Alexander RV	B47/28D	1988	Blue Triangle, Rainham, 2003
140	F140PHM	Volvo B10M-50 Citybus	Alexander RV	B47/28D	1988	Arriva London, 2003
144	F144PHM	Volvo B10M-50 Citybus	Alexander RV	B47/28D	1988	Blue Triangle, Rainham, 2003
148	G148TYT	Volvo B10M-50 Citybus	Alexander RV	B47/28D	1990	Arriva London, 2003
429u	UCW429X	Leyland Atlantean AN68C/1R	East Lancs	B43/31F	1982	Blackburn, 2002
492	N372EAK	Volvo B10M-62	Plaxton Première 350	C49FT	1996	Knowles, Paignton, 2001
493	YR02ZMY	Volvo B10M-62	Plaxton Paragon	C49FT	2002	
494	YN54WWR	Volvo B12B	Plaxton Panther	C49FT	2005	
531	YN53VCD	Volvo B7R	Plaxton Profile	C53F	2004	
532	S701RWG	Volvo B10M-61	Plaxton Première 350	C53F	1998	
571	H203CRH	Volvo B10M-60	Plaxton Expressliner	C57F	1991	York Pullman, 1998
574	YR52MDY	Volvo B7R	Plaxton Prima	C57F	2002	
791	PN05SYF	Volvo B7TL	East Lancs Vyking	NC47/32F	2005	
801	PN52XBP	Volvo B7TL	East Lancs Vyking	NC47/33F	2002	

Web: www.richardson-travel.demon.co.uk
Depot: Pitsham Lane, Midhurst

Two new Volvo B7TL double-deck buses have been added to the Richardson Travel fleet. The eighty-seat example, 801, PN52XBP, is seen in passing through Trafalgar Square in London while on a private hire. The East Lancs Vyking bodies built in Blackburn feature high-back seating. *Colin Lloyd*

SAFEGUARD COACHES

Safeguard Coaches - Farnham Coaches

Safeguard Coaches Ltd, Ridgemount, Guildford, GU2 7TH

	WPF926	Volvo B9M	Plaxton Paramount 3200 III	C39F	1988	
F	247FCG	Volvo B10M-60	Plaxton Paramount 3200 III	C53F	1990	Excelsior, Bournemouth, 1990
F	G520EFX	Volvo B10M-60	Plaxton Paramount 3200 III	C55F	1990	Excelsior, Bournemouth, 1991
	H577MOC	Dennis Dart 8.5m	Carlyle Dartline	B28F	1990	Boomerang Bus, Tewkesbury, 00
	L967RUB	Toyota Coaster HZB50R	Caetano Optimo III	C21F	1994	Applegate, Newport, 1998
F	196FCG	EOS E180Z	EOS 90	C49FT	1995	Landtourer, Farnham, 1997
F	277FCG	EOS E180Z	EOS 90	C49FT	1995	Landtourer, Farnham, 1997
	159FCG	Setra S250	Setra Special	C53F	1995	Limebourne, Battersea, 1999
	M388KVR	Dennis Dart 9.8m	Northern Counties Paladin	B39F	1995	Travel West Midlands, 1998
	N611WND	Dennis Dart 9.8m	Northern Counties Paladin	B39F	1995	Pink Elephant, Heathrow, 1998
F	531FCG	Volvo B10M-62	Plaxton Première 350	C53F	1996	
	DSK560	Dennis Javelin 12m	Plaxton Première 320	C53F	1996	
	DSK559	Volvo B10M-62	Van Hool Alizée	C49FT	1997	
	DSK558	Volvo B10M-62	Van Hool Alizée	C53F	1998	Park's of Hamilton, 2002
	XHY378	Volvo B10M-62	Van Hool Alizée	C49FT	1998	Park's of Hamilton, 2002
	S132PGB	Volvo B10M-62	Van Hool T9 Alizée	C49FT	1998	Clyde Coast, Ardrossan, 2003
	R433FWT	Volvo B10M-62	Plaxton Première 350	C53F	1998	Wallace Arnold, 2001
	S503UAK	Dennis Javelin	Plaxton Première 320	C57F	1998	
	T530EUB	Volvo B10M-62	Plaxton Première 350	C49FT	1999	Wallace Arnold, 2003
	515FCG	Mercedes-Benz O404-15R	Hispano Vita	C49FT	2000	Austin, Earlston, 2001
	W203YAP	Mercedes-Benz Vario 0814	Plaxton Cheetah	C29F	2000	Airlinks, West Drayton, 2001
F	W209YAP	Mercedes-Benz Vario 0814	Plaxton Cheetah	C29F	2000	Airlinks, West Drayton, 2003
F	538FCG	Setra S250	Setra Special	C48FT	2000	
F	W257UGX	Setra S315 GT-HD	Setra	C53F	2000	Redwing, Herne Hill, 2003

Safeguard operates a pair of Optare Excel low-floor buses on local services in Guildford. X307CBT is seen heading for Bellfields Estate on route 3. *Richard Godfrey*

Safeguard Coaches is an independent company, which has remained in the same family since its inception in 1924. In 2001 a heritage bus that was new to Safeguard was re-acquired and is used for weddings and similar special events. This 1956 AEC Reliance is seen here at the 2002 Showbus event. 200APB is fitted with Burlingham coachwork. The Safeguard livery employs red while the Farnham Coaches scheme is white, purple and pink. *Richard Godfrey*

F	W295UGX	Setra S315 GT-HD	Setra	C48FT	2000	Redwing, Herne Hill, 2004
	X307CBT	Optare Excel L1070	Optare	N39F	2000	Tillingbourne, Cranleigh, 2001
	X308CBT	Optare Excel L1070	Optare	N39F	2000	Tillingbourne, Cranleigh, 2001
F	Y161HWE	MAN 18.350	Neoplan Transliner	C49FT	2001	
F	Y162HWE	MAN 18.350	Neoplan Transliner	C49FT	2001	
	Y748HWT	Volvo B10M-62	Plaxton Paragon	C49FT	2001	Wallace Arnold, 2003
	Y758HWT	Volvo B10M-62	Plaxton Paragon	C53F	2001	Wallace Arnold, 2004
F	CN51XNO	Volvo B7R	Plaxton Prima	C57F	2001	Bebb, Llantwit Fardre, 2002
	VU02TTJ	Dennis Dart SLF 8.5m	Plaxton MPD	N29F	2002	
	RX03XKH	Dennis Javelin 12m	Plaxton Profile	BC70F	2003	
	YJ03UMM	Optare Excel L1150	Optare	N41F	2003	
	YN05HUY	Volvo B12M	Plaxton Paragon	C53F	2005	

Special Event vehicle:

	200APB	AEC Reliance MU3RV	Burlingham	B44F	1956	Rexquote, Norton Fitzwarren, 2001

Previous registrations:

159FCG	M974NFU		DSK558	LSK501, R410EOS
196FCG	M623RCP		DSK559	P46GPG
247FCG	G514EFX		DSK560	N562UPF
277FCG	M625RCP		H577MOC	H577MOC, WLT339, RIL9774
515FCG	W417HOB		L967RUB	L967RUB, A20EFA
531FCG	N561UPF		WPF926	F296RMH
538FCG	W354EOL		XHY378	LSK504, R398EOS

Web: www.safeguardcoaches.co.uk; www.farnhamcoaches.co.uk
Depots: Guildford Park Road, Guildford and Odiham Road, Farnham; (F = Farnham Coaches)

The South East Bus Handbook

SCOTLAND & BATES

DCR RM & GA Bates, Heath Road, Appledore, Ashford, TN26 2AJ

Reg	Chassis	Body	Type	Year	Notes
BKO447Y	Volvo B10M-61	Plaxton Supreme V	C53F	1982	
B98XKE	Volvo B10M-61	Plaxton Paramount 3200 II	C55F	1985	
C542GKP	Volvo B10M-61	Plaxton Paramount 3200 II	C55F	1986	
E129WKN	Volvo B10M-61	Plaxton Paramount 3500 III	C53F	1988	
F988JKL	Volvo B10M-60	Plaxton Paramount 3500 III	C53F	1989	
H155DJU	Volvo B10M-60	Plaxton Paramount 3500 III	C53F	1990	
H601UWR	Volvo B10M-60	Plaxton Paramount 3500 III	C53F	1991	Wallace Arnold, 1994
M420VYD	Volvo B10M-62	Van Hool Alizée	C53F	1995	
N756CYA	Volvo B10M-62	Van Hool Alizée	C51FT	1996	
P728JYA	Volvo B10M-62	Van Hool Alizée	C51FT	1997	
R634VYB	Volvo B10M-62	Van Hool T9 Alizée	C51FT	1998	
T760JYB	Volvo B10M-62	Van Hool T9 Alizée	C51FT	1999	
W567RYC	Volvo B10M-62	Van Hool T9 Alizée	C51FT	2000	
Y224NYA	Volvo B10M-62	Van Hool T9 Alizée	C51FT	2001	
WJ02KDN	Volvo B12M	Van Hool T9 Alizée	C49FT	2002	
WA03HPY	Volvo B12M	Van Hool T9 Alizée	C49FT	2003	
WA04EWR	Volvo B12M	Van Hool T9 Alizée	C49FT	2004	
WA54KTP	Volvo B12M	Van Hool T9 Alizée	C49FT	2004	

Web: www.scotlandandbates.co.uk

In 1995 Scotland & Bates changed from purchasing Plaxton-bodied coaches to Van Hool. The fleet, which comprises entirely of Volvo mid-engined products is represented here by its 1999 example, T760JYB. This coach features the T9 variant of the Alizée coach, a product that has been in production since the late 1970s, and the gradual evolution of the model since then upholds the value of the product with operators. *Colin Lloyd*

SEAVIEW SERVICES

Seaview Services Ltd, Seafield Garage, College Farm, Faulkner Lane, Sandown, PO36 9AZ

Reg	Chassis	Body	Seats	Year	History
UFX858S	Bristol VRT/SL3/6LXB	Eastern Coach Works	CO43/31F	1977	Newbus, Nettlestone, 2003
C680KDS	Volvo B10M-61	Caetano Algarve	C49F	1986	Bluebird, Weymouth, 2005
PDL230	Volvo B10M-61	Van Hool Alizée	C55F	1989	Andrews, Trudoxhill, 2000
JXI507	Volvo B10M-60	Van Hool Alizée	C49FT	1990	Chivers, Elstead, 2001
G144ULG	Volvo B10M-60	Jonckheere Jubilee P599	C51FT	1990	Barratts, Nantwich, 1998
YTP749	Volvo B10M-60	Van Hool Alizée	C49FT	1992	Shearings, 1999
ODL678	Volvo B10M-60	Van Hool Alizée HE	C51FT	1993	Courtney, Backnell, 2002
PDL298	Volvo B10M-62	Van Hool Alizée HE	C48FT	1995	Coliseum, West End, 2002
XDL696	Volvo B10M-62	Van Hool T9 Alizée	C46FT	1998	Shearings, 2005
XOI792	Toyota Coaster BB50R	Caetano Optimo IV	C22F	1999	National Express, 2004
W11OWT	Irisbus EuroRider 391.12.35	Beulas Stergo ε	C51FT	2000	IoW Tours, Lake, 2003
W21OWT	Irisbus EuroRider 391.12.35	Beulas Stergo ε	C51FT	2000	IoW Tours, Lake, 2003

Previous registrations:

JXI507	G872RNC, JIL3972	TDL856	
G144ULG	G653ONH, B3BCL, G144ULG, XDL696	XDL696	R921YBA
ODL678	K479VVR, K17CCL	XOI792	S764DOX
PDL230	F752ENE, YXI2715	YTP749	J302RNE
PDL298	MIB651, M592COR		

Web: www.seaview-services.com

In 1922 Seaview businessman Richard Newell, owner of Seafield Garage, introduced a bus service between Seaview and Ryde using a converted wartime ambulance. At the time the service ran under the name of 'Newell's Express Motor Service', but the company was later to become known as Seaview Services. XOI792 is an Caetano Optimo and is the smallest coach in the fleet.

SOLENT BLUE LINE

Solent Blue Line - Blue Star

Musterphantom Ltd, Barton Park, Eastleigh, SO50 6RR

129	XBZ7729	Dennis Dart 9.8m	Plaxton Pointer	B40F	1995	Thamesdown, Swindon, 2004
130	XBZ7730	Dennis Dart 9.8m	Plaxton Pointer	B40F	1995	Thamesdown, Swindon, 2004
229	R829GKX	Iveco TurboDaily 59.12	Marshall C31	B27F	1998	Iveco-Ford demonstrator, 1999
240	P240VDL	Iveco TurboDaily 59-12	Marshall C31	BC23F	1996	Southern Vectis, 2005
241	P241VDL	Iveco TurboDaily 59-12	Marshall C31	BC23F	1996	Southern Vectis, 2005
242	P242VDL	Iveco TurboDaily 59-12	Marshall C31	BC23F	1996	Southern Vectis, 2005
255	N255FOR	Iveco TurboDaily 59-12	Mellor	B29F	1995	
259	N259FOR	Iveco TurboDaily 59-12	Mellor	B29F	1995	
260	N260FOR	Iveco TurboDaily 59-12	Mellor	B29F	1995	
526	L526YDL	Volvo B10B	Alexander Strider	B51F	1994	
526	L526YDL	Volvo B10B	Alexander Strider	B51F	1994	
527	L527YDL	Volvo B10B	Alexander Strider	B51F	1994	
528	L528YDL	Volvo B10B	Alexander Strider	B51F	1994	

571-582		TransBus Dart 8.8m	TransBus Mini Pointer	N29F	2003	
571	SN03EBP	574	SN03EBX	577	SN03ECC	580 SN03LDK
572	SN03EBU	575	SN03EBZ	578	SN03ECD	581 SN03LDL
573	SN03EBV	576	SN03ECA	579	SN03LDJ	582 SN03LDU

583	XIL8583	Dennis Dart 8.5m	Plaxton Pointer	B28F	1992	Metroline, 2004
584	XIL8584	Dennis Dart 8.5m	Plaxton Pointer	B28F	1992	Metroline, 2004
585	K716PCN	Dennis Dart 9.8m	Alexander Dash	B40F	1992	Go-Ahead London, 2004
586	K719PCN	Dennis Dart 9.8m	Alexander Dash	BC32F	1992	Go-Ahead London, 2004
694	WDL894Y	Leyland Olympian ONLXB/1R	Eastern Coach Works	B45/30F	1983	Southern Vectis, 1990
697	A697DDL	Leyland Olympian ONLXB/1R	Eastern Coach Works	B45/30F	1984	Southern Vectis, 1990
699	A699DDL	Leyland Olympian ONLXB/1R	Eastern Coach Works	B45/30F	1984	Southern Vectis, 1990
703	A203MEL	Leyland Olympian ONLXB/1R	Eastern Coach Works	B45/30F	1984	Hampshire Bus, 1987
704	A204MEL	Leyland Olympian ONLXB/1R	Eastern Coach Works	B45/30F	1984	Hampshire Bus, 1987
706	F706RDL	Leyland Olympian ONCL10/1RZ	Leyland	BC39/29F	1989	
707	F707RDL	Leyland Olympian ONCL10/1RZ	Leyland	BC39/29F	1989	
708	F708SDL	Leyland Olympian ONCL10/1RZ	Leyland	BC39/29F	1989	
709	F709SDL	Leyland Olympian ONCL10/1RZ	Leyland	BC39/29F	1989	

In 2003 Solent Blue Line took delivery of twelve TransBus Mini Pointers. These feature the latest livery, and 580, SN03LDK, is seen passing Winchester Community Prison.
Richard Godfrey

721-734

Leyland Olympian ON2R50C13Z5 Leyland — B47/31F* 1989-91 *721/2 are BC39/29F

721	G721WDL	728	H728DDL	731	H731DDL	733	H733DDL	
722	G722WDL	729	H729DDL	732	H732DDL	734	H734DDL	

735	M735BBP	Volvo Olympian YN2RC16Z5	East Lancs	BC41/29F	1995	
736	M736BBP	Volvo Olympian YN2RV18Z4	East Lancs	BC41/29F	1995	
737	R737XRV	Volvo Olympian	Northern Counties Palatine	BC41/29F	1998	
738	R738XRV	Volvo Olympian	Northern Counties Palatine	BC41/29F	1998	
739	R739XRV	Volvo Olympian	Northern Counties Palatine	BC41/29F	1998	
741	R741XRV	Volvo Olympian	Northern Counties Palatine	BC41/29F	1998	

742-749

Dennis Trident — East Lancs Lolyne — N47/27F — 1999

742	T742JPO	744	T744JPO	746	T746JPO	748	T748JPO
743	T743JPO	745	T745JPO	747	T747JPO	749	T749JPO

750-757

Volvo B7TL — East Lancs Vyking — N46/27F — 2001

750	HX51ZRA	752	HX51ZRD	754	HX51ZRF	756	HX51ZRJ
751	HX51ZRC	753	HX51ZRE	755	HX51ZRG	757	HX51ZRK

817	F817URN	Leyland Olympian ONCL10/1RZ	Leyland	B47/31F	1989	Leyland demonstrator, 1990
818	N539LHG	Volvo Olympian YN2RV18Z4	Northern Counties	B47/27F	1996	Metrobus, 2004
819	N411JBV	Volvo Olympian YN2RV18Z4	Northern Counties	B47/30F	1996	Go-Ahead London, 2004
820	N413JBV	Volvo Olympian YN2RV18Z4	Northern Counties	B47/30F	1996	Go-Ahead London, 2004
901w	UFX857S	Bristol VRT/SL3/6LXB	Eastern Coach Works	CO43/31F	1977	Bath Bus Co, 2003
902w	WTG360T	Bristol VRT/SL3/6LXB	Alexander AL	CO43/31F	1979	Bath Bus Co, 2003

2511-2532

Optare MetroRider MR05 — Optare — B31F — 1992-93 — Wilts & Dorset, 2005

2511	J511RPR	2523	K523UJT	2531	K531UJT	2532	K532UJT
2515	J515RPR	2525	K525UJT				

Ancillary vehicles:

253	N253FOR	Iveco TurboDaily 59-12	Mellor	B29F	1995	
575	MIL9575	Dennis Javelin	Plaxton Paramount	TV	1989	Southern Vectis, 2005

Previous registrations:

K716PCN	K716PCN, NFX667	XBZ7729	MAN14A, M410XTC
K719PCN	K719PCN, XYK976	XIL8583	J393GKH
XBZ7729	MAN14A, M410XTC	XIL8584	J394GKH

Web: www.solentblueline.com
Depots: Barton Park, Eastleigh; Gang Warily, Blackfield and Premier Way, Romsey.

After production of Eastern Coach Works bodies ceased in Lowestoft, similar-styled buses were built at the Leyland National facility in Workington. These were produced under the Leyland name. Solent Blue Line 721, G721WDL, illustrates the style. *Mark Lyons*

SOULS

Soul Bros Ltd, 2 Stilebrook Road, Olney, MK46 5EA

1	Y5BUS	Setra S315 GT-HD	Setra	C49FT	2001	Buzzlines, Hythe, 2005
2	Y6BUS	Setra S315 GT-HD	Setra	C49FT	2001	Buzzlines, Hythe, 2005
3	Y3BUS	Setra S315 GT-HD	Setra	C49FT	2001	Buzzlines, Hythe, 2005
4	Y7BUS	Setra S315 GT-HD	Setra	C49FT	2001	Buzzlines, Hythe, 2005
5	UDN126	Volvo B10M-62	Plaxton Excalibur	C45FT	1997	Easson, Southampton, 2002
6	P60ULS	Volvo B10M-62	Plaxton Excalibur	C49FT	1997	Truronian, Truro, 2002
7	RBW396	Dennis Javelin 12m	Plaxton Première 320	C53F	1998	Burgundy Car, Bracknell, 2002
8	P60SOU	Volvo B10M-62	Plaxton Première 350	C53F	1997	Southern, Barrhead, 2003
9	P50SOU	Volvo B10M-62	Plaxton Première 320	C53F	1997	Southern, Barrhead, 2003
10	K50ULS	Dennis Javelin 12m	Plaxton Première 320	C53F	1996	Abbeyways, Hamson, 2001
11	MLZ4286	Volvo B10M-62	Jonckheere Mistral 50	C53F	1996	Clarkes of London, 2004
12	MLZ4290	Volvo B10M-62	Jonckheere Mistral 50	C53F	1996	Clarkes of London, 2004
13	MLZ4287	Volvo B10M-62	Jonckheere Mistral 50	C53F	1996	Clarkes of London, 2004
14	MLZ4288	Volvo B10M-62	Jonckheere Mistral 50	C53F	1996	Clarkes of London, 2004
15	MLZ4289	Volvo B10M-62	Jonckheere Mistral 50	C53F	1996	Clarkes of London, 2004
16	M50ULS	Volvo B10M-62	Plaxton Excalibur	C35FT	1996	Flights, Birmingham, 2000
17	PIW4127	Dennis Javelin 12m	Plaxton Première 320	C53F	1995	Metroline (Brents), 2001
18	239BUP	Dennis Javelin 12m	Plaxton Première 320	C53F	1995	Metroline (Brents), 2001
19	M5OUL	Volvo B10M-62	Plaxton Excalibur	C53F	1995	Excelsior, Bournemouth, 1998
20	L50ULS	Volvo B10M-60	Plaxton Excalibur	C53F	1994	Wallace Arnold, 1998
21	WJI6166	Dennis Javelin 12m	Plaxton Première 320	C70F	1993	Go-Felix, Stanley, 1998
22	130VBJ	Dennis Javelin 12m	Plaxton Première 320	C70F	1993	Vince's Cs, Burghdere, 2002
23	230WYA	Dennis Javelin 11m	Plaxton Paramount 3200 III	C53F	1991	JGS, Rotherham, 2000
24	ALZ2490	Volvo B10M-60	Plaxton Première 320	C53F	1993	Wallace Arnold, 1997
25	RAZ3785	Dennis Javelin 12m	Plaxton Paramount 3200 III	C53F	1992	Western Buses, 1998
26	675PBM	Volvo B10M-60	Plaxton Paramount 3500 III	C53F	1989	Classic Tours, Paignton, 1996
27	FAZ4494	Volvo B10M-60	Plaxton Première 320	C53F	1989	The Londoners, Nunhead, 1995
28	577HDV	Volvo B10M-60	Plaxton Première 350	C53F	1989	The Londoners, Nunhead, 1995
29	855GAC	Dennis Javelin 11m	Plaxton Paramount 3200 III	C53F	1988	JGS, Rotherham, 2000
30	821FHU	Volvo B10M-61	Plaxton Paramount 3500 III	C53F	1988	Wallace Arnold, 1991
31	HIL2386	Volvo B10M-61	Plaxton Paramount 3500 III	C53F	1988	Owens, Yateley, 1995
32	50DBD	Volvo B10M-61	Plaxton Paramount 3500 III	C53F	1988	Wallace Arnold, 1991
33	HIL2182	Volvo B10M-61	Plaxton Paramount 3500 III	C53F	1988	Lowland, 1993
34	KYU77	Volvo B10M-61	Plaxton Paramount 3500 III	C53F	1988	Wallace Arnold, 1991
35	VIJ4021	Volvo B10M-61	Plaxton Paramount 3500 III	C53F	1988	Addy & Bradley, Barnsley, 1997
36	459KBM	Volvo B10M-61	Plaxton Paramount 3500 III	C53F	1988	Premier Travel, 1992
37	751EKX	Volvo B10M-61	Plaxton Paramount 3500 III	C53F	1988	Wallace Arnold, 1992

Plaxton bodywork dominates Souls' coach fleet. Shown here is Paramount 3500 number 37, 751EKX, based on a Volvo B10M.

The Plaxton Excalibur featured a rearward-sloping front when compared with the Première. Souls operates three examples of the model represented by M5OUL which was taking break at Chessington when photographed. *Dave Heath*

38	966MBM	Volvo B10M-61	Plaxton Paramount 3500 III	C53F	1988	Lowland, 1993
39	VUD483	DAF SB2300	Plaxton Paramount 3200 II	C53F	1986	Smith, Alcester, 1987
40	872PYA	DAF SB2300	Plaxton Paramount 3200 II	C53F	1986	Smith, Alcester, 1987
41	IAZ5657	Volvo B10M-61	Plaxton Paramount 3200 II	C53F	1985	Safeguard, Guildford, 1996
42	LIL9811	Volvo B10M-61	Plaxton Paramount 3200 II	C53F	1985	Safeguard, Guildford, 1996
43	TAZ4495	Volvo B10M-61	Plaxton Paramount 3200	C53F	1984	Holt, Thornton-le-Dale, 2001

Previous registrations:

50DBD	E313UUB	K50ULS	N93FWJ
130VBJ	ENF557Y	KYU77	E312UUB
239BUP	N464BHE	L50ULS	L936NWW, TAZ4995
230WYA	H660AST	LIL9811	B907SPR
459KBM	E304UUB	LSV146	ENF556Y
577HDV	F414DUG, PIW4127	M5OUL	A3EXC, M680MRU
675PBM	F443DUG	M50ULS	FTG5, N389DRW
751EKX	E303UUB	MLZ4286	N545SJF
821FHU	E320UUB	MLZ4287	N549SJF
855GAC	F370MUT	MLZ4288	N551SJF
872PYA	C772MVH	MLZ4289	N552SJF
873DTU	-	MLZ4290	N555CLA
954CUH	-	P50ULS	P985NKU
966MBM	E308UUB	PIW4127	N20JET
A79ABD	A79ABD, 855GAC	RAZ3785	J13WSB
ALZ2490	K849HUM	RBW396	R138XWF
ENF552Y	ENF552Y, 873DTU	TAZ4995	A445YWG
ENF559Y	ENF559Y, 577HDV	UDN126	A7XEL, P731AAA
FAZ4494	F418DUG	VIJ4021	E310UUB
HIL2282	E314UUB	VUD483	C783MVH
HIL2386	E319UUB	WJI6166	L72MRA
IAZ5657	B906SPR		

Named Vehicles: 130VBJ *Hardmead*; 873DTU *Newport*; LSV146 *Astwood* ; RBW396 *Broughton*; 577HDV *Clifton*
Depots: Yardley Road, Olney and Quorn Road, Rushden.
Web: www.souls-coaches.co.uk

The South East Bus Handbook

SOUTHERN VECTIS

The Southern Vectis Omnibus Co Ltd, Nelson Road, Newport, PO30 1RD

100-106		Volvo B7TL		Plaxton President		N45/22F	2002		
100	HW52EPK	102	HW52EPN	104	HW52EPP			106	HW52EPV
101	HW52EPL	103	HW52EPO	105	HW52EPU				

244-247		Iveco TurboDaily 59-12		Marshall C31		BC23F	1996-97		
244	P244VDL	245	P245VDL	246	P246VDL			247	P247VDL

260	L445FFR	Iveco TurboDaily 59-12		Mellor Duet		B27F	1994	Stagecoach Devon, 2001	
300	HW52EPX	Dennis Dart SLF		Plaxton Pointer		N37F	2002		

301-314		Alexander Dennis Dart 8.8m		Alexander Dennis Mini Pointer		N27F	2004-05		
301	HW54BTU	305	HW54BTZ	309	HW54BUH			312	HW54BUP
302	HW54BTV	306	HW54BUA	310	HW54BUJ			313	HW54BUU
303	HW54BTX	307	HW54BUE	311	HW54BUO			314	HW54BUV
304	HW54BTY	308	HW54BUF						

503	XDL872	Bristol VRT/SL3/6LXB		Eastern Coach Works		CO43/31F	1977	Traditional Motor Bus Co., 1999
504	WDL655	Bristol VRT/SL3/6LXB		Eastern Coach Works		CO43/31F	1977	Traditional Motor Bus Co., 1999
681	ODL447	Bristol VRT/SL3/6LXB		Eastern Coach Works		O43/31F	1980	
682	VDL744	Bristol VRT/SL3/6LXB		Eastern Coach Works		O43/31F	1980	
683	934BDL	Bristol VRT/SL3/6LXB		Eastern Coach Works		B43/31F	1981	
710	TIL6710	Leyland Olympian ONCL10/1RZ		Leyland		BC41/29F	1989	
711	TIL6711	Leyland Olympian ONCL10/1RZ		Leyland		BC41/29F	1989	
712	TIL6712	Leyland Olympian ONCL10/1RZ		Leyland		BC41/29F	1989	

713-727		Leyland Olympian ON2R50C13Z5		Leyland		BC41/29F	1989-90		
713	TIL6713	716	TIL6716	719	TIL6719	724	TIL6724	726	TIL6726
714	TIL6714	717	TIL6717	720	TIL6720	725	TIL6725	727	TIL6727
715	TIL6715	718	TIL6718	723	TIL6723				

735-743		Leyland Olympian ON2R50C13Z5		Northern Counties		BC41/29F*	1993	*742/3 are O41/29F	
735	K735ODL	737	K737ODL	739	K739ODL	741	K741ODL	743	K743ODL
736	K736ODL	738	K738ODL	740	K740ODL	742	K742ODL		

Catering for the tourists to the Isle of Wight, Southern Vectis has converted to partial open-top two Olympians, 742 and 743. The former, K742ODL, is shown heading for Alum Bay.
Phillip Stephenson

Seen heading for Newport is one of Southern Vectis' latest batch of Alexander Dennis Mini Pointers. The modern livery carried by the batch is shown on 314, HW54BUV. *Mark Lyons*

744-751			Volvo Olympian YN2R50C18Z4		Northern Counties		BC41/29F	1995	
744	M744HDL	746	M746HDL	749	M749HDL	750	M750HDL	751	M751HDL
745	M745HDL	748	M748HDL						

752-759			Volvo Olympian		Northern Counties Palatine I		BC41/29F	1998	
752	R752GDL	754	R754GDL	756	R756GDL	758	R758GDL	759	R759GDL
753	R753GDL	755	R755GDL	757	R757GDL				

810-815			Dennis Dart 8.5m		UVG Urban Star		BC31F	1996	
810	N810PDL	812	N812PDL	813	N813PDL	814	N814PDL	815	N815PDL
811	N811PDL								

816	G516VYE	Dennis Dart 8.5m	Duple Dartline	B31F	1990	London United, 2000
817	G526VYE	Dennis Dart 8.5m	Duple Dartline	B31F	1990	London United, 2000
818	J382GKH	Dennis Dart 8.5m	Plaxton Pointer	B31F	1992	Rehill, Birstall, 2003
819	K244PAG	Dennis Dart 8.5m	Plaxton Pointer	B31F	1992	Rehill, Birstall, 2003

Heritage vehicle:

902	CDL899	Bristol K5G	Eastern Coach Works	O30/26R	1939	

Ancillary vehicle:

929	L227THP	Volvo B10B	Alexander Strider	TV	1993	Volvo demonstrator, 1994

Previous registrations:
VIL2754   E745JAY, KGL803

Depots: Princes Road, Freshwater; Nelson Road, Newport; Park Road, Ryde; Faulkner Lane, Sandown and Pier Street, Ventnor.
Web: www.svoc.co.uk

The South East Bus Handbook

TAPPINS

Tom Tappin Ltd, Collett Road, Southmead Park, Didcot, OX11 7ET

GJZ9571	Leyland Atlantean AN68/1R	Alexander AL	O45/33F	1973	Lothian Buses, 2002
GJZ9572	Leyland Atlantean AN68/1R	Alexander AL	O45/33F	1973	Guide Friday, 2002
GJZ9573	Leyland Atlantean AN68/1R	Alexander AL	O45/33F	1973	Guide Friday, 2002
GJZ9570	Leyland Atlantean AN68/1R	East Lancs	O47/32F	1974	Guide Friday, 2002
GJZ9576	Leyland Fleetline FE30AGR	Northern Counties	O47/33F	1978	Guide Friday, 2002
GJZ9574	Leyland Atlantean AN68A/1R	Roe	O47/28F	1979	Guide Friday, 2002
GJZ9575	Leyland Atlantean AN68A/1R	Roe	O47/28F	1979	Guide Friday, 2002
GSC664X	Leyland Atlantean AN68C/1R	Alexander AL	PO45/31F	1981	Lothian Buses, 1999
653GBU	Leyland National 2 NL116AL11/1R		B52F	1982	AERE, Harwell, 1991
461XPB	Volvo B10M-61	Plaxton Viewmaster IV	C51F	1982	
500EFC	Volvo B10M-61	Plaxton Viewmaster IV	C51F	1982	
AJZ9161	Volvo B10M-61	Plaxton Paramount 3500	C53F	1985	
RIL7163	Volvo B10M-61	Plaxton Paramount 3500	C53F	1985	
ANZ1323	Volvo B10M-61	Plaxton Paramount 3500 II	C53F	1986	
KUI5324	Volvo B10M-61	Plaxton Paramount 3500 II	C53F	1986	
ANZ1325	Volvo B10M-61	Plaxton Paramount 3500 II	C53F	1986	
YUE338	Volvo B10M-61	Plaxton Paramount 3500 II	C49F	1986	
TIL5973	Volvo B10M-61	Plaxton Paramount 3500 III	C53F	1987	
TIL5974	Volvo B10M-61	Plaxton Paramount 3500 III	C53F	1987	
TIL5975	Volvo B10M-61	Plaxton Paramount 3500 III	C53F	1987	
E471SON	MCW Metrobus DR102/63	MCW	B45/30F	1988	London Buses, 1992
YBZ3260	Volvo B10M-61	Plaxton Paramount 3500 III	C53F	1988	
LUI8400	Volvo B10M-60	Plaxton Paramount 3500 III	C49F	1989	Wallace Arnold, 1993
TIL7165	Volvo B10M-60	Plaxton Paramount 3500 III	C53F	1989	
LUI3166	Volvo B10M-60	Plaxton Paramount 3500 III	C53F	1989	

Tappins was founded around 1900, and has grown to be one of the largest coach operators in South-East England. In addition to the coaches, Tappins operates an Oxford open-top sightseeing tour fleet recently augmented by Olympians from Dublin. The latest coach livery is illustrated by Van Hool Alizée N176LHU, one of a large order delivered in 1996, seen here passing through Trafalgar Square. *Keith Grimes*

To meet the needs of small parties, two Toyota Coasters with Caetano Optimo bodies are in the fleet. The first of the pair, P414HRB, dating from 1997, is shown here. *Phillip Stephenson*

MUI7851	Leyland Olympian ONCL10/1RZ	Alexander RL	O47/27D	1990	Dublin Bus, 2003
MUI7852	Leyland Olympian ONCL10/1RZ	Alexander RL	O47/27D	1990	Dublin Bus, 2003
MUI7853	Leyland Olympian ONCL10/1RZ	Alexander RL	O47/27D	1990	Dublin Bus, 2003
MUI7854	Leyland Olympian ONCL10/1RZ	Alexander RL	O47/27D	1990	Dublin Bus, 2003
KUI9417	Volvo B10M-60	Plaxton Paramount 3500 III	C53F	1990	
KUI9418	Volvo B10M-60	Plaxton Paramount 3500 III	C53F	1990	
GLZ4419	Volvo B10M-60	Plaxton Paramount 3500 III	C53F	1990	
ECZ3504	Volvo B10M-60	Plaxton Paramount 3500 III	C49F	1990	Wallace Arnold, 1993
BNZ3505	Volvo B10M-60	Plaxton Paramount 3500 III	C49F	1990	Wallace Arnold, 1993
G506LWU	Volvo B10M-60	Plaxton Paramount 3500 III	C49F	1990	Wallace Arnold, 1993
ECZ3507	Volvo B10M-60	Plaxton Paramount 3500 III	C49F	1990	Wallace Arnold, 1993
TIL4508	Volvo B10M-60	Plaxton Paramount 3500 III	C49F	1990	Wallace Arnold, 1993
TIL7509	Volvo B10M-60	Plaxton Paramount 3500 III	C49F	1990	Wallace Arnold, 1993
TIL2510	Volvo B10M-60	Plaxton Paramount 3500 III	C53F	1990	Wallace Arnold, 1993
TIL2511	Volvo B10M-60	Plaxton Paramount 3500 III	C53F	1990	Wallace Arnold, 1993
SIL9512	Volvo B10M-60	Plaxton Paramount 3500 III	C50F	1990	Wallace Arnold, 1993
SIL9513	Volvo B10M-60	Plaxton Paramount 3500 III	C50F	1990	Wallace Arnold, 1993
RIL5261	Volvo B10M-60	Plaxton Paramount 3500 III	C53F	1991	
TIL9262	Volvo B10M-60	Plaxton Paramount 3500 III	C53F	1991	
LUI9301	Volvo B10M-60	Van Hool Alizée H	C49F	1993	
TIL9302	Volvo B10M-60	Van Hool Alizée H	C49F	1993	
TIL1184	Volvo B10M-55	Plaxton Derwent II	B55F	1993	Tillingbourne, Cranleigh, 2001
L540XJU	Mazda E2200	Howletts	M8	1993	
N171LHU	Volvo B10M-62	Van Hool Alizée HE	C53F	1996	
N172LHU	Volvo B10M-62	Van Hool Alizée HE	C53F	1996	
N173LHU	Volvo B10M-62	Van Hool Alizée HE	C53F	1996	
N174LHU	Volvo B10M-62	Van Hool Alizée HE	C53F	1996	
N175LHU	Volvo B10M-62	Van Hool Alizée HE	C53F	1996	
N176LHU	Volvo B10M-62	Van Hool Alizée HE	C53F	1996	
N177LHU	Volvo B10M-62	Van Hool Alizée HE	C53F	1996	
N178LHU	Volvo B10M-62	Van Hool Alizée HE	C53F	1996	
N179LHU	Volvo B10M-62	Van Hool Alizée HE	C53F	1996	
N180LHU	Volvo B10M-62	Van Hool Alizée HE	C53F	1996	

The South East Bus Handbook

As we go to press a new, partial open-top East Lancs Vyking double-deck has entered service. If its layout, designed to allow use on school contact work as well as tour duties, is successful, others may be expected to displace older Atlanteans of which GJZ9574, with Roe bodywork, and seen earlier in 2005, may well be one. *Dave Heath*

P414HRB	Toyota Coaster BB50R	Caetano Optimo IV	C21F	1997	
P415HRB	Toyota Coaster BB50R	Caetano Optimo IV	C21F	1997	
R184VSJ	Volvo B10M-62	Van Hool T9 Alizée	C49FT	1998	Clyde Coast, Ardrossan, 2002
T4GLF	Volvo B10M-62	Van Hool T9 Alizée	C49FT	1999	Clyde Coast, Ardrossan, 2002
S810MCC	Volvo B10M-62	Van Hool T9 Alizée	C49FT	1999	Clynnog & Trefor, Trefor, 2005
PO55NXU	Volvo B7TL	East Lancs Vyking	PO--/--F	2005	

Previous registrations:

461XPB	NBL904X		
500EFC	NBL905X	LUI9301	K301GDT
653GBU	WBW735X	MUI7851	90D1013, G907FVX
AJZ9161	B161FWJ	MUI7852	90D1014, G919FVX
ANZ1323	C323UFP	MUI7853	90D1012, G951FVX
ANZ1325	C325UFP	MUI7854	90D1010, G963FVX
BNZ3505	G505LWU	RIL5261	H261GRY
ECZ3504	G504LWU	RIL7163	B163FWJ
ECZ3507	G507LWU	S810MCC	S810MCC, XSU653
GLZ4419	G419YAY	SIL9512	G512LWU
GLZ9570	OTO549M	SIL9513	G513LWU
GJZ9571	BFS14L	TIL1184	K101XPA
GJZ9572	BFS39L	TIL2510	G510LWU
GJZ9573	OSF928M	TIL2511	G511LWU
GJZ9574	STK124T	TIL4508	G508LWU
GJZ9575	STK129T	TIL5973	D73HRU
GJZ9576	UTV217S	TIL5974	D74HRU
IIL1832	E480YWJ	TIL5975	D75HRU
KBZ7145	D826UTF	TIL7165	F165XLJ
KUI5324	C324UFP	TIL7509	G509LWU
KUI9417	G417VAY	TIL9262	H262GRY
KUI9418	G418VAY	TIL9302	K302GDT
LUI3166	F166XLJ	YUE338	C326UFP
LUI8400	F400DUG	YBZ3260	E260PEL

Depots: Station Road, Didcot; Collett Road, Southmead Park, Didcot and Osney Mead, Oxford.
Web: www.tappins.co.uk

THAMES TRAVEL

Thames Travel (Wokingham) Ltd; Thames Travel (Wallingford) Ltd; Wyndham House, Lester Way, Wallingford, OX10 9TD

WWL208X	Leyland Olympian ONLXB/1R	Eastern Coach Works	B47/28D	1982	City Line, Oxford, 2002
M501VJO	Dennis Dart 9.8m	Marshall C37	B36D	1995	City Line, Oxford, 2002
R846JGD	Mercedes-Benz Vario O814	Plaxton Beaver 2	B31F	1998	
R847JGD	Mercedes-Benz Vario O814	Plaxton Beaver 2	B27F	1998	
R848JGD	Mercedes-Benz Vario O814	Plaxton Beaver 2	B31F	1998	
V67SVY	Volvo B10BLE	Alexander ALX300	NC41F	1999	First, 2004
X49VVY	Optare Solo M850	Optare	N27F	2001	
X383VVY	Optare Solo M850	Optare	N27F	2001	
Y313KDP	Volvo B6BLE	East Lancs Flyte	N36F	2001	Chiltern Queens, Woodcote, 2002
Y877KDP	Volvo B6BLE	East Lancs Flyte	N31F	2001	Chiltern Queens, Woodcote, 2002
Y972GPN	Dennis Dart SLF 8.5m	Plaxton MPD	N29F	2001	
Y973GPN	Dennis Dart SLF 8.5m	Plaxton MPD	N29F	2001	
KP51SXU	Dennis Dart SLF 8.5m	Plaxton MPD	N29F	2002	Chiltern Queens, Woodcote, 2002
KP51UFB	Dennis Dart SLF 8.5m	Plaxton MPD	N29F	2002	
KP51UFC	Dennis Dart SLF 8.5m	Plaxton MPD	N29F	2002	
KP51UFG	Dennis Dart SLF 8.5m	Plaxton MPD	N29F	2002	
KP51UFH	Dennis Dart SLF 8.5m	Plaxton MPD	N29F	2002	
KP51UFK	Dennis Dart SLF 10.1m	Plaxton Pointer 2	N36F	2002	
KP51UFL	Dennis Dart SLF 10.1m	Plaxton Pointer 2	N36F	2002	
BD02HDV	Mercedes-Benz Sprinter 413 CDi	Frank Guy	M13	2002	
BX02CMF	Mercedes-Benz Sprinter 413 CDi	Frank Guy	M13	2002	
KU52RXF	Dennis Dart SLF 8.5m	Plaxton MPD	N29F	2003	
KU52RXG	Dennis Dart SLF 8.5m	Plaxton MPD	N29F	2003	
KU52RXR	Dennis Dart SLF 8.5m	Plaxton MPD	N29F	2003	
KU52RXS	Dennis Dart SLF 8.5m	Plaxton MPD	N29F	2003	
KX53SGV	Optare Solo M850	Optare	N26F	2003	
KX53SGY	Optare Solo M850	Optare	N26F	2003	
KX53SGZ	Optare Solo M850	Optare	N26F	2003	
OU04FMV	TransBus Dart 8.8m	TransBus Mini Pointer	N29F	2004	
OU54PGZ	Scania OmniDekka N94UD	East Lancs	N47/33F	2005	
AE05EUX	MAN 14.220	MCV Evolution	N40F	2005	
AE05EUZ	MAN 14.220	MCV Evolution	N40F	2005	
OU05LWP	Mercedes-Benz Vario O616	Mellor	B25F	2005	

Previous registrations:
OU04FMV   SN04EFW   V67SVY   V3JJL

Web: www.busbook.co.uk

2005 saw the arrival of a double-deck to the Thames Travel fleet. Fitted with high-back seating, Scania OmniDekka 154, OU54PGZ, is seen on route X20 to Henley and Windsor. Fleet numbers are carried which match numbers in older registration while new index marks are sequences as 1 of 54, 254 etc.
Dave Heath

133

TIMETRAK

J A Appleford, 109 Upper Halliford Road, Shepperton, TW17 8SH

JDK911P	Bristol RESL6G	East Lancs	BC42F	1975	Bromyard Omnibus, 2001
WSV498	Volvo B58-61	Van Hool	C52F	1980	Classic Coaches, Booker, 2000
FDV818V	Bristol VRT/SL3/6LXB	Eastern Coach Works	B43/31F	1980	Classic Coaches, Booker, 2000
B122UUD	Leyland Tiger TRCTL11/3RH	Plaxton Paramount 3500 II E	C50F	1985	Swanbrook, Cheltenham, 2002
L618LJM	Optare MetroRider MR17	Optare	B25F	1994	Leggs, Cobham, 2004
J272SOC	Dennis Dart 9.8m	Carlyle Dartline	B43F	1994	Compass Buses, Newark, 2003

Previous registration:
WSV498   DSJ302V

Timetrak's double-deck is a Bristol VR that was new to the Cornish operator, Western National. Carrying a Cornish cream base colour, FDV818V was taking part in an enthusiasts' transport rally. *Phillip Stephenson*

TOUREX

Tourex - Nostalgia Travel - The School Bus Company

Tourex Ltd, Ruskin Cottage, North Hinksey, Oxford, OX2 0NA

22	558BWL	Leyland Tiger TRCTL11/3R	Marshall Campaigner	BC54F	1983	MoD (20KB65), 1995
23	YJN166	Leyland Tiger TRCTL11/3R	Marshall Campaigner	BC54F	1983	MoD (20KB44), 1995
24	A734YOX	Leyland Tiger TRCTL11/3R	Marshall Campaigner	BC54F	1983	MoD (20KB67), 1996
25	A788YOX	Leyland Tiger TRCTL11/3R	Marshall Campaigner	BC54F	1983	MoD (20KB52), 1996
27	D527DPM	Leyland Tiger TRCTL11/3RZ	Plaxton Derwent 2	BC54F	1987	MoD (82KF40), 1997
28	A359TBW	Leyland Tiger TRCTL11/3R	Marshall Campaigner	BC54F	1984	MoD (20KB49), 1999
30	A49VDE	Leyland Tiger TRCTL11/3R	Marshall Campaigner	BC54F	1984	Davies Bros, Pencader, 1999
33	CBD899T	Bristol VRT/SL3/6LXB	Eastern Coach Works	B43/31F	1978	Arriva The Shires, 2001
34	C259GUH	Lcyland Tiger TRCTL11/3RH	Plaxton Paramount 3500 II	C48FT	1986	Andy James, Tetbury, 2001
35	F86TDL	Leyland Tiger TRCTL11/3R	Marshall Campaigner	BC53F	1983	Southern Vectis, 2001
37	EBW107Y	Leyland Tiger TRCTL11/3R	Duple Dominant IV Express	C50F	1983	Chiltern Queens, Woodcote, 2002
41	PIL6578	Volvo B10M-61	Plaxton Paramount 3200 II	C53F	1986	Chiltern Queens, Woodcote, 2002
42	PIL6579	Volvo B10M-61	Plaxton Paramount 3200 III	C53F	1987	Chiltern Queens, Woodcote, 2002
43	PIL6576	Volvo B10M-61	Plaxton Paramount 3200 II	C53F	1985	Chiltern Queens, Woodcote, 2002
45	C454GKE	Leyland Olympian ONTL11/2RHSp	Eastern Coach Works	C45/28F	1986	Weavaway, Newbury, 2003
46	966MKE	Leyland Tiger TRCTL11/3ARZM	Plaxton Paramount 3200	C53F	1990	Matthews Blue, Shouldham, 2005
50	C17OST	Leyland Tiger TRCL10/3ARZA	Plaxton Paramount 3200 III	C70F	1991	Lewis Meridian, Greenwich, 2005
51	A642WDT	Leyland Olympian ONLXB/1R	Eastern Coach Works	B43/31F	1984	Yorkshire Traction, 2005
79	786AFC	Leyland Leopard PSU3F/5R	Plaxton Supreme IV Express	C53F	1981	Percival's, Oxford, 1987
80	VWL96	Leyland Leopard PSU3F/5R	Plaxton Supreme IV Express	C53F	1981	Percival's, Oxford, 1987

Heritage vehicles:

07	LYB941	Bedford OB	Duple Vista	C29F	1948	Longstaff, Carlton, 1989
15	FJB739C	Bristol Lodekka FLF6G	Eastern Coach Works	H38/32F	1965	Percivals, Oxford, 1991

Previous registrations:

512AUO	YPD107Y
558BWL	A484YOX
786AFC	LWL743W
966MKE	F704ENE, YMF752, F620HWE
A49VDE	20KB64
C17OST	J796CNN, 65RTO
C259GUH	C259GUH, 86TS330
C454GKE	C454GKE, B10MLT
F86TDL	20KB78, A550DPA
PIL6576	B911SPR
PIL6578	C644SJM
PIL6579	D262HFX
VWL96	LWL744W
YJN166	A537YOX

Depot: Swannybrook Farm, Kingston Bagpuize, Abingdon

Tourex' principal operation involves school services in Oxfordshire. Typical of the fleet is Leyland Tiger 28, A359TBW, one of many Marshall Campaigner-boded buses formerly with the MoD and now converted for civilian work.
Bill Potter

TRUEMANS TRAVEL

Truemans Coaches (Fleet) Ltd, Truemans End, Lynchford Road, Ash Vale, GU12 5PQ

J13TRU	Volvo B10M-60	Van Hool Alizée	C53F	1992	Fleet Coaches, 2000
J14TRU	Volvo B10M-60	Van Hool Alizée	C53F	1992	Fleet Coaches, 2000
J16TRU	Volvo B10M-60	Van Hool Alizée	C53F	1992	Fleet Coaches, 2000
J17TRU	DAF SB3000	Van Hool Alizée HE	C53F	1996	
2448RU	Iveco EuroRider 391E.12.35	Beulas Stergo ε	C52F	1999	
J18TRU	Irisbus EuroRider 391E.12.35	Beulas El Mundo	C51FT	2001	
J19TRU	Irisbus EuroRider 391E.12.35	Beulas Stergo ε	C53F	2001	
1287RU	Irisbus EuroRider 391E.12.35	Beulas Stergo ε	C52F	2001	
1116RU	Irisbus EuroRider 391E.12.35	Beulas El Mundo	C49FT	2001	
4227RU	Irisbus EuroRider 391E.12.35	Beulas El Mundo	C49FT	2001	
2003RU	Irisbus EuroRider 391E.12.35	Beulas El Mundo	C49FT	2003	
J20TRU	Irisbus EuroRider 391E.12.35	Beulas El Mundo	C49FT	2003	
2439RU	Irisbus EuroRider 391E.12.35	Beulas Stergo ε	C49FT	2003	
J30TRU	Irisbus EuroRider 391E.12.35	Beulas Stergo ε	C53F	2003	
J33TRU	Irisbus EuroRider 391E.12.35	Beulas Stergo ε	C53F	2003	

Previous registrations:

1116RU	From new		J16TRU	K811EET
1287RU	From new		J18TRU	Y812YBC
2003RU	From new		J19TRU	Y813YBC
2439RU	From new		J20TRU	FG03JBZ
4227RU	From new		J30TRU	FG03JBX
J13TRU	J411AWF		J33TRU	FG03JBY
J14TRU	J412AWF			

The Truemans Travel and Truemans Coaches names are used for this fleet. All the coaches with RU plates are Truemans Travel while TRU plates relate to Truemans Coaches. The Irisbus EuroRider has been selected for sales this century, though the body style has been divided between the Stergo ε (3.6m high) and El Mundo (3.78m high). One of the former, J30TRU is illustrated. *Colin Lloyd*

W & H MOTORS

AG & GM Heron, Kelvin Centre, Kelvin Way, Crawley, RH10 9SF

G555BPJ	Leyland Swift LBM6T/2RA	Wadham Stringer Vanguard II	B39F	1989		
G392NPW	Van Hool T815	Van Hool Acron	C49FT	1990	Silver Knight, Wickford, 1999	
G901ANR	Van Hool T815	Van Hool Acron	C49FT	1990	Castleways, Winchcombe, '99	
K232WNH	MAN 16.290	Jonckheere Deauville P599	C51FT	1993	Marchwood Motorways, 1999	
K233WNH	MAN 16.290	Jonckheere Deauville P599	C51FT	1993	Marchwood Motorways, 1999	
R260GNJ	Iveco TurboDaily 59.12	Marshall C31	BC29F	1997		
W146ULT	Toyota Coaster BB50R	Caetano Optimo IV	C22F	2000		
W771AAY	MAN 24.400	Noge Catalan 370	C49FT	2000		
W547RNB	Ayats Bravo A3E/BR1	Ayats	C57/16DT	2000	Waterhouse, Polegate, 2001	
WH02WOW	Ayats Bravo A3E/BR1	Ayats	C55/16DT	2000		
YN03AWM	MAN 18.360	Noge Catalan 350	C51FT	2003		
YN03AWP	MAN 18.360	Noge Catalan 350	C51FT	2003		
FJ05AOG	Volvo B12B	Sunsundegui Sideral	C49FT	2005		
FJ05AOH	Volvo B12B	Sunsundegui Sideral	C49FT	2005		
FN05DGE	Volvo B12B	Sunsundegui Sideral	C49FT	2005		

Previous registrations:
G392NPW   G515LPW, A10BCT   G901ANR   G901ANR, 86JBF

Web: www.wandhgroup.co.uk

Following on from a MAN 24.400 tri-axle double-deck coach, two single-deck Noge Catalan coaches joined the W H tours fleet in 2003. Illustrating the Noge 350 model is YN03AWM. *Dave Heath.*

WARRENS

Warrens Coaches (Kent & Sussex) Ltd, High Street, Ticehurst, Wadhurst, TN5 7AN

UBK606	Mercedes-Benz 0303/15R	Mercedes-Benz	C53F	1986	Solent, New Milton, 1997
KBZ2276	Volvo B10M-61	Plaxton Paramount 3500 III	C53F	1988	Rye Coaches, 1991
J84OKK	Setra S215HD	Setra Tornado	C49FT	1992	
XBZ7723	Volvo B10M-60	Jonckheere Deauville 45	C53F	1993	West Coast Motors, 2000
P170ANR	Toyota Coaster HZB50R	Caetano Optimo III	C21F	1996	
R870SDT	Scania L94IB	Irizar InterCentury 12.32	C53F	1997	
V202EAL	Iveco EuroRider 391E.12.29	Beulas Stergo ε	C53F	1999	
V203EAL	Iveco EuroRider 391E.12.35	Beulas Stergo ε	C53F	1999	
W657SJF	Irisbus EuroRider 391E.12.29	Beulas Stergo ε	C49FT	2000	
W658SJF	Irisbus EuroRider 391E.12.29	Beulas Stergo ε	C49FT	2000	
GN53AJU	Irisbus EuroRider 391E.12.35	Beulas Stergo ε	C32FT	2003	

Previous registration:

KBZ2276	E218GCG		UBK606	D27CAC, 5505ML, SIW1934, D27CAC
			XBZ7723	K200WCM, K462SSU

Web: www.warrens.uk.com

Latterly with West Coast Motors, Jonckheere Deauville 45 XBZ7723 is seen in Warrens livery. *Dave Heath*

WEAVAWAY

Weavaway - Newbury & District - Noah Vale

L & S Weaver, 169 Main Street, Newbury, RG19 6HN

	Reg	Chassis	Body	Seats	Year	History
	W197ESO	Bova FHD 12.370	Bova Futura	C49FT	2000	
	B10MSC	MCW Metrobus DR115/5	MCW	B63/43D	1988	New World First Bus, 2001
	B10MSE	MCW Metrobus DR115/5	MCW	B63/43D	1988	New World First Bus, 2001
	B10MDC	Dennis Condor DDA1702	Duple Metsec	B63/43D	1989	New World First Bus, 2002
w	B10MFC	Dennis Condor DDA1702	Duple Metsec	B63/43D	1989	New World First Bus, 2002
w	B10MKC	Dennis Condor DDA1702	Duple Metsec	B63/43D	1989	New World First Bus, 2002
w	B10MKF	Dennis Condor DDA1702	Duple Metsec	B63/43D	1989	New World First Bus, 2002
w	B10MWA	Dennis Condor DDA1702	Duple Metsec	B63/43D	1989	New World First Bus, 2002
w	B10MWC	Dennis Condor DDA1702	Duple Metsec	B63/43D	1989	New World First Bus, 2002
	S222AJW	DAF SB220	Optare Delta	B49F	1998	Airlinks, 2002
	V79JKG	Optare Excel L1070	Optare	N38F	1999	Bebb, Llantwit Fardre, 2004
	OO02TEN	Bova FHD 12.340	Bova Futura	C49FT	2002	
	WT52EBG	MAN 24.400	Noge Catalan	C49FT	2002	
	WA03UDY	Bova FHD 12.340	Bova Futura	C53F	2003	
	WA03UDZ	Bova FHD 12.340	Bova Futura	C53F	2003	
	WA53FDG	Bova FHD 12.340	Bova Futura	C49FT	2004	
	WA53FDJ	Bova FHD 12.340	Bova Futura	C49FT	2004	
	YN53EHZ	Volvo B7R	TransBus Profile	BC70F	2003	
	NBZ70	Volvo B7R	TransBus Profile	BC70F	2004	
	NDZ70	Volvo B7R	TransBus Profile	BC70F	2004	
	WA05DFG	VDL Bova FHD 13.340	VDL Bova Futura	C53FT	2005	
	WA05DFJ	VDL Bova FHD 13.340	VDL Bova Futura	C53FT	2005	
	OU05AVB	Volvo B9TL	East Lancs Vyking	BC63/39F	2005	
	OU05AVD	Volvo B9TL	East Lancs Vyking	BC63/39F	2005	

Weavaway also use the Newbury & District and Noah Vale names. Pictured in the former colours is Optare Solo YN03NEF.
Dave Heath
check - not on fleet list

In 2005 Bova joined VDL Groupe, the Dutch manufacturer. Two early sales were to Weavaway, one of which is WA03UDY, seen parked on London's Embankment. *Colin Lloyd*

OU05AVY	Volvo B9TL	East Lancs Vyking	BC63/39F	2005
OU05AWJ	Volvo B9TL	East Lancs Vyking	BC63/39F	2005
OU05KKB	Volvo B9TL	East Lancs Vyking	BC63/39F	2005
OU05KLA	Volvo B9TL	East Lancs Vyking	BC63/39F	2005
SN05FNW	Mercedes-Benz Vario 0814	Plaxton Beaver 2	BC31F	2005
-	Scania K124EB6	Irizar PB	C53FT	On order
-	Scania K124EB6	Irizar PB	C53FT	On order
-	Scania K124EB6	Irizar PB	C	On order
-	Scania K124EB6	Irizar PB	C	On order
-	Scania K94IB4	Irizar S-Kool	BC70F	On order
-	Scania K94IB4	Irizar S-Kool	BC70F	On order
-	Scania K94IB4	Irizar S-Kool	BC70F	On order

Previous registrations:

B10MBD	EH9604(HK), G659FVX	B10MSE	DY8312(HK), F215UJN
B10MDC	EJ3194(HK), G839FVX	B10MWA	EG5131(HK), F330UJN
B10MFC	EH2014(HK), G859FVX	B10MWC	EH6403(HK), G807FVX
B10MKC	EE9168(HK), F287UJN	NBZ70	YN04WTC
B10MKF	EG7583(HK), G708FVX	NDZ70	YN04WTD
B10MSC	EA1844(HK), F214UJN	S222AJW	S610JUA
		W197ESO	W11WAY

Depots: New Greenham Park, Newbury and Great Knollys Street, Reading

WEST KENT BUSES

S Gilkes, The Coach Station, London Road, West Kingsdown, TN15 6AR

VDV123S	Bristol VRT/SL3/6LXB	Eastern Coach Works	B43/33F	1978	Moffat & Williamson, Gauldry, '03
FYD864T	AEC Reliance 6U3ZR	Plaxton Supreme IV	C53F	1979	preservation, 2005
KYV329X	Leyland Titan TNLXB2RR	Leyland	B44/32F	1981	London Central, 2000
KYV370X	Leyland Titan TNLXB2RR	Leyland	B44/32F	1981	Tilley, Orpington, 2005
KYV442X	Leyland Titan TNLXB2RR	Leyland	B44/32F	1981	Stagecoach South, 2002
NUW671Y	Leyland Titan TNLXB2RR	Leyland	B44/32F	1982	Stagecoach South, 2000
A871SUL	Leyland Titan TNLXB2RR	Leyland	B44/32F	1983	London Central, 2000
B124WUV	Leyland Titan TNLXB2RR	Leyland	B44/32F	1984	Stagecoach South, 2002
B906RVF	Leyland Tiger TRCTL11/3RH	Plaxton Paramount 3200 II E	C55F	1985	Thompson, Parkgate, 2004

Special event vehicles:

WKG287	AEC Reliance 2MU3RA	Willowbrook	B41F	1961	Quantock Motor Services, 2004
KOW901F	AEC Regent V 3D2RA	Neepsend	B40/30R	1967	B&B Location Diners, 2005

Ancillary vehicle:

OFS911M	Leyland Atlantean AN68	Alexander AL	O45/33D	1973	Guide Friday, Stratford, 2003

Previous registration:
KYV370X   KYV370X, TAZ4062

Surrounded by an array of spot-lights and cameras, Titan A871SUL displays the colours of West Kent Buses. The vehicle was employed on rail replacement duties when the bus was pictured in Ashford bus station. *Bob Hawkes*

WHEELERS TRAVEL

Wheelers Travel Ltd, Merrie Mead, Rownham's Lane, North Baddesley, SO52 9HR

Reg	Chassis	Body	Seating	Year	Notes
TJT182X	Leyland Olympian ONLXB/1R	Marshall	B47/31F	1982	
KHF131	Volvo B10M-61	Duple	C51FT	1983	Sansome, Southampton, 2003
YIL2185	Volvo B10M-60	Plaxton Paramount 3200 III	C49FT	1984	Sansome, Southampton, 2003
OLW503	Volvo B10M-61	Plaxton Paramount 3500 II	C53F	1985	Mitchell, Hedge End, 2001
E175OMU	Volvo B10M-61	Duple 340	C53F	1988	
XIB1906	Volvo B10M-60	Plaxton Paramount 3500 III	C53F	1989	Sansome, Southampton, 2003
YXI9256	Volvo B10M-61	Van Hool Alizée H	C53F	1989	Sansome, Southampton, 2003
G483BJT	Ford Transit VE6	Bristol Street	M3L	1989	Home James, Totton, 2001
GLZ4406	Mercedes-Benz 811D	PMT Ami	C33F	1989	Mustapha, Enfield, 2000
LIL3057	Mercedes-Benz 609D	Crystals	BC26F	1989	Sansome, Southampton, 2003
WLT702	DAF SBR3000	Plaxton Paramount 4000 III	C55/19CT	1990	Poynter's, Rye, 2003
H987ERV	Renault Trafic	?	M8	1990	?, 2002
RIL8251	Mercedes-Benz 408D	Made-to-Measure	M16	1991	Norman, Braishfield, 2000
LUI7865	Scania K113CRB	Berkhof Excellence 2000	C53F	1992	Applebys, Grimsby, 2002
J4HSL	Toyota Coaster	Caetano Optimo III	C18F	1992	Holt Services, Henfield, 2003
MLZ9698	Volvo B10M-61	Van Hool Alizée H	C49FT	1992	Sansome, Southampton, 2003
A1YET	Volvo B10M-61	Van Hool Alizée H	C49FT	1992	Sansome, Southampton, 2003
L628VUS	LDV 400	LDV	M8L	1993	Glasgow MBC, 2002
FCZ9151	Volkswagen Transporter	AVB	M12	1993	
HCZ1821	Renault Master	Made-to-Measure	M13	1993	Cooper, Hamble, 2001
MBZ8369	Mercedes-Benz 814D	Autobus Classiqoe	C33F	1993	CS&GB, South Newton, 2002
L38LRC	Mercedes-Benz 814D	Autobus Classiqoe	C24F	1993	Sansome, Southampton, 2001
SIL9041	Mercedes-Benz 609D	PVB	BC24F	1994	Norman, Braishfield, 2000
N745DBD	Ford Transit VE6	Ford	M14	1995	private owner, 2003
N576WAW	Ford Transit VE6	Ford	M8	1995	private owner, 2002
N495DOR	LDV 400	LDV	M16	1995	Trent Valley, Rugeley, 2001
N222TAY	Dennis Javelin GX 12m	Berkhof Excellence	C53F	1995	
P881FMO	Dennis Javelin GX 12m	Berkhof Axial 50	C53F	1997	Impact, Hanwell, 2004
P904FMO	Dennis Javelin GX 12m	Berkhof Axial 50	C53F	1997	Impact, Hanwell, 2004
P905FMO	Dennis Javelin GX 12m	Berkhof Axial 50	C53F	1997	Impact, Hanwell, 2004
P906FMO	Dennis Javelin GX 12m	Berkhof Axial 50	C53F	1997	Impact, Hanwell, 2004
NIL7251	Dennis Javelin 12m	Plaxton Première 320	C53F	1997	?, 2004
R919XTP	Ford Transit VE6	Mayflower	M16	1998	
R167EOO	Ford Transit VE6	Ford	M8	1998	private owner, 2002
S167UBU	Iveco Daily 49.10	Mellor	N16FL	1998	TLS, 1998
T492RCE	LDV Convoy	LDV	M14	1999	van, 2003
V390KCA	LDV Convoy	LDV	M14	2000	van, 2000
BU03YTE	BMC Probus 850RE	BMC	C35F	2003	

Previous registrations:

A1YET	J227NNC	MLZ9698	J226NNC
E175OMU	E175OMU, 9682FH	PLW503	B162FWJ
FCZ9151	?	RIL8251	J440MDB, USV680
GLZ4406	G41PFSF	SIL9041	M966WTR, USV678
HCZ1821	K990XND, 64GWC	WBZ8369	L476JEE
J4HSL	J721FGP	WLT702	G776HOV
JIL3715	F601GET	XIB1906	F439DUG
KHF131	A298RSU	YIL2185	G375REG
LIL357	F130COE	YXI9256	F750ENE
LUI7865	J677LVL, 388XYC		

Depots: Baddersley Road, Annefield; Upper Northam Drive, Hedge End; Romsey Road, Ower and Roley Farm, Fair Oak, Southampton.

WHITE BUS SERVICES

C E Jeatt & Sons Ltd, North Street Garage, North Street, Winkfield, Windsor, SL4 4TF

JMJ633V	Bedford YMT	Plaxton Supreme IV Express	C53F	1979	Moore, Windsor, 1987
JNM747Y	Bedford YNT	Plaxton Paramount 3200	C53F	1983	Grey of Ely, 1997
B633DDW	Bedford YNT	Plaxton Paramount 3200 II	C53F	1985	Fernhill Travel, Bracknell, 1995
B542OJF	Bedford YNT	Duple Laser	C53F	1985	Victoria, Tean, 1997
B30MSF	Bedford YNT	Duple Laser 2	C53F	1985	Glyn Evans, Manmoel, 1998
C668WRT	Bedford YNT	Duple Dominant	B63F	1986	Chambers, Bures, 1995
E849AAO	Bedford YNV Venturer	Plaxton Paramount 3200 III	C55F	1987	Reynolds, Watford, 1999
L561ASU	Dennis Javelin 12m	Wadham Stringer Vanguard II	BC70F	1995	MoD (77KK25), 2005
L523MJB	Dennis Javelin 12m	Wadham Stringer Vanguard II	BC70F	1995	MoD (47KL48), 2005
P131RWR	DAF SB220	Optare Delta	B49F	1987	Luton Airport, 2004
R89GNW	DAF SB220	Optare Delta	B53F	1998	Flyerbus, Dublin, 2003
R674OEB	Dennis Javelin 12m	Berkhof Excellence 1000LD	C57F	1998	Greys of Ely, 2005
S158JUA	DAF SB220	Optare Delta	B53F	1998	National Express, W Drayton, '03
L715FPE	MAN 18.370	Berkhof Excellence 1000LD	C53F	1994	Hodge's, Sandhurst, 2003
L522MDP	MAN 18.370	Berkhof Excellence 1000LD	C53F	1994	Hodge's, Sandhurst, 2003
W808AAY	Irisbus EuroRider 391E.12.35	Beulas Stergo ε	C49FT	2000	Fernhill, Bracknell, 2005

Previous registrations:

E849AAO	E849AAO, FSU739		L715FPE	L715FPE, 5881PH
JNM747Y	JNM747Y, ESU307		R674OEB	ESU350
L522MDP	1598PH, L522MDP		R89GNW	?

White Bus Services operates three Optare Delta buses in, as one would expect, an all-white livery. Seen heading for Ascot, R89GNW, which was one of the last Delta buses to be built, joined the fleet after a period in Dublin. *Richard Godfrey*

WIGHT BUS

Isle of Wight Council, 21 Whitcombe Road, Newport, PO30 1YS

5801	HW04DFN	TransBus Javelin 12m	TransBus Profile	BC70F	2004
5803	HW54DCU	Alexander Dennis Dart 10.1m	Alexander Dennis Pointer	N37F	2004
5804	HW54DCO	Alexander Dennis Dart 10.1m	Alexander Dennis Pointer	N37F	2004
5805	HW54DCF	Alexander Dennis Dart 10.1m	Alexander Dennis Pointer	N37F	2004
5816	P81VDL	Dennis Javelin 12m	UVG Unistar	B72F	1997
5817	P82VDL	Dennis Javelin 12m	UVG Unistar	B72F	1997
5818	P83VDL	Dennis Javelin 12m	UVG Unistar	B72F	1997
5819	J142JDL	Dennis Javelin 11m	Wadham Stringer	B67F	1991
5821	R301BDL	Mercedes-Benz Vario O814	UVG CitiStar	B30FL	1997
5825	P231TDL	Mercedes-Benz 811D	UVG CitiStar	B33F	1996
5827	R302BDL	Mercedes-Benz Vario O814	UVG CitiStar	B30FL	1997
5828	R303BDL	Mercedes-Benz Vario O814	UVG CitiStar	B30FL	1997
5834	R304BDL	Mercedes-Benz Vario O814	UVG CitiStar	B30FL	1997
5841	P124TDL	Dennis Javelin GX 12m	Caetano Algarve II	C57F	1996
5842	P125TDL	Dennis Javelin GX 12m	Caetano Algarve II	C57F	1996
5843	P137TDL	Dennis Dart 9.8m	UVG Urban Star	B43F	1996
5844	P138TDL	Dennis Dart 9.8m	UVG Urban Star	B43F	1996
5845	P139TDL	Dennis Dart 9.8m	UVG Urban Star	B43F	1996
5846	P140TDL	Dennis Dart 9.8m	UVG Urban Star	B43F	1996
5847	P141TDL	Dennis Dart 9.8m	UVG Urban Star	B43F	1996
5848	P142TDL	Dennis Dart 9.8m	UVG Urban Star	B43F	1996
5862	HW54DCE	Alexander Dennis Dart 8.8m	Alexander Dennis Mini Pointer	N29F	2004
5863	HW54DBZ	Alexander Dennis Dart 8.8m	Alexander Dennis Mini Pointer	N29F	2004
5864	X172BNH	Mercedes-Benz Vario O814	Plaxton Beaver 2	B32F	2000
5871	KF02ZWK	Mercedes-Benz Sprinter 413CDi	UVG	B16FL	2002
5872	KF02ZWL	Mercedes-Benz Sprinter 413CDi	UVG	B16FL	2002
5873	KF02ZWM	Mercedes-Benz Sprinter 413CDi	UVG	B16FL	2002
5874	KF02ZWN	Mercedes-Benz Sprinter 413CDi	UVG	B16FL	2002
5875	KF02ZWR	Mercedes-Benz Sprinter 413CDi	UVG	B16FL	2002
5877	KE04EAK	Mercedes-Benz Sprinter 413CDi	UVG	B16FL	2004
6202	M975DNJ	LDV 400	SEM	M10L	1995
6206	X758LOK	LDV Convoy	LDV	M11	2000
6214	R492BDL	LDV Convoy	Lonsdale	M11L	1997
6217	R493BDL	LDV Convoy	Lonsdale	M11L	1997

Depots: Whitcombe Road, Newport; Faulkner Lane, Sandown and on various school premises.

Wightbus is the trading name of the Isle of Wight Council which operates an ever increasing fleet of buses. Showing the livery used is 5848, P142TDL, a Dart with UVG Urban Star bodywork. *Phillip Stephenson*

WILTAX

Wiltax Buses Ltd, 41 Manor Road, Ashford, TW15 2SL

LA1	G171YUR	Leyland Olympian ONLXB/1R	Alexander RH	B45/31F	1999	Mullany, Watford, 2005
LA2	C652LFT	Leyland Olympian ONLXB/1R	Alexander RH	B45/31F	1986	Stagecoach 2005
L34	C34CHM	Leyland Olympian ONLXB/1R	Eastern Coach Works	B42/30F	1986	Arriva London, 2005
L164	D164FYM	Leyland Olympian ONLXB/1R	Eastern Coach Works	B42/26D	1986	Arriva London, 2005
MM265	N132XEG	MAN 11.220	Marshall C37	B38F	1996	Metroline, 2005
M429	VLT191	MCW Metrobus DR101/12	MCW	B43/28D	1980	Metroline, 2004
M449	VLT177	MCW Metrobus DR101/12	MCW	B43/28D	1980	Metroline, 2004
M609	KYO609X	MCW Metrobus DR101/14	MCW	B43/28D	1981	Arriva OLST, 2004
M659	KYV659X	MCW Metrobus DR101/12	MCW	B43/28D	1981	Arriva OLST, 2004
M1283	VLT23	MCW Metrobus DR101/12	MCW	B43/28F	1985	Day, Chale, 2003
M1428	VLT87	MCW Metrobus DR101/12	MCW	B43/28D	1986	Metroline, 2004
M1438	C436BUV	MCW Metrobus DR101/12	MCW	B43/28D	1986	Abbey Coaches, 2005

Previous registrations:

VLT23	B283WUL		VLT171	GYE449W
VLT87	C428BUV		VLT191	GYE429W

Web: www.wiltaxbuses.com

The mostly double-deck fleet of Wiltax's operation is concentrated on rail-replacement services. Seen undertaking such duties is Metrobus KYV659X, which also retains its former London Buses number M659. *Dave Heath*

WOOTTENS

Opperman (1990) Ltd, The Coach Yard, Lycrome Road, Lye Green, Chesham, HP5 3LG

JIL2199	Leyland National 11351A/1R	East Lancs Greenway (1994)	B49F	1977	British Bus Sales, Cobham, 2004
WJI2849	Bristol VRT/SL3/680 (6LXB)	Eastern Coach Works	B43/31F	1981	Brighton & Hove, 2000
ABW310X	Leyland Leopard PSU3G/4R	Willowbrook Warrior (1990)	B48F	1982	Cityline, Oxford, 2002
BBW214Y	Leyland Olympian ONLXB/1R	Eastern Coach Works	B47/28D	1982	Cityline, Oxford, 2003
760BUS	Leyland Olympian ONTL11/2RSp	Eastern Coach Works	BC45/31F	1985	Jackson, Bicknacre, 2003
C64HOM	Leyland Lynx LX1126LXCTFR1	Leyland Lynx	B51F	1986	Cityline, Oxford, 2004
E227CFC	Leyland Olympian ONLXB/1RH	Alexander RL	B47/30F	1988	Arriva The Shires, 2003
N903ABL	Volvo B10M-62	Berkhof Excellence	C53F	1996	Truemans, Fleet, 2003
N289OYE	Volvo B10M-62	Plaxton Première 350	C53F	1996	Redwing, Camberwell, 2000
P288ENT	Volvo B10M-62	Plaxton Première 350	C53F	1997	Bysiau Cwm Taf, Whitand, 2005
P822GBA	Volvo B10M-62	Van Hool T9 Alizée	C53F	1997	Shearings, 2005
R186TKU	Volvo B10M-62	Plaxton Première 350	C53F	1998	JGS, Rotherham, 2005
R551TKV	Volvo B10M-62	Plaxton Première 350	C57F	1998	Country Lion, Northampton, 2005
FE02FCA	Volvo B7R	Jonckheere Modulo	C57FT	2002	
W100TEN	Volvo B12M	Jonckheere Mistral 50	C51FT	2002	
FE52HFW	Irisbus EuroMidi CC95.9E18F	Indcar Maxim 2	C29F	2003	
FN52GVE	Irisbus EuroRider 391E.12.35	Beulas Stergo ε	C49FT	2002	
FN52GVF	Irisbus EuroRider 391E.12.35	Beulas Stergo ε	C53F	2002	
FG03JAU	Irisbus EuroRider 391E.12.35	Beulas Stergo ε	C49FT	2003	
FG03JBU	Irisbus EuroRider 391E.12.35	Beulas Stergo ε	C53F	2003	
FG03JCU	Irisbus EuroRider 391E.12.35	Beulas Stergo ε	C49FT	2003	

Previous registrations:

760BUS	B107LPH, B111WAT, B782FOG	W100TEN	FE02FCC
ABW310X	VUD33X	WJI2849	JWV273X
JIL2199	UHG736R		
R551TKV	A20CLC		

Web: www.woottens.co.uk

Woottens has now taken five Irisbus EuroRiders with Beulas Stergo ε bodywork into the fleet, along with an Irisbus EuroMidi. Illustrating the Beulas Stergo ε is FN52GVF. *Colin Lloyd*

WORTH'S

Worths Motor Services Ltd, The Garage, Oxford Road, Enstone, Chipping Norton, OX7 4LQ

JWL322W	Volvo B58-61	Plaxton Supreme IV	C57F	1980	
BBW216Y	Leyland Olympian ONLXB/1R	Eastern Coach Works	B47/28D	1982	Cityline, Oxford, 1999
CUD220Y	Leyland Olympian ONLXB/1R	Eastern Coach Works	B47/28D	1983	Cityline, Oxford, 2002
SKG406Y	Volvo B10M-61	Plaxton Paramount 3200	C53F	1983	K&P John, Llanharry, 1990
SIL6722	Volvo B10M-61	Plaxton Paramount 3500 II	C53F	1986	Wallace Arnold, 1991
774YPG	Volvo B10M-61	Plaxton Paramount 3200 III	C49FT	1988	
XSK144	Volvo B10M-61	Plaxton Paramount 3200 III	C57F	1988	
KAZ2755	Volvo B10M-61	Plaxton Paramount 3200 III	C57F	1989	
IUI6722	Volvo B10M-60	Plaxton Paramount 3200 III	C57F	1989	Independent, Horsforth, 1994
G844VAY	Volvo B10M-60	Duple 320	C57F	1989	Crawford, Neilston, 1992
G780WFC	Optare MetroRider MR09	Optare	BC25F	1990	Cityline, Oxford, 1999
WJI2322	Volvo B10M-60	Jonckheere Deauville P599	C53F	1990	Harris, Catshill, 1995
DCZ2322	Volvo B10M-60	Plaxton Paramount 3200 III	C57F	1990	Bere Regis & District, 1993
L150HUD	Volvo B10M-62	Plaxton Première 350	C53F	1993	Oxford Bus Company, 2001
L151HUD	Volvo B10M-62	Plaxton Première 350	C53F	1993	Oxford Bus Company, 2001
L154HUD	Volvo B10M-62	Plaxton Première 350	C53F	1993	Oxford Bus Company, 2001
P7WMS	Volvo B10M-62	Berkhof Axial	C51FT	1997	
R8WMS	Volvo B10M-62	Plaxton Excalibur	C53F	1998	
S6WMS	Volvo B10M-62	Plaxton Excalibur	C53F	1998	
S2WMS	Dennis Dart SLF	Plaxton Pointer 2	N39F	1999	
V9WMS	Volvo B10M-62	Plaxton Première 320	C53F	1999	
W5WMS	Volvo B10M-62	Plaxton Première 320	C53F	1999	
Y363YOM	Mercedes-Benz Vita 412D	Mercedes-Benz	M10	2001	
Y4WMS	Dennis Dart SLF	Plaxton MPD	N29F	2001	
BU53ZWZ	Mercedes-Benz Citaro O530	Mercedes-Benz	N42F	2004	
TW53WMS	Volvo B12M	Jonckheere Mistral 50	C53F	2004	

Heritage vehicle:

LUD606	Bedford SBG	Duple Bella Vega	C41F	1957	

Previous registrations:

774YPG	F318GWL	SIL6722	C121DWR, 551DJB
DCZ2322	H443JLJ	WJI2322	G144MNH
IUI6722	F464WFX	XSK144	F396HFC
KAZ2755	F322MFC		

Web: www.worthscoaches.co.uk

Worth's fleet comprises many Plaxton-bodied Volvo coaches. Representing the fleet is L150HUD, a Volvo B10M with a Première 350 body and one of three that were latterly used on Oxford Citybus services, and which thus feature destination indicators.
Dave Heath

147

Vehicle Index

1FTO	Flights-Hallmark	1045MM	Marchwood M'ways	6967PH	Hodge's	A19LTG		Lucketts
50DBD		1108AP	Autopoint	7107PH	Hodge's	A19TKF	The King's Ferry
52CLC	Crawley	1 SRU	Truemans	7209RU	Heyfordian	A20HLC	Lucketts
58DAF	C&S C	1168BY	Heritage Travel	7298RU	Heyfordian	A20HOF	Hellyers
90WFC	Motts Travel	1194PO	Heritage Travel	7396LJ	Heyfordian	A70THX	Newnham
98CLJ	Grayline	1287RU	Truemans	7572MW	Heritage Travel	A102SUU	Nu-Venture
130VBJ	Souls	1435VZ	Heyfordian	7634AP	Autopoint	A113MUD	Charlton Services
159FCG	Safeguard	1455MV	Heritage Travel	7693AP	Autopoint	A135SMA	Countryliner
160CLT	Edward Thomas	1509AP	Autopoint	7855PU	Heritage Travel	A203MEL	Solent Blue Line
171CLC	Crawley Luxury	1521YG	Heritage Travel	7958NU	Heyfordian	A204MEL	Solent Blue Line
196FCG	Safeguard	1598PH	Hodge's	8015MM	Marchwood M'ways	A249SVW	Redroute
200APB	Safeguard	1725LJ	Crawley Luxury	8216FN	Heyfordian	A252TAG	Rebound
225ASV	Marchwood M'ways	1746MT	Motts Travel	8357KV	Heritage Travel	A305MKJ	Ham's Travel
230WYA	Souls	1924RH	Rambler	8421RU	Nu-Venture	A359TBW	Tourex
247FCG	Safeguard	2003RU	Truemans	8447RU	Nu-Venture	A385XGG	Black & White
267PPH	Edward Thomas	2185NU	Heyfordian	8466PH	Hodge's	A405BHL	Emsworth & District
277FCG	Safeguard	2317AP	Autopoint	8548VF	Heyfordian	A494JEC	Rebound
317LDV	Compass Travel	239BUP	Souls	8665UB	Heritage Travel	A49VDE	Tourex
435SFC	Coliseum	2439RU	Truemans	8779XV	Heyfordian	A616THV	Renown
435UPD	Edward Thomas	2448RU	Truemans	8874PH	Hodge's	A640BCN	Eastonways
447ECR	Black & White	2448UE	Poynter's	8896PH	Hodge's	A642WDT	Tourex
459KBM	Souls	2480PH	Hodge's	8903AP	Autopoint	A681KDV	Countryliner
461XPB	Tappins	2482NX	Heyfordian	8957FN	Heritage Travel	A697DDL	Solent Blue Line
481HYE	Heyfordian	2568PH	Hodge's	8990PH	Hodge's	A699DDL	Solent Blue Line
491NFC	Flights-Hallmark	2622NU	Heyfordian	9022KV	Heritage Travel	A734YOX	Tourex
494WYA	Redroute	2719DT	Heritage Travel	9041PU	Heritage Travel	A788YOX	Tourex
500EFC	Tappins	2779AP	Autopoint	9415AP	Autopoint	A829SUL	Emsworth & District
515FCG	Safeguard	2851NX	Heritage Travel	9467MU	Heyfordian	A857SUL	Nu-Venture
531FCG	Safeguard	2941VU	Heritage Travel	9489PH	Hodge's	A864SUL	Cheney
538FCG	Safeguard	3069AP	Autopoint	9649PH	Hodge's	A867SUL	Nu-Venture
558BWL	Tourex	3103PH	Charlton Services	9682FH	Heyfordian	A871SUL	West Kent Buses
576DXC	Edward Thomas	3442AP	Autopoint	9775MT	Motts Travel	A873SUL	Nu-Venture
577HDV	Souls	3544FH	Heritage Travel	9785SM	Cheney	A883SUL	Emsworth & District
636VHX	Coliseum	3556PH	Hodge's	9925AP	Autopoint	A889FPM	Emsworth & District
653GBU	Tappins	3558RU	Nu-Venture	A1YET	Wheelers Travel	A916SYE	Cheney
666VMX	Lucketts	3900PH	Hodge's	A3HFU	Hellyers	A933SYE	Ham's Travel
670DHO	Marchwood M'ways	4078NU	Heyfordian	A4FPK	Crawley Luxury	A975SYE	Nu-Venture
675PBM	Souls	4227RU	Truemans	A4HFY	Hellyers	ABW310X	Woottens
685CLC	Crawley Luxury	4402PH	Hodge's	A4TKF	The King's Ferry	AE04PJY	OFJ
687CLC	Crawley Luxury	4442MT	Motts Travel	A6HFN	Hellyers	AE04PKA	OFJ
741UKL	Mervyns	4631PH	Hodge's	A6TKF	The King's Ferry	AE05EUX	Thames Travel
751EKX	Souls	4638UG	Heritage Travel	A7HLC	Lucketts	AE05EUZ	Thames Travel
760BUS	Woottens	4754RU	Heritage Travel	A8FTG	Flights-Hallmark	AE05UVB	OFJ
774YPG	Worth's	4827WD	Heyfordian	A8HOF	Hellyers	AE54HYT	OFJ
776WME	Countryliner	4885UR	Heritage Travel	A8TKF	The King's Ferry	AE54HYU	OFJ
784CLC	Crawley Luxury	5134PH	Hodge's	A11HOU	Countryliner	AE54HYV	OFJ
786AFC	Tourex	5184MM	Marchwood M'ways	A11UFB	John Pike	AF03HOF	Hellyers
789CLC	Crawley Luxury	5226PH	Hodge's	A12GPS	Centra	AFY184X	The King's Ferry
809AOU	Cardinal	5300RU	John Pike	A12HLC	Lucketts	AHC411	Eastbourne Buses
820GXC	Cheney	5501AP	Autopoint	A12HOF	Hellyers	AHZ1253	Eastbourne Buses
821FHU	Souls	5536AP	Autopoint	A13HLC	Lucketts	AJB635	Mervyns
855GAC	Souls	5705MT	Motts Travel	A13HOF	Hellyers	AJZ9161	Tappins
868AVO	Heyfordian	5723MT	Motts Travel	A14GPS	Centra	AK52LWF	Eastonways
872PYA	Souls	5752AP	Autopoint	A14TKF	The King's Ferry	ALZ2490	Souls
934BDL	Southern Vectis	5812MT	Motts Travel	A15TKF	The King's Ferry	ALZ3054	Charlton Services
940HFJ	Grayline	5874MT	Motts Travel	A16HLC	Lucketts	ANA3T	Cardinal
943YKN	Heyfordian	6170PX	Heritage Travel	A16HOF	Hellyers	ANZ1323	Tappins
944BKT	Autocar	6247MT	Motts Travel	A16TKF	The King's Ferry	ANZ1325	Tappins
947CBK	Grayline	6300RU	Heritage Travel	A17HLC	Lucketts	ASV440	Crawley Luxury
966MBM	Souls	6595KV	Heyfordian	A17HOF	Hellyers	AUP356W	Accord
966MKE	Tourex	6601MT	Motts Travel	A17TKF	The King's Ferry	B8JHN	Crawley Luxury
978VYD	Crawley Luxury	6775DDL	Black & White	A18HOF	Hellyers	B10HOF	Hellyers
9920MT	Motts Travel	6787MT	Motts Travel	A18TKF	The King's Ferry	B10MDC	Weavaway
997GAT	Altonian	6957MT	Motts Travel	A19HOF	Hellyers	B10MFC	Weavaway

The South East Bus Handbook

B10MKC	Weavaway	BU04EYK	Hotelink	CEL105T	Marchwood M'ways	E65ELT	British Airways
B10MKF	Weavaway	BU04EYL	Hotelink	CH05BAN	Banstead Coaches	E109JYV	Kent CC
B10MMT	Motts Travel	BU04EYM	Hotelink	CHZ1784	Cruisers	E129WKN	Scotland & Bates
B10MSC	Weavaway	BU04EYP	Hotelink	CHZ2815	Cruisers	E153OMD	Motts Travel
B10MSE	Weavaway	BU51AYC	Fleetwing	CHZ2889	Cruisers	E1750MU	Wheelers Travel
B10MWA	Weavaway	BU51BUZ	Buzzlines	CHZ2948	Cruisers	E227CFC	Woottens
B10MWC	Weavaway	BU53AXH	Flights-Hallmark	CHZ5934	Cruisers	E232GPH	Mervyns
B12RMT	Motts Travel	BU53AXJ	Flights-Hallmark	CHZ5936	Cruisers	E247	Reading Buses
B30MSF	White Bus	BU53AYA	Flights-Hallmark	CHZ5937	Cruisers	EC	Ham's Travel
B42KAL	Compass Travel	BU53POV	Centra	CHZ5938	Cruisers	E30	Mervyns
B44HAM	Ham's Travel	BU53ZWZ	Worth's	CHZ5942	Cruisers	E154SON	Reading Buses
B66GHR	Newnham	BVR59T	Black & White	CHZ5981	Cruisers	E456SON	Reading Buses
B68GHR	Newnham	BW03UWH	Flights-Hallmark	CJ02XZK	OFJ	E457SON	Reading Buses
B90WUL	Carousel	BW03UWJ	Flights-Hallmark	CL52CCL	Courtney	E458SON	Reading Buses
B97WUV	Nu-Venture	BW03ZUD	Flights-Hallmark	CL5561	Crawley Luxury	E459ANC	Emsworth & District
B100WUL	Carousel	BW05LGW	Flights-Hallmark	CLC145	Crawley Luxury	E459SON	Reading Buses
B101WUL	Carousel	BX02CMF	Thames Travel	CLV84X	Heritage Travel	E460SON	Reading Buses
B108KPF	Autocar	BX02UPW	OFJ	CN51XNO	Safeguard	E462SON	Reading Buses
B120WUL	Amberlee	BX05AKK	Regent Coaches	CR04RAM	Rambler	E463SON	Reading Buses
B122UUD	Timetracker	BX05DNU	Regent Coaches	CSU432	Charlton Services	E464SON	Reading Buses
B124WUV	West Kent Buses	BX05DOA	Regent Coaches	CUB539Y	Motts Travel	E465SON	Reading Buses
B148EDP	Redroute	BX05DVA	Regent Coaches	CUD220Y	Worth's	E466SON	Reading Buses
B149EDP	Redroute	BX54EBP	Countryliner	CUL162V	Ham's Travel	E467SON	Reading Buses
B182CBW	Rebound	BXI2563	Nu-Venture	CUV198C	Carousel	E468SON	Reading Buses
B184BLG	Rebound	BYX247V	Eastonways	CUV322C	Redroute	E469SON	Reading Buses
B213WUL	Amberlee	BYX258V	Carousel	CYJ375Y	Heritage Travel	E470YWJ	Rebound
B229WUL	Redroute	BYX283V	Carousel	D72HRU	Banstead Coaches	E471SON	Tappins
B240XHM	Eastonways	BYX290V	Eastonways	D82UTF	Reading Buses	E849AAO	White Bus
B272WUL	Carousel	C8LEA	Emsworth & District	D101NDW	Nu-Venture	E857DPN	Eastbourne Buses
B497CBD	Compass Travel	C170ST	Tourex	D104NDW	Nu-Venture	E858DPN	Eastbourne Buses
B518HAM	Ham's Travel	C25CHM	Renown	D110NDW	Nu-Venture	E911DRD	Reading Buses
B522HAM	Ham's Travel	C34CHM	Wiltax	D156FYM	ASD Bus	E912DRD	Reading Buses
B542HAM	Ham's Travel	C37CHM	Renown	D162FYM	Renown	E913DRD	Reading Buses
B542OJF	White Bus	C64HOM	Woottens	D164FYM	Wiltax	E914DRD	Reading Buses
B586EGT	Cheney	C113CHM	ASD Bus	D180FYM	Renown	E915DRD	Reading Buses
B633DDW	White Bus	C259GUH	Tourex	D214FYM	Renown	E916DRD	Reading Buses
B637LJU	Renown	C286LOX	Amberlee	D255FYM	Flights-Hallmark	E917DRD	Reading Buses
B739GCN	Heyfordian	C337VRY	Marchwood M'ways	D303PEV	Red Rose	E968KDP	Rambler
B743GCN	Amberlee	C345BUV	Carousel	D527DPM	Tourex	EBW107Y	Tourex
B747GCN	Amberlee	C347BUV	Redroute	D602RGJ	Emsworth & District	ECZ3504	Tappins
B906RVF	West Kent Buses	C348DND	Cardinal 2	D718CLC	Crawley Luxury	ECZ3507	Tappins
B98XKE	Scotland & Bates	C351BUV	Carousel	D785GCD	Kingsman	ECZ9142	The King's Ferry
B999CUS	Emsworth & District	C356BUV	Carousel	D982JJD	Edward Thomas	ES05PBS	Buddens
BAZ7296	Eastonways	C386BUV	Carousel	DBK264W	Black & White	ESU940	Heyfordian
BBW214Y	Woottens	C391BUV	Amberlee	DCZ2316	Black & White	ET0585	Edward Thomas
BBW216Y	Worth's	C393BUV	Carousel	DCZ2322	Worth's	EU03XOJ	Ham's Travel
BBW217Y	Charlton Services	C432BUV	Carousel	DDY222	Rambler	EYE322V	Redroute
BD02HDV	Thames Travel	C436BUV	Wiltax	DDY557	Rambler	EYE336V	Carousel
BDY389	Rambler	C454GKE	Tourex	DE52OLJ	Hertz	F43XPR	RDH Services
BEP968V	Brijan	C521DND	Ham's Travel	DE52OLK	Hertz	F49ENF	Red Rose
BF03HOF	Hellyers	C521LJR	Renown	DHC782E	Eastbourne Buses	F75DDA	Carousel
BHO442V	Redroute	C542GKP	Scotland & Bates	DJI654	Crawley Luxury	F77DDA	Amberlee
BJ03JHU	Hertz	C650LJR	Amberlee	DK264W	Black & White	F78DDA	Carousel
BJ03JHV	Hertz	C652LFT	Wiltax	DSK558	Safeguard	F86TDL	Tourex
BJZ2804	Heritage Travel	C652LJR	Redroute	DSK559	Safeguard	F116PHM	MK Metro
BKE848T	Redroute	C665LJR	Amberlee	DSK560	Safeguard	F120PHM	Richardson Travel
BKO447Y	Scotland & Bates	C668WRT	White Bus	DW05HAM	Ham's Travel	F124PHM	MK Metro
BL51BUZ	Buzzlines	C670LJR	Redroute	DW52HAM	Ham's Travel	F136PHM	MK Metro
BNZ3466	Heritage Travel	C680KDS	Seaview Services	DW54HAM	Ham's Travel	F139PHM	Richardson Travel
BNZ3505	Tappins	C724JTL	Rebound	DYA93A	Charlton Services	F140PHM	Richardson Travel
BPA66Y	Redroute	C820BYY	Flights-Hallmark	E21ECH	Centra	F141PHM	Crawley Luxury
BT05BJT	Brijan	C983PUF	British Airways	E25UNE	Motts Travel	F143PHM	Crawley Luxury
BU03LXV	Countryliner	CAZ1066	Empress Coaches	E26UNE	Motts Travel	F144PHM	Richardson Travel
BU03LXW	Countryliner	CB51BUS	Carousel	E27UNE	Motts Travel	F165OOW	Kingsman
BU03LYG	RDH Services	CB52BUS	Carousel	E28UNE	Motts Travel	F166SMT	Nu-Venture
BU03YTE	Wheelers Travel	CB53BUS	Carousel	E29UNE	Motts Travel	F167SMT	Kent CC
BU04EXR	Countryliner	CB54BUS	Carousel	E30UNE	Motts Travel	F168SMT	Kent CC
BU04EXS	Flights-Hallmark	CBD899T	Tourex	E31UNE	Autocar	F239CNY	Amberlee
BU04EYH	Hotelink	CDL899	Southern Vectis	E32UNE	Autocar	F246RJX	Marchwood M'ways
BU04EYJ	Hotelink	CE02MDJ	Accord	E61MDT	Amberlee	F247RJX	Marchwood M'ways

The South East Bus Handbook

F248RJX	Marchwood M'ways	FN05DGE	W&H Motors	G722WDL	Solent Blue Line	GN03TYB	The King's Ferry
F254HAM	Ham's Travel	FN52GVE	Woottens	G727RGA	Emsworth & District	GN04PKC	Kent CC
F267OFJ	Kingsman	FN52GVF	Woottens	G767CDU	Emsworth & District	GN04PKD	Kent CC
F393DHL	MK Metro	FN54FLC	Renown	G778WFC	Redroute	GN04PLX	Kent CC
F548WGL	Altonian	FOR35T	Flights-Hallmark	G779WFC	Redroute	GN04PLZ	Kent CC
F558NJM	Carousel	FS05PBS	Buddens	G780WFC	Worth's	GN05DZU	Kent Coach
F559NJM	Carousel	FSK598	Countryliner	G783WFC	Charlton Services	GN51DFU	Kent CC
F605RPG	Newnham	FTN708W	ASD Bus	G788URY	Crosskeys	GN51DGU	Kent CC
F649PLW	Cruisers	FYD864T	West Kent Buses	G792URY	Crosskeys	GN51UNY	The King's Ferry
F655HVM	Regent Coaches	G22UWL	Cheney	G793URY	Crosskeys	GN51WCA	The King's Ferry
F706RDL	Solent Blue Line	G25YRY	Poynter's	G794URY	Crosskeys	GN53AJU	Warrens
F707RDL	Solent Blue Line	G39TGW	Emsworth & District	G844VAY	Worth's	GN53YUF	Nu-Venture
F708SDL	Solent Blue Line	G54BEL	RDH Services	G865KKY	Crosskeys	GN54SBX	Kent Coach
F709SDL	Solent Blue Line	G73UYV	Poynter's	G866WGW	Renown	GO04BAN	Banstead Coaches
F763EKM	Motts Travel	G74UYV	Poynter's	G867WGW	Renown	GOG138W	Amberlee
F766EKM	Motts Travel	G75UYV	Poynter's	G887VNA	C&S Coaches	GS54PBS	Buddens
F817URN	Solent Blue Line	G77UYV	Poynter's	G901ANR	W&H Motors	GSC664X	Tappins
F865LCU	Ham's Travel	G78UYV	Redroute	G905TYR	Redroute	GT03MTT	Motts Travel
F894SMU	Crawley Luxury	G79BLD	C&S Coaches	G936MYG	Poynter's	GT05MTT	Motts Travel
F988JKL	Scotland & Bates	G91VMM	Country Rider	G937MYG	Poynter's	GU52HAO	Coastal
FAZ1066	Empress Coaches	G102NGN	Farleigh Coaches	G960ATP	Altonian	GU52HAX	Coastal
FAZ4494	Souls	G119NGN	Flights-Hallmark	GAZ8573	Charlton Services	GU52HJY	Coastal
FC0314	Rambler	G126NGN	Renown	GB03MTT	Motts Travel	GU52HKA	Coastal
FCZ9151	Wheelers Travel	G127NGN	Renown	GB04EBL	Eastbourne Buses	GU52HKB	Coastal
FD03YOG	Regent Coaches	G133PGK	Renown	GDY493	Rambler	GU52HKC	Coastal
FD54DHL	The King's Ferry	G138PGK	Renown	GDY500X	Rambler	GU52HKD	Coastal
FD54DHM	The King's Ferry	G140GOJ	Charlton Services	GIL5976	Accord	GU52HXM	Courtney
FDV818V	Timetrack	G144ULG	Seaview Services	GJ02JJF	Kingsman	GX02AED	Rambler
FDY83	Rambler	G148TYT	Richardson Travel	GJ02JJL	The King's Ferry	GX02AEE	Rambler
FE02FBF	Flights-Hallmark	G171YUR	Wiltax	GJ02LUZ	The King's Ferry	GX02WXS	Eastbourne Buses
FE02FBG	Flights-Hallmark	G191BLM	British Airways	GJ52GYD	Kent Coach	GX02WXT	Eastbourne Buses
FE02FBJ	Flights-Hallmark	G192BLM	British Airways	GJ52MUV	The King's Ferry	GX02WXU	Eastbourne Buses
FE02FBK	Flights-Hallmark	G193BLM	British Airways	GJ520MZ	The King's Ferry	GX02WXV	Eastbourne Buses
FE02FBL	Flights-Hallmark	G194BLM	British Airways	GJI7173	Charlton Services	GX02WXW	Eastbourne Buses
FE02FBN	Flights-Hallmark	G195BLM	British Airways	GJZ9570	Tappins	GX02WXY	Eastbourne Buses
FE02FBO	Flights-Hallmark	G196BLM	British Airways	GJZ9571	Tappins	GX03AZJ	Compass Travel
FE02FBU	Flights-Hallmark	G197BLM	British Airways	GJZ9572	Tappins	GX03AZL	Compass Travel
FE02FCA	Woottens	G198BLM	British Airways	GJZ9573	Tappins	GX04ASU	Coastal
FE51RDO	Flights-Hallmark	G199BLM	British Airways	GJZ9574	Tappins	GX04AZA	Compass Travel
FE51RGO	Regent Coaches	G227YLU	Pearce	GJZ9575	Tappins	GX04BXN	Compass Travel
FE51RGX	McLeans	G252EHD	Poynter's	GJZ9576	Tappins	GX04LWR	Eastbourne Buses
FE51RGZ	McLeans	G258TSL	Brijan	GK02OLA	Kent CC	GX04LWS	Eastbourne Buses
FE52HFW	Woottens	G283EOG	Carousel	GK02WCY	Cardinal	GX04LWT	Eastbourne Buses
FG03JAU	Woottens	G316YHJ	Menzies	GK02WDJ	Kent CC	GX04LWU	Eastbourne Buses
FG03JBU	Woottens	G356PNN	Cheney	GK02YKY	Kent CC	GX04LWV	Eastbourne Buses
FG03JCJ	Regent Coaches	G362YUR	Eastbourne Buses	GK02YKZ	Kent CC	GX04LWW	Eastbourne Buses
FG03JCU	Woottens	G363YUR	Eastbourne Buses	GK04CWP	Kent Coach	GX05AOP	Coastal
FIL6689	Charlton Services	G392NPW	W&H Motors	GK51FHL	Kent CC	GYE524W	Carousel
FIL7617	Heritage Travel	G456MGG	Autocar	GK51FHN	Kent CC	GYE586W	Amberlee
FIL7662	Heyfordian	G483BJT	Wheelers Travel	GK51FHO	Kent CC	GYE598W	Carousel
FIL7664	Heyfordian	G501XBL	Reading Buses	GK51FHP	Kent CC	H2KFC	The King's Ferry
FIL8317	Heyfordian	G502XBL	Reading Buses	GK52KLA	Accord	H36YCW	Emsworth & District
FIL8441	Heyfordian	G503XBL	Reading Buses	GK52KLC	Accord	H37SAK	Charlton Services
FJ03VMT	McLeans	G504XBL	Reading Buses	GK52OLN	Accord	H37YCW	Emsworth & District
FJ03VMU	McLeans	G505XBL	Reading Buses	GK53AFU	Kent CC	H115THE	Renown
FJ04SNF	Accord	G505XLO	Emsworth & District	GK53AFV	Kent CC	H120THE	Eastonways
FJ05ANV	The King's Ferry	G506LWU	Tappins	GK53CUA	Kent CC	H124THE	Ham's Travel
FJ05AOD	The King's Ferry	G506XBL	Reading Buses	GK53CUC	Kent CC	H127THE	Eastonways
FJ05AOG	W&H Motors	G507XBL	Reading Buses	GK53CUG	Kent CC	H155DJU	Scotland & Bates
FJ05AOH	W&H Motors	G508XBL	Reading Buses	GK53CUH	Kent CC	H169WWT	Eastonways
FJ53KZF	The King's Ferry	G509XBL	Reading Buses	GK53CUJ	Kent CC	H172WWT	Redroute
FJ53VDE	McLeans	G510XBL	Reading Buses	GK53DLD	Kent CC	H185DVM	C&S Coaches
FJ53VDF	McLeans	G516VYE	Southern Vectis	GK53DLE	Kent CC	H186EJF	Countywide
FKM304V	Redroute	G520EFX	Safeguard	GK53ETZ	Crosskeys	H201DVM	Emsworth & District
FKX279T	Kingsman	G526VYE	Southern Vectis	GK53FHR	Kent CC	H203CRH	Richardson Travel
FLY747T	British Airways	G555BPJ	W&H Motors	GLZ4406	Wheelers Travel	H204DVM	Emsworth & District
FN02RXF	McLeans	G621CPS	Countryliner	GLZ4419	Tappins	H220LOM	ASD Bus
FN02RXG	McLeans	G625VNX	Charlton Services	GN02XCU	Kent CC	H226ECX	Emsworth & District
FN02VBD	The King's Ferry	G638REG	Nu-Venture	GN03EHP	Kent CC	H281NRF	The King's Ferry
FN02VBE	The King's Ferry	G721WDL	Solent Blue Line	GN03EHR	Kent CC	H310ECK	Rebound

H312HLB	British Airways	HN54OBE	Centra	HX51ZRC	Solent Blue Line	J582CUB		Redroute
H312HPF	Edward Thomas	HN54WMO	Centra	HX51ZRD	Solent Blue Line	J705CGK		Nu-Venture
H313HLB	British Airways	HN54WMP	Centra	HX51ZRE	Solent Blue Line	J739CWT		Fleetwing
H314HLB	British Airways	HOD75	Mervyns	HX51ZRF	Solent Blue Line	J742CWT		Fleetwing
H315HLB	British Airways	HPK504N	Baileys Buses	HX51ZRG	Solent Blue Line	J743CWT		Fleetwing
H317HLB	British Airways	HS51PBS	Buddens	HX51ZRJ	Solent Blue Line	J744CWT		Fleetwing
H319HLB	British Airways	HSV989	Heritage Travel	HX51ZRK	Solent Blue Line	J745CWT		Fleetwing
H389KPY	Empress Coaches	HT02BJT	Brijan	HXI3012	Newnham	J786KHD		Reading Buses
H390KPY	Empress Coaches	HTR557P	Black & White	IAZ4816	Hellyers	J788KHD		Reading Buses
H421GPM	Emsworth & District	HUD479S	Farleigh Coaches	IAZ5657	Souls	J823KRH		C&S Coaches
H435GVL	Farleigh Coaches	HV52WSJ	Centra	IAZ6421	Rebound	J851MLC		British Airways
H510BND	Regent Coaches	HV52WSK	Centra	IAZ8156	Autocar	J852MLC		British Airways
H536XGK	Grayline	HV52WSL	Centra	IIL1355	Cheney	J855MLC		British Airways
H550XGK	RDH Services	HV52WSN	Centra	IIL3505	Poynter's	J856MLC		British Airways
H554GKX	Carousel	HV52WSO	Centra	IUI2138	Nu-Venture	J857MLC		British Airways
H556GKX	Carousel	HV52WSU	Centra	IUI2139	Nu-Venture	J858MLC		British Airways
H562FLE	Cheney	HV52WSW	Centra	IUI2140	Nu-Venture	J941MFT		MK Metro
H563GKX	Carousel	HV52WSX	Centra	IUI2142	Nu-Venture	J962JNL		Eastonways
H564GKX	Carousel	HV52WSY	Centra	IUI5035	John Pike	J974JNL		Eastonways
H577MOC	Safeguard	HV52WSZ	Centra	IUI5036	John Pike	J975JNL		Eastonways
H580VWB	Newnham	HV52WTA	Centra	IUI5037	John Pike	JAZ1066		Empress Coaches
H601UWR	Scotland & Bates	HV52WTG	Centra	IUI5045	John Pike	JBZ5056		Heritage Travel
H613NJB	Redroute	HV52WTJ	Centra	IUI6722	Worth's	JDK911P		Timetrack
H670ATN	Eastonways	HV52WTK	Centra	J4HSL	Wheelers Travel	JDY673		Rambler
H672LCF	Regent Coaches	HW04DFN	Wight Bus	J8ASD	ASD Bus	JDY888Y		Rambler
H690JDB	Buzzlines	HW52EPK	Southern Vectis	J10CLC	Crawley Luxury	JF04HOF		Hellyers
H712LOL	RDH Services	HW52EPL	Southern Vectis	J13TRU	Truemans	JG04RAM		Rambler
H728DDL	Solent Blue Line	HW52EPN	Southern Vectis	J14TRY	Truemans	JG54RAM		Rambler
H729DDL	Solent Blue Line	HW52EPO	Southern Vectis	J16TRU	Truemans	JHT122		Black & White
H731DDL	Solent Blue Line	HW52EPP	Southern Vectis	J17TRU	Truemans	JIL1066		Empress Coaches
H732DDL	Solent Blue Line	HW52EPU	Southern Vectis	J18TRU	Truemans	JIL2199		Woottens
H733DDL	Solent Blue Line	HW52EPV	Southern Vectis	J19TRU	Truemans	JIL3969		C&S Coaches
H734DDL	Solent Blue Line	HW52EPX	Southern Vectis	J20TRU	Truemans	JIL6396		C&S Coaches
H758DTM	Altonian	HW54BTU	Southern Vectis	J26YHJ	Cruisers	JIL6397		C&S Coaches
H787JFC	Cheney	HW54BTV	Southern Vectis	J30TRU	Truemans	JIL6399		C&S Coaches
H787RWJ	C&S Coaches	HW54BTX	Southern Vectis	J33TRU	Truemans	JIL7705		C&S Coaches
H792PTW	Nu-Venture	HW54BTY	Southern Vectis	J34YHJ	Cruisers	JIL8213		Eastonways
H793PTW	Nu-Venture	HW54BTZ	Southern Vectis	J45GCX	Marchwood M'ways	JIL8230		Coliseum
H838PTW	Nu-Venture	HW54BUA	Southern Vectis	J84OKK	Warrens	JJD445D		Redroute
H848DNJ	RDH Services	HW54BUE	Southern Vectis	J1000FC	Pearce	JJD535D		Amberlee
H858NOC	MK Metro	HW54BUF	Southern Vectis	J100SOU	Compass Travel	JJI3616		Charlton Services
H929DRJ	Altonian	HW54BUH	Southern Vectis	J116WSC	Countryliner	JMJ633V		White Bus
H952DRJ	Crawley Luxury	HW54BUJ	Southern Vectis	J122FUF	Eastbourne Buses	JNM747Y		White Bus
H956DRJ	The King's Ferry	HW54BUO	Southern Vectis	J124FUF	Red Rose	JS51PBS		Buddens
H971FKE	Cheney	HW54BUP	Southern Vectis	J137LLK	Countywide	JUD597W		Pearce
H987ERV	Wheelers Travel	HW54BUU	Southern Vectis	J142JDL	Wight Bus	JUI4377		RDH Services
HAM496N	Ham's Travel	HW54BUV	Southern Vectis	J221FUF	Eastbourne Buses	JUO983		Marchwood M'ways
HC6422	Flights-Hallmark	HW54DBZ	Wight Bus	J223XKY	C&S Coaches	JWL322W		Worth's
HCZ1821	Wheelers Travel	HW54DCE	Wight Bus	J224XKY	C&S Coaches	JWV265W		John Pike
HDD654	Black & White	HW54DCF	Wight Bus	J227HMY	Renown	JXI507		Seaview Services
HDY405	Rambler	HW54DCO	Wight Bus	J229HGY	Ham's Travel	K2CLC		Crawley Luxury
HDY565	Rambler	HW54DCU	Wight Bus	J246NNC	C&S Coaches	K3CLC		Crawley Luxury
HDZ2604	MK Metro	HX03BYT	Lucketts	J247NNC	C&S Coaches	K5CLC		Crawley Luxury
HDZ2605	MK Metro	HX04JLV	Accord	J248LLK	British Airways	K7GPH		Charlton Services
HDZ2606	MK Metro	HX04VRT	Accord	J248NNC	C&S Coaches	K11CLC		Crawley Luxury
HDZ2607	MK Metro	HX04VRU	Accord	J252NNC	C&S Coaches	K14KFC		The King's Ferry
HDZ2611	MK Metro	HX04VRW	Accord	J254NNC	C&S Coaches	K44PBS		Buddens
HF03HOF	Hellyers	HX04VRY	Accord	J256NNC	C&S Coaches	K50ULS		Souls
HIL2279	Renown	HX51LPE	Flights-Hallmark	J272SOC	Timetrack	K55PBS		Buddens
HIL2282	Souls	HX51LPJ	Accord	J275LLK	British Airways	K66PBS		Buddens
HIL2386	Souls	HX51LPK	Accord	J310WHJ	Carousel	K77PBS		Buddens
HIL3207	Edward Thomas	HX51LPL	Accord	J311LLK	British Airways	K88PBS		Buddens
HIL3455	Heritage Travel	HX51LPN	Accord	J35UHP	Buddens	K99PBS		Buddens
HIL3670	John Pike	HX51LPO	Accord	J382GKH	Southern Vectis	K170FYG		Reading Buses
HIL4017	Edward Thomas	HX51LPU	Accord	J412AOO	Cruisers	K171YVC		Autopoint
HIL4415	Compass Travel	HX51LPV	Accord	J504GCD	Emsworth & District	K200SAS		Renown
HIL7978	Coliseum	HX51LPY	Accord	J511RPR	Solent Blue Line	K232WNH		W&H Motors
HJ52OKK	Countywide	HX51LPZ	Accord	J515RPR	Solent Blue Line	K233WNH		W&H Motors
HJ52OKL	Countywide	HX51LSO	MK Metro	J528WTW	Altonian	K244PAG		Southern Vectis
HJB635W	Crawley Luxury	HX51ZRA	Solent Blue Line	J539GCD	Emsworth & District	K302FYG		MK Metro

The South East Bus Handbook

K316???	British Airways	KBZ2276	Warrens	KP54BYK	Flights-Hallmark	KX53SGZ	Thames Travel
K317???	British Airways	KCT255	Kent Coach	KP54BYL	Flights-Hallmark	KX53SHJ	Centra
K318SLF	British Airways	KCT353	Kent Coach	KP54BYM	Flights-Hallmark	KX53SJV	Flights-Hallmark
K319SLF	British Airways	KCT415	Kent Coach	KP54BYN	Flights-Hallmark	KX54AVD	MK Metro
K320SLF	British Airways	KCT638	Kent Coach	KP54BYO	Flights-Hallmark	KX54AVE	MK Metro
K321SLF	British Airways	KCT986	Kent Coach	KP54BYR	Flights-Hallmark	KX54NKJ	Centra
K323CVX	Carousel	KDZ5803	Eastonways	KP54BYT	Flights-Hallmark	KX54NKK	Centra
K341RBB	John Pike	KE03ZFB	Centra	KP54BYU	Flights-Hallmark	KX54NKL	Centra
K373HHK	Cheney	KE03ZFC	Centra	KP54BYV	Flights-Hallmark	KX54NKM	Centra
K376RTY	RDH Services	KE03ZFD	Centra	KP54BYW	Flights-Hallmark	KX54NKN	Centra
K377RTY	RDH Services	KE04DZM	Centra	KP54BYX	Flights-Hallmark	KX54NKO	Centra
K379RTY	MK Metro	KE04EAK	Wight Bus	KP54BYY	Flights-Hallmark	KX54NKP	Centra
K419FAV	MK Metro	KE04OLK	Centra	KP54BYZ	Flights-Hallmark	KX54NKR	Centra
K426FAV	MK Metro	KE04WBD	MK Metro	KP54BZA	Flights-Hallmark	KX54NKT	Centra
K428FAV	MK Metro	KE04WBF	MK Metro	KPJ271W	Newnham	KX54NKU	Centra
K479JHJ	RDH Services	KE04WBG	MK Metro	KPJ271W	Newnham	KX54NLA	Courtney
K480OKH	RDH Services	KE04WBJ	MK Metro	KS51PBS	Buddens	KX54NLC	Courtney
K523UJT	Solent Blue Line	KE04WBK	MK Metro	KT03BUS	Kingsman	KX54NLD	Courtney
K525UJT	Solent Blue Line	KE04WBL	MK Metro	KT04BUS	Kingsman	KX5UDG	Buzzlines
K531UJT	Solent Blue Line	KE04WBM	MK Metro	KU02YBA	Centra	KY0609X	Wiltax
K532UJT	Solent Blue Line	KE04WBN	MK Metro	KU02YBB	Centra	KYU77	Souls
K576MGT	Eastonways	KE04WBP	MK Metro	KU02YBC	Centra	KYV312X	Ham's Travel
K589SUP	Amberley	KE04WBT	MK Metro	KU02YBD	Centra	KYV329X	West Kent Buses
K616HVV	MK Metro	KE05KXX	Flights-Hallmark	KU02YBE	Centra	KYV370X	West Kent Buses
K623PGO	Grayley	KE05KXZ	Flights-Hallmark	KU02YBF	Centra	KYV432X	Ham's Travel
K631GVX	Cardinal	KE05MMF	Flights-Hallmark	KU02YBG	Centra	KYV442X	West Kent Buses
K702BBL	Reading Buses	KE05MMJ	Flights-Hallmark	KU52RXF	Thames Travel	KYV455X	Nu-Venture
K716PCN	Solent Blue Line	KE05MPX	Flights-Hallmark	KU52RXG	Thames Travel	KYV481X	Ham's Travel
K719PCN	Solent Blue Line	KEN959	Coliseum	KU52RXN	Thames Travel	KYV488X	Poynter's
K725HUG	Compass Travel	KF02ZWH	Centra	KU52RXS	Thames Travel	KYV529X	Poynter's
K735ODL	Southern Vectis	KF02ZWK	Wight Bus	KU52RXX	Countryliner	KYV659X	Wiltax
K736ODL	Southern Vectis	KF02ZWL	Wight Bus	KUI5157	Cheney	KYV703X	Carousel
K737ODL	Southern Vectis	KF02ZWM	Wight Bus	KUI5158	Cheney	KYV737X	Carousel
K738ODL	Southern Vectis	KF02ZWN	Wight Bus	KUI5159	Cheney	KYV758X	Carousel
K739ODL	Southern Vectis	KF02ZWR	Wight Bus	KUI5160	Cheney	KYV771X	Redroute
K740ODL	Southern Vectis	KF02ZWS	Centra	KUI5324	Tappins	KYW335	Mervyns
K741ODL	Southern Vectis	KF02ZWT	Centra	KUI9417	Tappins	L6CLC	Crawley Luxury
K742ODL	Southern Vectis	KF02ZWY	Menzies	KUI9418	Tappins	L6HAM	Ham's Travel
K743ODL	Southern Vectis	KF02ZXB	Flights-Hallmark	KV03ZFZ	Flights-Hallmark	L8KFC	The King's Ferry
K797EPU	Regent Coaches	KF05HOF	Hellyers	KV03ZGA	Flights-Hallmark	L9CLC	Crawley Luxury
K809PLX	British Airways	KF52TZV	Centra	KV03ZGB	Flights-Hallmark	L11VWL	Pearce
K810PLX	British Airways	KF52TZW	Centra	KV03ZGC	Flights-Hallmark	L26CAY	Heyfordian
K811PLX	British Airways	KF52UAG	Menzies	KV03ZGK	Reading Buses	L38LRC	Wheelers Travel
K812PLX	British Airways	KF52UAN	Menzies	KV03ZGL	Reading Buses	L50ULS	Souls
K813PLX	British Airways	KHF131	Wheelers Travel	KV03ZGM	Reading Buses	L58YJF	British Airways
K814PLX	British Airways	KIW1066	Empress Coaches	KV03ZGN	Reading Buses	L103DNX	RDH Services
K815PLX	British Airways	KIW5196	Kent CC	KV4644	Heritage Travel	L109HHV	Carousel
K816PLX	British Airways	KJ02JXT	MK Metro	KV51KZC	Flights-Hallmark	L116HHV	Redroute
K817PLX	British Airways	KLB596	Black & White	KV51KZJ	Countryliner	L119YFH	Cruisers
K818PLX	British Airways	KM02BEO	Centra	KX04HRA	Courtney	L126YFH	Cruisers
K819PLX	British Airways	KM51BFL	Centra	KX04HRC	Flights-Hallmark	L150HUD	Worth's
K820PLX	British Airways	KM51BFN	Centra	KX04HTD	Flights-Hallmark	L151HUD	Worth's
K821PLX	British Airways	KM51BFO	Centra	KX04HTE	Flights-Hallmark	L153WAG	Carousel
K822PLX	British Airways	KM51BFP	Centra	KX05KDZ	Flights-Hallmark	L154HUD	Worth's
K823PLX	British Airways	KM51BFU	Centra	KX05KFC	Flights-Hallmark	L164PDT	Banstead Coaches
K824PLX	British Airways	KM51BFV	Centra	KX05KFD	Flights-Hallmark	L189MAU	Compass Travel
K825PLX	British Airways	KM51BFX	Centra	KX05KFE	Flights-Hallmark	L191MAU	Compass Travel
K826PLX	British Airways	KM51BFY	Centra	KX05KFF	Flights-Hallmark	L221ULU	British Airways
K848EEC	Amberley	KN52KOH	Accord	KX51UCR	Flights-Hallmark	L223ULU	British Airways
K860BOL	RDH Services	KOW901F	West Kent Buses	KX51UCS	Centra	L224ULU	British Airways
K861BOL	RDH Services	KP02BVA	Flights-Hallmark	KX51UCT	Centra	L225ULU	British Airways
K864LGN	RDH Services	KP51SXU	Countryliner	KX51UCU	Centra	L226ULU	British Airways
K864ODY	ASD Bus	KP51SXU	Thames Travel	KX51UCV	Centra	L227THP	Southern Vectis
K867BOL	RDH Services	KP51UFB	Thames Travel	KX53SBY	Courtney	L228ULU	British Airways
K871ANT	Eastonways	KP51UFC	Thames Travel	KX53SBZ	Courtney	L229ULU	British Airways
K873GOO	Cruisers	KP51UFG	Thames Travel	KX53SCV	Courtney	L230ULU	British Airways
K874ODY	ASD Bus	KP51UFH	Thames Travel	KX53SCZ	Courtney	L231ULU	British Airways
K987SCU	Eastonways	KP51UFK	Thames Travel	KX53SDO	Courtney	L232ULU	British Airways
K990CBO	Eastonways	KP51UFL	Thames Travel	KX53SGV	Thames Travel	L233ULU	British Airways
KAZ2755	Worth's	KP54BYJ	Flights-Hallmark	KX53SGY	Thames Travel	L234ULU	British Airways

Reg	Operator	Reg	Operator	Reg	Operator	Reg	Operator
L235ULU	British Airways	L933JFU	Regent Coaches	M141MPL	British Airways	M6100RJ	Cheney
L275HJD	Centra	L948NWW	Horseman	M142MPL	British Airways	M6140RJ	Cheney
L319YAM	Cheney	L951NWW	Horseman	M143MPL	British Airways	M615RCP	C&S Coaches
L325YDU	Eastbourne Buses	L952NWW	Horseman	M144KPA	Crawley Luxury	M618DPN	Centra
L330YKV	Eastbourne Buses	L954NWW	Horseman	M144MPL	British Airways	M618YGH	Accord
L388ULX	British Airways	L955NWW	Horseman	M145MPL	British Airways	M619DPN	Centra
L389ULX	British Airways	L957NWW	Horseman	M146MPL	British Airways	M619RCP	C&S Coaches
L390ULX	British Airways	L958NWW	Horseman	M148MPL	British Airways	M628RCP	C&S Coaches
L391ULX	British Airways	L959NWW	Horseman	M149MPL	British Airways	M633RCP	C&S Coaches
L392ULX	British Airways	L960NWW	Horseman	M150MPL	British Airways	M634KVU	Heyfordian
L409GPY	Heyfordian	L961NWW	Horseman	M151MPL	British Airways	M636RCP	C&S Coaches
L417UUF	Eastbourne Buses	L967RUB	Safeguard	M152MPL	British Airways	M639KVU	Heyfordian
L445FFR	Southern Vectis	LA02WMZ	Centra	M153MPL	British Airways	M650RCP	C&S Coaches
L452UEB	Emsworth & District	LBZ2577	Crawley Luxury	M154MPL	British Airways	M659SBL	Horseman
L509EHD	Marchwood M'ways	LDY173	Rambler	M156MPL	British Airways	M664KVU	Hellyers
L510EHD	Marchwood M'ways	LDZ2502	Heyfordian	M157MPL	British Airways	M67UKL	Cruisers
L522MDP	White Bus	LDZ2503	Heyfordian	M158MPL	British Airways	M683DGN	OFJ
L523MJB	White Bus	LFR873X	Farleigh Coaches	M159MPL	British Airways	M735BBP	Solent Blue Line
L526YDL	Solent Blue Line	LIB1066	Empress Coaches	M165NJW	Cruisers	M736BBP	Solent Blue Line
L526YDL	Solent Blue Line	LIL2180	Fleetwing	M193UAN	OFJ	M738KCU	Rebound
L527YDL	Solent Blue Line	LIL3057	Wheelers Travel	M194UAN	OFJ	M744HDL	Southern Vectis
L528YDL	Solent Blue Line	LIL7230	Motts Travel	M196UAN	OFJ	M745HDL	Southern Vectis
L529EHD	Reading Buses	LIL9811	Souls	M212EGF	Accord	M745RCP	C&S Coaches
L531BDH	Cruisers	LIL9970	RDH Services	M214UYD	Hellyers	M746HDL	Southern Vectis
L540XJU	Tappins	LJ53LDD	OFJ	M251XWS	Fleetwing	M748HDL	Southern Vectis
L542XUT	Compass Travel	LJ53LDF	OFJ	M260VEJ	Red Rose	M749HDL	Southern Vectis
L561ASU	White Bus	LJ53LDG	OFJ	M292SBT	Compass Travel	M750HDL	Southern Vectis
L565FND	Cheney	LJ53LDV	OFJ	M300MFC	Pearce	M751HDL	Southern Vectis
L579JSA	Heyfordian	LM0193X	Reading Buses	M365VUD	Rebound	M770MKO	Cruisers
L584JSA	Heyfordian	LOI8643	Ham's Travel	M388KVR	Safeguard	M771BHU	John Pike
L585JSA	Heyfordian	LS51PBS	Buddens	M392EGF	Hotelink	M775XHW	Fleetwing
L587JSA	Heyfordian	LT04CTV	OFJ	M403MPD	Regent Coaches	M778XHW	Fleetwing
L600CLA	Charlton Services	LT04CWL	OFJ	M420VYD	Scotland & Bates	M780XHW	Fleetwing
L616LJM	Charlton Services	LUA272V	Black & White	M425PVN	Redroute	M794VJ0	Kent CC
L618LJM	Timetrack	LUA287V	Redroute	M427WAK	Banstead Coaches	M8010JW	MK Metro
L628VUS	Wheelers Travel	LUI3166	Tappins	M429RDC	ASD Bus	M802RCP	C&S Coaches
L639HKL	Cruisers	LUI7865	Wheelers Travel	M432RDC	ASD Bus	M803RCP	C&S Coaches
L662MSF	Flights-Hallmark	LUI8400	Tappins	M440AVG	Compass Travel	M804PRA	Kent Coach
L667MSF	Flights-Hallmark	LUI8402	Mervyns	M441CCD	Eastbourne Buses	M804RCP	C&S Coaches
L6720HL	McLeans	LUI9301	Tappins	M463KFJ	Cruisers	M809RCP	C&S Coaches
L6730HL	McLeans	LU0393	Crawley Luxury	M477UYA	Hellyers	M833HNS	Heyfordian
L697CNR	British Airways	LV02LLA	Grayline	M501VJ0	Thames Travel	M846LFP	Marchwood M'ways
L705FRD	Reading Buses	LVS441V	Hellyers	M509VJ0	RDH Services	M846RCP	Marchwood M'ways
L706FRD	Reading Buses	LVS442V	Hellyers	M511PDP	Reading Buses	M84MYM	Ham's Travel
L707LJM	Reading Buses	LX03KPE	Countryliner	M512PDP	Reading Buses	M9030VR	Poynter's
L709JUD	MK Metro	LX510PC	Accord	M513PDP	Reading Buses	M906EGK	Hotelink
L711JUD	MK Metro	LX510PD	Accord	M514VJ0	RDH Services	M907EGK	Hotelink
L713JUD	MK Metro	M3KFC	Emsworth & District	M528DPN	Eastbourne Buses	M9160VR	Poynter's
L715FPE	White Bus	M8BSL	Banstead Coaches	M529DPN	Eastbourne Buses	M930TYG	Reading Buses
L7170MV	Compass Travel	M10CLA	MK Metro	M530DPN	Eastbourne Buses	M968RWL	Pearce
L7180MV	Compass Travel	M43AOT	Accord	M539PKR	Cruisers	M971CVG	Motts Travel
L7190MV	Compass Travel	M50ULS	Souls	M565BLC	British Airways	M975DNJ	Wight Bus
L740YGE	Heyfordian	M53PRA	MK Metro	M566BLC	British Airways	M993HHS	Heyfordian
L743YGE	Heyfordian	M50UL	Souls	M572BLC	British Airways	M995ALR	British Airways
L745YGE	Heyfordian	M70TGM	MK Metro	M572RCP	C&S Coaches	M996CYS	Compass Travel
L752YGE	Heyfordian	M71AKA	Countywide	M573BLC	British Airways	MBU534L	Black & White
L808TFY	Compass Travel	M73AKA	Countywide	M574BLC	British Airways	MBZ8369	Wheelers Travel
L809TFY	Compass Travel	M74AKA	Countywide	M578BLC	British Airways	MC52HAM	Ham's Travel
L813SAE	Cardinal	M78HHB	Flights-Hallmark	M579BLC	British Airways	MCY188M	Redroute
L835CDG	Eastonways	M82MYM	Flights-Hallmark	M579RCP	Altonian	MDY797	Rambler
L838MWT	Eastonways	M83MYM	Flights-Hallmark	M580BLC	British Airways	MFX778	Coliseum
L840MWT	Compass Travel	M91MYM	Ham's Travel	M591BLC	British Airways	MHS5P	Nu-Venture
L881MWB	ASD Bus	M95DLN	Cruisers	M592BLC	British Airways	MIB5354	Ham's Travel
L881YVK	Renown	M101ECV	Poynter's	M593BLC	British Airways	MIB650	Coliseum
L901NWW	Horseman	M104BPX	Marchwood M'ways	M594BLC	British Airways	MIB651	Coliseum
L902NWW	Horseman	M104NKR	Cruisers	M595BLC	British Airways	MIB652	Coliseum
L903NWW	Horseman	M109JHB	Nu-Venture	M596BLC	British Airways	MIL4690	Amberlee
L904NWW	Horseman	M138MPL	British Airways	M6030RJ	Cheney	MIL8332	Flights-Hallmark
L905NWW	Horseman	M139MPL	British Airways	M6040RJ	Cheney	MIL9575	Solent Blue Line
L933ABJ	Eastonways	M140MPL	British Airways	M6090RJ	Cheney	MJG416R	Crosskeys

MJI1678	Grayline	N150BOF	Compass Travel	N413JBV	Solent Blue Line	N745DBD	Wheelers Travel
MJI1679	Grayline	N151BOF	Compass Travel	N439XDV	Renown	N756CYA	Scotland & Bates
MK02BUS	MK Metro	N171LHU	Tappins	N452VPM	British Airways	N784JBM	Red Rose
MK02HAO	Regent Coaches	N172LHU	Tappins	N453VPM	British Airways	N802GRV	Red Rose
MK52UGP	OFJ	N173LHU	Tappins	N469VPJ	British Airways	N802NHS	Heyfordian
MKZ2030	C&S Coaches	N174LHU	Tappins	N469WDA	Compass Travel	N803GRV	Red Rose
MLH304L	Redroute	N175LHU	Tappins	N470VPJ	British Airways	N803NHS	Heyfordian
MLZ4286	Souls	N176LCK	Amberlee	N472VPJ	British Airways	N805NHS	Renown
MLZ4287	Souls	N176LHU	Tappins	N473VPJ	British Airways	N808NHS	Heyfordian
MLZ4288	Souls	N177LCK	Amberlee	N475VPJ	British Airways	N809NHS	Heyfordian
MLZ4289	Souls	N177LHU	Tappins	N477VPJ	British Airways	N810PDL	Southern Vectis
MLZ4290	Souls	N178LCK	Amberlee	N478VPJ	British Airways	N811PDL	Southern Vectis
MLZ9698	Wheelers Travel	N178LHU	Tappins	N495DOR	Wheelers Travel	N812PDL	Southern Vectis
MRD1	Reading Buses	N178OUT	Accord	N506LUA	Compass Travel	N813PDL	Southern Vectis
MSV412	Black & White	N179LCK	Amberlee	N511YHN	The King's Ferry	N814PDL	Southern Vectis
MT02MTT	Motts Travel	N179LHU	Tappins	N514YTF	Reading Buses	N815PDL	Southern Vectis
MT03MTT	Motts Travel	N179UPG	British Airways	N515YTF	Reading Buses	N901HWY	Nu-Venture
MT04MTT	Motts Travel	N180LCK	Amberlee	N516YTF	Reading Buses	N902HWY	Red Rose
MT05MTT	Motts Travel	N180LHU	Tappins	N517YTF	Reading Buses	N903ABL	Woottens
MT51MTT	Motts Travel	N182FLR	British Airways	N518LUF	Eastbourne Buses	N903HWY	Nu-Venture
MUI5922	Banstead Coaches	N183FLR	British Airways	N518YTF	Reading Buses	N904HWY	Countryliner
MUI7851	Tappins	N184FLR	British Airways	N519YTF	Reading Buses	N905HWY	Nu-Venture
MUI7852	Tappins	N195DYB	Crosskeys	N520YTF	Reading Buses	N906HWY	Nu-Venture
MUI7853	Tappins	N196FLR	British Airways	N529LHG	Centra	N917ETM	Brijan
MUI7854	Tappins	N198FLR	British Airways	N531LHG	Centra	N959UJT	Parking Express
MUK739R	Black & White	N203HLN	British Airways	N531RJR	ASD Bus	N974WJH	British Airways
MUY253X	Edward Thomas	N204FLR	British Airways	N532LHG	Centra	N976WJH	British Airways
MX03EHC	Centra	N205HLN	British Airways	N539LHG	Solent Blue Line	N986FWT	Baileys Buses
MX03EJY	Red Rose	N209WMS	British Airways	N572GRH	ASD Bus	NBZ2248	Buzzlines
MX03YDC	Kent CC	N219HBK	Red Rose	N576WAW	Wheelers Travel	NBZ70	Weavaway
MX05CZW	Regent Coaches	N222TAY	Wheelers Travel	N581GBW	Banstead Coaches	NDG172	Black & White
MX05CZY	Regent Coaches	N246HLN	British Airways	N593DOR	Marchwood M'ways	NDY820	Rambler
MY02BAN	Banstead Coaches	N253FOR	Solent Blue Line	N605JGP	Heyfordian	NDY962	Rambler
MY52BAN	Banstead Coaches	N255FOR	Solent Blue Line	N611WND	Safeguard	NDZ4521	MK Metro
N1HAM	Ham's Travel	N259FOR	Solent Blue Line	N613FLR	British Airways	NDZ70	Weavaway
N1VWL	Pearce	N260FOR	Solent Blue Line	N614FLR	British Airways	NDZ7918	MK Metro
N1VWL	Charlton Services	N272HLA	British Airways	N615FLR	British Airways	NDZ7919	MK Metro
N2FPK	Nu-Venture	N273HLN	British Airways	N616FLR	British Airways	NDZ7926	MK Metro
N3FPK	Nu-Venture	N274HLN	British Airways	N624ATF	Reading Buses	NDZ7933	MK Metro
N4PUS	Charlton Services	N275DWY	Compass Travel	N631CDY	Eastbourne Buses	NDZ7935	MK Metro
N5BJT	Brijan	N278HLA	British Airways	N660VJB	Horseman	NFM46	Black & White
N7CLC	Crawley Luxury	N278HLN	British Airways	N661VJB	Horseman	NG2414	Rambler
N11HAM	Ham's Travel	N279HLA	British Airways	N662FLR	ASD Bus	NHM465X	Ham's Travel
N12CLC	Crawley Luxury	N283HLA	British Airways	N662VJB	Horseman	NIB7625	Countywide
N26FWU	Eastbourne Buses	N283HLN	British Airways	N663VJB	Horseman	NIL4762	Poynter's
N27FWU	Eastbourne Buses	N284HLA	British Airways	N664VJB	Horseman	NIL7251	Wheelers Travel
N30BAN	Banstead Coaches	N284HLN	British Airways	N665VJB	Horseman	NIW6509	Fleetwing
N50HAM	Ham's Travel	N285HLN	British Airways	N669FLR	ASD Bus	NIW6510	Fleetwing
N81FWU	C&S Coaches	N286HLN	British Airways	N669VJB	Horseman	NIW6512	Fleetwing
N84FWU	C&S Coaches	N288HLN	British Airways	N670VJB	Horseman	NIW6518	Cheney
N86FWU	C&S Coaches	N2890YE	Woottens	N672VJB	Horseman	NJ51TXH	John Pike
N94WOM	Compass Travel	N301FOR	Marchwood M'ways	N673VJB	Horseman	NJI4304	Charlton Services
N95WOM	Compass Travel	N303HLA	British Airways	N692YJB	British Airways	NJV995	Black & White
N101CKN	Nu-Venture	N304FOR	Marchwood M'ways	N722UVR	Heyfordian	NKZ8970	C&S Coaches
N102BMM	Cruisers	N305FOR	Countywide	N724UVR	Heyfordian	NNS235V	Buzzlines
N102CKN	Nu-Venture	N342HLN	British Airways	N726UVR	Heyfordian	NSU914	Cheney
N114VPJ	British Airways	N343HLN	British Airways	N727UVR	Heyfordian	NUW595Y	Farleigh Coaches
N115VPJ	British Airways	N347UJB	British Airways	N728UVR	Heyfordian	NUW614Y	Nu-Venture
N121FLR	British Airways	N348HLN	British Airways	N729EOT	Accord	NUW638Y	Poynter's
N122FLR	British Airways	N348UJB	British Airways	N730EOT	Accord	NUW652Y	Nu-Venture
N123FLR	British Airways	N349HLN	British Airways	N731EOT	Accord	NUW671Y	West Kent Buses
N129MBW	Brijan	N349UJB	British Airways	N731UVR	Heyfordian	NUW672Y	Edward Thomas
N132XEG	Wiltax	N356ETM	Brijan	N732EOT	Accord	NYH161Y	Emsworth & District
N133FLR	British Airways	N359WHH	Fleetwing	N732UVR	Heyfordian	ODL447	Southern Vectis
N133XND	MK Metro	N372EAK	Richardson Travel	N733EOT	Accord	ODL678	Seaview Services
N134FLR	British Airways	N388VPB	British Airways	N733UVR	Heyfordian	ODU856G	Pearce
N134XND	MK Metro	N399LEW	Cheney	N734EOT	Accord	ODY395	Rambler
N137FLR	British Airways	N401SPA	Flights-Hallmark	N734UVR	Heyfordian	ODY607	Rambler
N138FLR	British Airways	N411DRH	ASD Bus	N735EOT	Accord	OE02WAU	Pearce
N149FLR	British Airways	N411JBV	Solent Blue Line	N735UVR	Heyfordian	OFJ580	OFJ

OFJ581	OFJ	P138TDL	Wight Bus	P695RUU	Renown	PN52XBP	Richardson Travel
OFJ582	OFJ	P139TDL	Wight Bus	P699RUU	Renown	PO51WNF	Reading Buses
OFS911M	West Kent Buses	P140TDL	Wight Bus	P7100DA	Countryliner	PO51WNG	Reading Buses
OGL849	Cheney	P141TDL	Wight Bus	P712RWU	Amberlee	PO51WNJ	Reading Buses
OIB3513	RDH Services	P142NLR	British Airways	P713RWU	Amberlee	PO51WNK	Reading Buses
OIB3514	RDH Services	P142TDL	Wight Bus	P714RWU	Amberlee	PO51WNL	Reading Buses
OJI3907	Charlton Services	P143NLR	British Airways	P715RWU	Amberlee	PO51WNM	Reading Buses
OK51BUZ	Buzzlines	P144GHE	Eastbourne Buses	P719FDY	Eastbourne Buses	Q255GRW	Crosskeys
OLW503	Wheelers Travel	P144NLR	British Airways	P728JYA	Scotland & Bates	R2BAN	Banstead Coaches
O002BUZ	Buzzlines	P148NLR	British Airways	P746HND	Compass Travel	R4HLC	Lucketts
O002TEN	Weavaway	P168RWR	The King's Ferry	P762BDD	Cheney	R5HLC	Lucketts
ORJ72W	Amberlee	P170ANR	Warrens	P822GBA	Woottens	R8WMS	Worth's
OSJ1X	Autocar	P170NLA	British Airways	P827MTR	Accord	R9BJT	Brijan
OSR197R	Black & White	P190PBP	Marchwood M'ways	P849BPB	British Airways	R10APT	Brijan
OU04FMV	Thames Travel	P191PBP	Marchwood M'ways	P851JKK	OFJ	R10HLC	Lucketts
OU04KMX	Pearce	P202CAY	Avis	P881FMO	Wheelers Travel	R16HAM	Ham's Travel
OU05AVB	Weavaway	P208RWR	C&S Coaches	P886PWW	Marchwood M'ways	R17HAM	Ham's Travel
OU05AVD	Weavaway	P209CAY	Avis	P887PWW	Marchwood M'ways	R20CLC	Crawley Luxury
OU05AVY	Weavaway	P209RWR	C&S Coaches	P901EGM	Reading Buses	R40TGM	Countryliner
OU05AWJ	Weavaway	P20SOU	Souls	P902EGM	Reading Buses	R50MTT	Motts Travel
OU05KKB	Weavaway	P211CAY	Avis	P903EGM	Reading Buses	R81EDW	Compass Travel
OU05KLA	Weavaway	P212CAY	Avis	P904EGM	Reading Buses	R83EDW	Brijan
OU05LWP	Thames Travel	P214CAY	Avis	P904FMO	Wheelers Travel	R84NNJ	Country Rider
OU54PGZ	Thames Travel	P215RUU	Rebound	P905EGM	Reading Buses	R89GNW	White Bus
OUC45R	Emsworth & District	P218VGN	OFJ	P905FMO	Wheelers Travel	R107DNV	MK Metro
OV5100A	Grayline	P231TDL	Wight Bus	P905PWW	Eastbourne Buses	R108DNV	MK Metro
OV5100B	Grayline	P237AUT	John Pike	P906EGM	Reading Buses	R109DNV	MK Metro
OV5100C	Grayline	P240VDL	Solent Blue Line	P906FMO	Wheelers Travel	R110DNV	MK Metro
OXI9100	Charlton Services	P241VDL	Solent Blue Line	P906PWW	Eastbourne Buses	R112DNV	MK Metro
OYD693	Countryliner	P242VDL	Solent Blue Line	P907EGM	Reading Buses	R113DNV	MK Metro
P1FTG	Flights-Hallmark	P244VDL	Southern Vectis	P908EGM	Reading Buses	R114GNW	Countywide
P1RWL	Pearce	P244WWX	Cardinal	P909EGM	Reading Buses	R115GNW	Eastbourne Buses
P2FTG	Flights-Hallmark	P245VDL	Southern Vectis	P910EGM	Reading Buses	R116DNV	MK Metro
P2RDJ	Crosskeys	P246VDL	Southern Vectis	P910PWW	Eastbourne Buses	R117DNV	MK Metro
P2TYR	Nu-Venture	P247VDL	Southern Vectis	P911GJM	Reading Buses	R118DNV	MK Metro
P3FTG	Flights-Hallmark	P288ENT	Woottens	P912GJM	Reading Buses	R119DNV	MK Metro
P3RDJ	Crosskeys	P288MLY	British Airways	P912SUM	Parking Express	R120DNV	MK Metro
P4BAN	Banstead Coaches	P290MLD	Eastonways	P913GJM	Reading Buses	R121DNV	MK Metro
P4FTG	Flights-Hallmark	P293MLD	Poynter's	P914GJM	Reading Buses	R125CMY	Accord
P5FTG	Flights-Hallmark	P297MLD	McLeans	P914XUG	Reading Buses	R127CMY	Accord
P6FTG	Flights-Hallmark	P321MLY	British Airways	P915GJM	Reading Buses	R128CMY	Accord
P6SYD	Compass Travel	P339ROO	Flights-Hallmark	P933KYC	Hellyers	R146COR	Hellyers
P7FTG	Flights-Hallmark	P373XGG	Motts Travel	P943EBB	Fleetwing	R163GNW	Countywide
P7WMS	Worth's	P37JCR	Accord	P943YSB	Fleetwing	R164GNW	Countywide
P8FTG	Flights-Hallmark	P38JCR	Accord	P953DNR	Hellyers	R167EOO	Wheelers Travel
P9FTG	Flights-Hallmark	P39JCR	Accord	P971PNG	OFJ	R173YLL	British Airways
P10FTG	Flights-Hallmark	P414HRB	Tappins	P975HWF	RDH Services	R180BDT	Altonian
P14CLC	Crawley Luxury	P415HRB	Tappins	P982HWF	RDH Services	R184VSJ	Tappins
P15CLC	Crawley Luxury	P417LLU	British Airways	P984JKP	Regent Coaches	R186TKU	Woottens
P36JCR	Accord	P423HNT	Fleetwing	P985JKP	Regent Coaches	R204STF	Horseman
P49JJU	Hellyers	P424PBP	Brijan	PA52HAM	Ham's Travel	R206DKG	Eastbourne Buses
P50SOU	Souls	P433LLU	British Airways	PAX466F	MK Metro	R207DKG	Eastbourne Buses
P60ULS	Souls	P451FVV	Cruisers	PAZ1066	Empress Coaches	R208DKG	Eastbourne Buses
P70FTG	Flights-Hallmark	P480LLU	British Airways	PDL230	Seaview Services	R209DKG	Eastbourne Buses
P73VWO	Brijan	P490LLU	British Airways	PDL298	Seaview Services	R210DKG	Eastbourne Buses
P77FTG	Flights-Hallmark	P507NWU	Red Rose	PDN873	Cheney	R211DKG	Eastbourne Buses
P81VDL	Wight Bus	P524XBB	Poynter's	PDY272	Rambler	R212DKG	Eastbourne Buses
P82VDL	Wight Bus	P529BLJ	Cheney	PDY42	Rambler	R213DKG	Eastbourne Buses
P83VDL	Wight Bus	P535YEU	OFJ	PG04HOF	Hellyers	R214DKG	Eastbourne Buses
P118RSF	The King's Ferry	P545RBX	Altonian	PIB5891	Heritage Travel	R215DKG	Eastbourne Buses
P119RSF	The King's Ferry	P591MTR	Marchwood M'ways	PIL3500	Charlton Services	R218DNT	Cruisers
P124RWR	Marchwood M'ways	P616LTP	Countywide	PIL6576	Tourex	R246YLL	British Airways
P124TDL	Wight Bus	P618MLE	British Airways	PIL6578	Tourex	R260GNJ	W&H Motors
P125RWR	Marchwood M'ways	P619MLE	British Airways	PIL6579	Tourex	R301BDL	Wight Bus
P125TDL	Wight Bus	P620MLE	British Airways	PIW4127	Souls	R302BDL	Wight Bus
P126RWR	Marchwood M'ways	P631MLD	British Airways	PJI1861	Heritage Travel	R303BDL	Wight Bus
P131RWR	White Bus	P682RWU	Countryliner	PJI5627	Heritage Travel	R304BDL	Wight Bus
P132YEL	John Pike	P686RWU	Countryliner	PMK106V	Black & White	R329VJO	Pearce
P137TDL	Wight Bus	P688RWU	Countryliner	PMY177W	Nu-Venture	R334FVW	Regent Coaches
P138NLR	British Airways	P690RUU	Renown	PN05SYF	Richardson Travel	R348FYJ	Accord

The South East Bus Handbook

R351FYJ	Accord	R916SJH	Reading Buses	S9BJT	Brijan	S701RWG	Richardson Travel
R355FYJ	Accord	R919XTP	Wheelers Travel	S20MTT	Motts Travel	S705CMA	OFJ
R37GNW	Reading Buses	R931AMB	Kent CC	S35KRV	Brijan	S706CMA	OFJ
R415EOS	Heyfordian	R943YNF	Charlton Services	S36UBO	Buzzlines	S721KNV	Menzies
R433FWT	Safeguard	R949AMB	MK Metro	S45UBO	Buzzlines	S723KNV	Menzies
R440TLB	British Airways	R955TLD	Kingsman	S46UBO	Buzzlines	S729SKE	Kent CC
R487YKM	Kent CC	R976FNW	Carousel	S47UBO	Buzzlines	S747XYA	Crosskeys
R492BDL	Wight Bus	R977FNW	Baileys Buses	S48UBO	Buzzlines	S757CKO	Edward Thomas
R493BDL	Wight Bus	R979FNW	Baileys Buses	S51KNW	Eastbourne Buses	S766SKK	Kent CC
R511WDC	Countryliner	R984FNW	Carousel	S51UBO	Flights-Hallmark	S775RNE	Kent CC
R517NTF	MK Metro	R986FNW	Carousel	S101KNR	Kent CC	S776RNE	Kent CC
R524EUD	Grayline	R988FNW	Carousel	S101LBL	Reading Buses	S778RNE	Kent CC
R527YRP	Menzies	R991FNW	Carousel	S102LBL	Reading Buses	S793RRL	Menzies
R530YRP	Menzies	R998KKO	Heyfordian	S103LBL	Reading Buses	S794XUG	Country Rider
R551TKV	Woottens	RA53BLK	OFJ	S104LBL	Reading Buses	S810MCC	Tappins
R560GRN	Rebound	RAN646R	Black & White	S105LBL	Reading Buses	S835DPN	Eastbourne Buses
R625GKO	The King's Ferry	RAZ3785	Souls	S106LBL	Reading Buses	S844BUF	Accord
R626GKO	The King's Ferry	RBW396	Souls	S107LBL	Reading Buses	S847DGX	Courtney
R627SJM	Reading Buses	RDG304G	Black & White	S122KBD	MK Metro	S853DGX	Courtney
R629SJM	Reading Buses	RE02NKT	OFJ	S129LLN	British Airways	S854DGX	Courtney
R634VYB	Scotland & Bates	RE02NKU	OFJ	S130LLN	British Airways	S857DGX	Courtney
R63GNW	Marchwood M'ways	RIL1024	Cheney	S131SET	Altonian	S876BYJ	Reading Buses
R670EWV	Accord	RIL4956	Cheney	S132LLN	British Airways	S877BYJ	Reading Buses
R672NFR	Courtney	RIL5261	Tappins	S132PGB	Safeguard	S878BYJ	Reading Buses
R674OEB	White Bus	RIL7163	Tappins	S133LLN	British Airways	S879BYJ	Reading Buses
R685HGX	Accord	RIL7974	Cheney	S134LLN	British Airways	S880BYJ	Reading Buses
R686HGX	Accord	RIL8251	Wheelers Travel	S135LLN	British Airways	S881BYJ	Reading Buses
R703XAL	Avis	RIW4098	Charlton Services	S136LLN	British Airways	S903DUB	MK Metro
R704XAL	Avis	RJI6611	Rebound	S151JUA	The King's Ferry	S925LBL	Reading Buses
R706XAL	Avis	RJI6612	Rebound	S152JUA	The King's Ferry	S926LBL	Reading Buses
R710XAL	Avis	RJI6860	Heritage Travel	S158JUA	White Bus	S927LBL	Reading Buses
R716KHN	Cruisers	RJI7972	Rebound	S167UBU	Wheelers Travel	S928LBL	Reading Buses
R718BNF	Nu-Venture	RL51CVZ	Countywide	S190VKM	Kent CC	S929LBL	Reading Buses
R720BNF	Nu-Venture	RL51CWA	Countywide	S192WAN	Horseman	S930LBL	Reading Buses
R720LDY	Eastbourne Buses	RL51CXB	Countryliner	S193WAN	Horseman	S931LBL	Reading Buses
R737XRV	Solent Blue Line	RL51CXC	Countryliner	S222AJW	Weavaway	SA02UGN	Hellyers
R738XRV	Solent Blue Line	RL51CXD	Countryliner	S228LLT	OFJ	SAD189	Black & White
R739XRV	Solent Blue Line	RL51ZLN	Countywide	S295WOA	Flights-Hallmark	SDY788	Rambler
R741XRV	Solent Blue Line	RL51ZLO	Countywide	S296WOA	Flights-Hallmark	SF05HOF	Hellyers
R752GDL	Southern Vectis	RMO75Y	Reading Buses	S297UBU	OFJ	SF53KUP	Cruisers
R753GDL	Southern Vectis	RMO77Y	Reading Buses	S297WOA	Flights-Hallmark	SIB6713	Eastonways
R754GDL	Southern Vectis	RMO78Y	Reading Buses	S298WOA	Flights-Hallmark	SIL2890	Nu-Venture
R755GDL	Southern Vectis	RO03JVA	Courtney	S300MTT	Motts Travel	SIL6719	Cheney
R756GDL	Southern Vectis	RO03JVD	Courtney	S303UBU	OFJ	SIL6722	Worth's
R757GDL	Southern Vectis	RO03JVL	Courtney	S340NVP	Cruisers	SIL8756	Cheney
R758GDL	Southern Vectis	RR02BUS	Red Rose	S340SET	MK Metro	SIL8757	Cheney
R759GDL	Southern Vectis	RR03BUS	Red Rose	S345NVP	Cruisers	SIL9041	Wheelers Travel
R796GSF	Red Rose	RX03XKH	Safeguard	S364OOB	Flights-Hallmark	SIL9512	Tappins
R813WJA	Menzies	RX05EOU	Hotelink	S365OOB	Flights-Hallmark	SIL9513	Tappins
R816WJA	Menzies	RX05EOW	Hotelink	S370SET	Buddens	SJ03EFA	Rebound
R824MJU	MK Metro	RX05EOY	Hotelink	S373SET	The King's Ferry	SJI2586	Hodge's
R825MJU	MK Metro	RX05EOZ	Hotelink	S377PGB	Countywide	SJI4428	Heyfordian
R826MJU	MK Metro	RX51EXM	Horseman	S394LLT	OFJ	SJI7466	Renown
R827WBC	MK Metro	RX51EXN	Horseman	S396HVV	Flights-Hallmark	SJI8094	Edward Thomas
R829GKX	Solent Blue Line	RX51EXO	Horseman	S401ERP	MK Metro	SJI8124	Buddens
R843FWW	Red Rose	RX51EXP	Horseman	S402ERP	MK Metro	SJI8128	Heritage Travel
R846JGD	Thames Travel	RX51XXL	Countywide	S403ERP	MK Metro	SK52USS	Reading Buses
R847JGD	Thames Travel	RX53LBJ	OFJ	S404ERP	MK Metro	SKG406Y	Worth's
R848JGD	Thames Travel	RX53LFH	Countywide	S417RLH	British Airways	SKL680X	John Pike
R870MDY	Eastbourne Buses	RX53LNH	Countywide	S484KJT	Horseman	SLJ387X	Countywide
R870SDT	Warrens	RX53LNJ	Countywide	S490UAK	Motts Travel	SN03EBP	Solent Blue Line
R871MDY	Eastbourne Buses	RX53RYW	MK Metro	S497UAK	McLeans	SN03EBU	Solent Blue Line
R871SDT	The King's Ferry	RX55DUV	Courtney	S503UAK	Safeguard	SN03EBV	Solent Blue Line
R872MDY	Eastbourne Buses	RY03DDU	Menzies	S507KJU	Kent CC	SN03EBX	Solent Blue Line
R873MDY	Eastbourne Buses	RY03DDV	Menzies	S540RKL	Kent CC	SN03EBZ	Solent Blue Line
R874MDY	Eastbourne Buses	S2WMS	Worth's	S551BNV	Menzies	SN03ECA	Solent Blue Line
R875MDY	Eastbourne Buses	S3HAM	Ham's Travel	S551KNW	Eastbourne Buses	SN03ECC	Solent Blue Line
R882SDT	The King's Ferry	S4HAM	Ham's Travel	S556BNV	Menzies	SN03ECD	Solent Blue Line
R901EDO	Reading Buses	S5MTT	Motts Travel	S602KUT	Marchwood M'ways	SN03LDJ	Solent Blue Line
R902GJO	Pearce	S6WMS	Worth's	S603KUT	Marchwood M'ways	SN03LDK	Solent Blue Line

SN03LDL	Solent Blue Line	T173AUA	British Airways	T723UOS	Heyfordian	TIL4754		Brijan
SN03LDU	Solent Blue Line	T186AUA	Marchwood M'ways	T725UOS	Heyfordian	TIL5973		Tappins
SN04EFH	Flights-Hallmark	T186RJD	OFJ	T728JHE	Buddens	TIL5974		Tappins
SN04EFL	Renown	T187AUA	Marchwood M'ways	T729JHE	Buddens	TIL5975		Tappins
SN05FNW	Weavaway	T189RJD	OFJ	T730JHE	Buddens	TIL6710		Southern Vectis
SN53ETK	Compass Travel	T191RJD	OFJ	T731JHE	Buddens	TIL6711		Southern Vectis
SN53ETL	Compass Travel	T192RJD	OFJ	T739JHE	Parking Express	TIL6712		Southern Vectis
SN53ETO	Compass Travel	T193RJD	OFJ	T742JPO	Solent Blue Line	TIL6713		Southern Vectis
SN53ETR	Compass Travel	T194RJD	OFJ	T743JHE	Parking Express	TIL6714		Southern Vectis
SN53LWM	Nu-Venture	T195RJD	OFJ	T743JPO	Solent Blue Line	TIL6715		Southern Vectis
SN53LWO	Nu-Venture	T196RJD	OFJ	T744JPO	Solent Blue Line	TIL6716		Southern Vectis
SN53LWP	Nu-Venture	T197RJD	OFJ	T745JPO	Solent Blue Line	TIL6717		Southern Vectis
SN55DUV	Courtney	T214BBR	MK Metro	T746JHE	Parking Express	TIL6718		Southern Vectis
SN55DUY	Courtney	T222ADY	Rambler	T746JPO	Solent Blue Line	TIL6719		Southern Vectis
SN55DVA	Courtney	T285CGU	Grayline	T747JPO	Solent Blue Line	TIL6720		Southern Vectis
SN55DVB	Courtney	T341FWR	Red Rose	T748JPO	Solent Blue Line	TIL6723		Southern Vectis
SND710X	Tourex	T354JWA	Parking Express	T749JPO	Solent Blue Line	TIL6724		Southern Vectis
SPV860	Grayline	T356JWA	Parking Express	T759JYB	Hellyers	TIL6725		Southern Vectis
SV9314	Heritage Travel	T357JWA	Parking Express	T75WGH	Centra	TIL6726		Southern Vectis
SVS617	Flights-Hallmark	T362JWA	Parking Express	T760JYB	Scotland & Bates	TIL6727		Southern Vectis
T2CCL	Courtney	T364JWA	Parking Express	T763JYB	Hellyers	TIL7165		Tappins
T3HLC	Lucketts	T365JWA	Parking Express	T781KNW	Menzies	TIL7509		Tappins
T4GLF	Tappins	T367JWA	Parking Express	T781LNT	Accord	TIL8271		Edward Thomas
T4HMC	Flights-Hallmark	T368JWA	Parking Express	T782KNW	Menzies	TIL8272		Edward Thomas
T5BUS	Flights-Hallmark	T374JWA	Parking Express	T783KNW	Menzies	TIL9262		Tappins
T6HMC	Flights-Hallmark	T401OWA	The King's Ferry	T784KNW	Menzies	TIL9302		Tappins
T7HLC	Lucketts	T403BFC	Pearce	T785KNW	Menzies	TJI1688		Renown
T7MTT	Motts Travel	T405ENV	MK Metro	T787KNW	Menzies	TJI4926		Hellyers
T9MTT	Motts Travel	T406ENV	MK Metro	T788KNW	Menzies	TJI6278		Charlton Services
T10DMB	Horseman	T407ENV	MK Metro	T789KNW	ASD Bus	TJI6313		Kent CC
T16CLC	Crawley Luxury	T408ENV	MK Metro	T801FRU	John Pike	TJI8792		Emsworth & District
T20DMB	Horseman	T409ENV	MK Metro	T805FGT	Centra	TJR715Y		Redroute
T39APO	John Pike	T410ENV	MK Metro	T806FGT	Centra	TJR719Y		Redroute
T45KAW	MK Metro	T414VVW	Regent Coaches	T816RVA	ASD Bus	TJT182X		Wheelers Travel
T49CNN	Buzzlines	T421ADN	Compass Travel	T875HGT	Centra	TND409X		Emsworth & District
T50BAN	Banstead Coaches	T422ADN	Compass Travel	T876HGT	Centra	TPD103X		Nu-Venture
T59MLL	Motts Travel	T443CBC	Menzies	T877HGT	Centra	TPD125X		Flights-Hallmark
T70HAM	Ham's Travel	T446EBD	Parking Express	T880HGT	Centra	TRN468V		Newnham
T72JBA	Countryliner	T454HNH	Menzies	T883JBC	British Airways	TW53WMS		Worth's
T73JBO	Compass Travel	T455HNH	Menzies	T932EAN	Reading Buses	TWH698T		Black & White
T75JBO	Compass Travel	T456HNH	Menzies	T933EAN	Reading Buses	UBK606		Warrens
T76JBO	Compass Travel	T467EGT	Eastbourne Buses	T934EAN	Reading Buses	UCW429X		Richardson Travel
T78JBA	Countryliner	T468EGT	Eastbourne Buses	T935EAN	Reading Buses	UDN126		Souls
T80HAM	Ham's Travel	T492RCE	Wheelers Travel	T936EAN	Reading Buses	UDY512		Rambler
T87LJC	British Airways	T497KLF	British Airways	T936WWV	Eastbourne Buses	UDY910		Rambler
T90HAM	Ham's Travel	T504KLF	British Airways	T937AYJ	Eastbourne Buses	UDZ7334		Countywide
T92LJC	British Airways	T530EUB	Safeguard	T962LLB	British Airways	UF03HOF		Hellyers
T93JBA	MK Metro	T532EUB	John Pike	T972LLB	British Airways	UFX857S		Solent Blue Line
T95GGO	Centra	T538EUB	Crawley Luxury	T980WPN	Hotelink	UFX858S		Seaview Services
T100MTT	Motts Travel	T546HNH	Thames Travel	T981LLB	British Airways	UG1066		Empress Coaches
T125LRP	MK Metro	T550HNH	Countryliner	T981WPN	Hotelink	UHY374		Black & White
T126LRP	MK Metro	T553ADN	Reading Buses	T982WPN	Hotelink	UIL2720		Cheney
T127LRP	MK Metro	T554ADN	Reading Buses	T983WPN	Hotelink	UIL2721		Cheney
T130AUA	Buzzlines	T556ADN	Reading Buses	T984RJE	Cruisers	UIL2722		Cheney
T131AUA	Centra	T556UOX	The King's Ferry	T984WPN	Hotelink	UIL2723		Cheney
T132AUA	Buzzlines	T570LKM	The King's Ferry	T985WPN	Hotelink	UIL2725		Cheney
T133AUA	Buzzlines	T571JND	Altonian	TAZ4495	Souls	UIL2726		Cheney
T134AUA	Buzzlines	T587KGB	MK Metro	TAZ4988	Cheney	UIL7821		Cheney
T137AUA	Buzzlines	T594CGT	Countryliner	TAZ4990	Cheney	UIL7822		Cheney
T138AUA	Buzzlines	T606LKL	Kent CC	TDY388	Rambler	UIL7823		Cheney
T139AUA	Buzzlines	T607LKL	Kent CC	TDY946	Rambler	UIL7824		Cheney
T151OGC	Centra	T622RBX	MK Metro	TG04HOF	Hellyers	UIL9043		Poynter's
T152OGC	Centra	T643NTW	OFJ	THX105S	Redroute	UN02BUZ		Buzzlines
T152OGC	Centra	T692LNV	MK Metro	TIB4922	RDH Services	UNA844S		Edward Thomas
T154OGC	Centra	T696OCR	Countywide	TIL1184	Tappins	UNJ408		Crawley Luxury
T156OGC	Centra	T701RBX	MK Metro	TIL1188	Compass Travel	UOI2609		Kingsman
T157OGC	Centra	T702RBX	MK Metro	TIL2510	Tappins	UOI2679		Emsworth & District
T158OGC	Centra	T703RBX	MK Metro	TIL2511	Tappins	UPB331S		Crosskeys
T159OGC	Centra	T704RBX	MK Metro	TIL4508	Tappins	UPT680V		Redroute
T172AUA	British Airways	T705RBX	MK Metro	TIL4557	Brijan	URT682		Cheney

The South East Bus Handbook

Reg	Operator	Reg	Operator	Reg	Operator	Reg	Operator
UTC872	Rebound	V899LOH	The King's Ferry	W141WGT	Centra	W656FUM	Crawley Luxury
UVY412	Brijan	V931VUB	Country Rider	W142WGT	Centra	W657SJF	Warrens
V1PKF	The King's Ferry	V932VUB	Country Rider	W143WGT	Centra	W658SJF	Warrens
V3BLU	The King's Ferry	V933VUB	Country Rider	W144WGT	Centra	W681DDN	MK Metro
V4BLU	The King's Ferry	V934VUB	Country Rider	W146ULT	W&H Motors	W689TNV	RDH Services
V7PCL	Autocar	V935VUB	Country Rider	W146WGT	Centra	W754URD	Country Rider
V9WMS	Worth's	V941DCF	Reading Buses	W147WGT	Centra	W771AAY	W&H Motors
V22CLC	Crawley Luxury	V942DCF	Reading Buses	W149WGT	Centra	W773URP	Countryliner
V57KGT	OFJ	V946DCF	Reading Buses	W181CDN	Marchwood M'ways	W808AAY	White Bus
V67SVY	Thames Travel	V951DKK	Country Rider	W182CDN	Marchwood M'ways	W845UVV	Centra
V79JKG	Weavaway	V962ENJ	British Airways	W184CDN	Marchwood M'ways	W851VHB	Country Rider
V82EVU	MK Metro	V963ENJ	British Airways	W197ESO	Weavaway	W869VGY	The King's Ferry
V87SOT	Marchwood M'ways	V998JKK	The King's Ferry	W200MTT	Motts Travel	W876ULH	British Airways
V101LKN	Country Rider	VCA461W	Eastonways	W203YAP	Safeguard	W903XKR	The King's Ferry
V108DCF	Reading Buses	VDL744	Southern Vectis	W207KNH	Regent Coaches	W904XKR	The King's Ferry
V108LVH	Red Rose	VDV123S	West Kent Buses	W209YAP	Safeguard	W908MDT	Buddens
V109DCF	Reading Buses	VFB617T	Countywide	W231CDN	Marchwood M'ways	W918XGH	Centra
V110DCF	Reading Buses	VFJ687	Coliseum	W232CDN	Marchwood M'ways	W919XGH	Centra
V112DCF	Reading Buses	VIB8319	Redroute	W248OLA	Avis	W921JNF	Countryliner
V113DCF	Reading Buses	VIJ4021	Souls	W249OLA	Avis	W928PLA	British Airways
V114DCF	Reading Buses	VIL4766	Crawley Luxury	W252UGX	Buzzlines	W936JNF	Renown
V115DCF	Reading Buses	VJY139V	Edward Thomas	W253UGX	Buzzlines	W937JNF	Countryliner
V128UNH	MK Metro	VJY141V	Edward Thomas	W257UGX	Safeguard	W954PLA	British Airways
V200RAD	Eastbourne Buses	VLT23	Wiltax	W258UGX	Buzzlines	W963JNF	Countywide
V202EAL	Warrens	VLT87	Wiltax	W259UGX	Buzzlines	W964JNF	Countywide
V203EAL	Warrens	VLT177	Wiltax	W261OLA	Avis	W977ULD	British Airways
V222PDY	Rambler	VLT191	Wiltax	W262OLA	Avis	W986WDS	MK Metro
V224LWU	OFJ	VSF438	Heyfordian	W263OLA	Avis	W989PLA	British Airways
V241LKN	Country Rider	VU02TTJ	Safeguard	W264OLA	Avis	W991XGH	Flights-Hallmark
V247BNV	Countryliner	VUD483	Souls	W265OLA	Avis	W992XGH	Flights-Hallmark
V252BNV	Menzies	VWL96	Tourex	W289EYG	Courtney	WA03HPY	Scotland & Bates
V257BNV	Countryliner	W2HLC	Lucketts	W295UGX	Safeguard	WA03UDY	Weavaway
V270BNV	Thames Travel	W2HOF	Hellyers	W298ULY	British Airways	WA03UDZ	Weavaway
V308DHC	Centra	W3CTS	MK Metro	W302NUF	British Airways	WA04EWR	Scotland & Bates
V365ECD	British Airways	W3HLC	Lucketts	W343MKY	Eastbourne Buses	WA05DFG	Weavaway
V383SVV	Parking Express	W5HAM	Ham's Travel	W358EOL	Grayline	WA05DFJ	Weavaway
V385SVV	Menzies	W5HLC	Lucketts	W359EOL	The King's Ferry	WA53FDG	Weavaway
V386MKJ	Kent CC	W5WMS	Worth's	W361ABD	Flights-Hallmark	WA53FDJ	Weavaway
V386SVV	Menzies	W7BAN	Banstead Coaches	W364ABD	Countryliner	WA54KTP	Scotland & Bates
V387MKJ	Kent CC	W110WT	Seaview Services	W367EOL	Amberlee	WCR474	Coliseum
V387SVV	Buzzlines	W210WT	Seaview Services	W367EOL	Menzies	WCR833	Coliseum
V387SVV	Menzies	W30CLC	Crawley Luxury	W368EOL	Amberlee	WDL655	Southern Vectis
V390KCA	Wheelers Travel	W38RLA	British Airways	W368EOL	Menzies	WDL693Y	Countryliner
V392SVV	Menzies	W40CLC	Crawley Luxury	W382KBE	Altonian	WDL694Y	Solent Blue Line
V407KKM	Country Rider	W56SJH	Horseman	W414KNH	MK Metro	WDL695Y	Countryliner
V412UNH	MK Metro	W57SJH	Horseman	W415KNH	MK Metro	WDL696Y	Countryliner
V413UNH	MK Metro	W59SJH	Horseman	W416KNH	MK Metro	WH02WOW	W&H Motors
V447EAL	Flights-Hallmark	W67RLA	British Airways	W452AKN	The King's Ferry	WIB1118	Autocar
V448EAL	Flights-Hallmark	W84XKP	Kent Coach	W453AKN	The King's Ferry	WIL1066	Empress Coaches
V480NKK	Regent Coaches	W100TEN	Woottens	W485ASB	Fleetwing	WIW4748	Poynter's
V490NKK	Regent Coaches	W112WGT	Centra	W487ASB	Fleetwing	WJ02KDN	Scotland & Bates
V540JBH	Centra	W114WGT	Centra	W488ASB	Fleetwing	WJ51BOU	Crosskeys
V544JBH	Centra	W116SRX	Reading Buses	W492ASB	Fleetwing	WJI2322	Worth's
V546JBH	Centra	W116WGT	Centra	W518NNJ	Hotelink	WJI2849	Woottens
V547JBH	Centra	W117SRX	Reading Buses	W519NNJ	Hotelink	WJI3814	The King's Ferry
V549JBH	Centra	W117WGT	Centra	W521NNJ	Hotelink	WJI6166	Souls
V585MKK	The King's Ferry	W118WGT	Centra	W522NNJ	Hotelink	WJI7696	Renown
V594DSM	Compass Travel	W119WGT	Centra	W523NNJ	Hotelink	WKG287	West Kent Buses
V625ENJ	British Airways	W122WGT	Centra	W524NNJ	Hotelink	WLT702	Wheelers Travel
V626ENJ	British Airways	W124WGT	Centra	W526NNJ	Hotelink	W002BUZ	Buzzlines
V66BJT	Brijan	W126WGT	Centra	W527NNJ	Hotelink	WP02XYG	OFJ
V672LWT	OFJ	W126YOR	Accord	W533YKN	The King's Ferry	WPF926	Safeguard
V673LWT	OFJ	W127WGT	Centra	W547RNB	W&H Motors	WPH134Y	Edward Thomas
V687MDA	John Pike	W128WGT	Centra	W552PPC	Accord	WR53VYW	Ham's Travel
V710LWT	Marchwood M'ways	W132WGT	Centra	W558JVV	RDH Services	WSV498	Timetrack
V762MKK	The King's Ferry	W133WGT	Centra	W558RYC	The King's Ferry	WT52EBG	Weavaway
V803DDY	British Airways	W134WGT	Centra	W567RYC	Scotland & Bates	WTG360T	Solent Blue Line
V804DDY	British Airways	W136WGT	Centra	W605FUM	McLeans	WWL208X	Thames Travel
V805DDY	British Airways	W137WGT	Centra	W626FUM	John Pike	WX04GXB	Accord
V806DDY	British Airways	W138WGT	Centra	W638FUM	McLeans	WX530XZ	Country Rider

Reg	Operator	Reg	Operator	Reg	Operator	Reg	Operator
WXI5864	Cheney	X964BPA	Reading Buses	Y252KNB	Compass Travel	YAY537	Heyfordian
WYV64T	Ham's Travel	XBZ7723	Warrens	Y252OHC	Brijan	YBO16T	Farleigh Coaches
WYW57T	Carousel	XBZ7729	Solent Blue Line	Y253KNB	Compass Travel	YBZ3260	Tappins
WYW59T	Black & White	XBZ7730	Solent Blue Line	Y253OHC	Brijan	YDL674T	Newnham
X3PBS	Buddens	XCT550	Heyfordian	Y254KNB	Compass Travel	YE52FGX	Courtney
X4PBS	Buddens	XDL696	Seaview Services	Y313KDP	Thames Travel	YE52FGZ	Eastbourne Buses
X7HAM	Ham's Travel	XDL872	Southern Vectis	Y331UKN	Kent CC	YE52FGZ	Eastbourne Buses
X8HAM	Ham's Travel	XFG29Y	Nu-Venture	Y332HWT	Kent CC	YE52FHD	Courtney
X9CCL	Courtney	XHY378	Safeguard	Y334AUT	Centra	YE52FHF	Reading Buses
X9HAM	Ham's Travel	XIB1906	Wheelers Travel	Y335AUT	Centra	YE52FHG	Reading Buses
X49VVY	Thames Travel	XIL1273	Renown	Y336UKN	Country Rider	YE52KPP	Courtney
X50CLC	Crawley Luxury	XIL1274	Renown	Y338FNH	Amberlee	YE52KPR	Courtney
X77CCH	The King's Ferry	XIL8583	Solent Blue Line	Y353CKR	Kent Coach	YE52KPT	Courtney
X94FOR	Cheney	XIL8584	Solent Blue Line	Y358LCK	Red Rose	YE52KPU	Courtney
X106MGN	Centra	XJI5691	Edward Thomas	Y359LCK	Red Rose	YF02SKN	Cardinal
X109MGN	Centra	XJJ663V	John Pike	Y363YOM	Worth's	YG02FVV	Reading Buses
X109MGN	Flights-Hallmark	XJJ668V	Brijan	Y447TKN	The King's Ferry	YG02FVW	Reading Buses
X113MGN	Centra	XJJ669V	John Pike	Y448TKN	The King's Ferry	YG02FVX	Reading Buses
X114MGN	Flights-Hallmark	XOI792	Seaview Services	Y449TKN	The King's Ferry	YG02FVY	Reading Buses
X117MGN	Flights-Hallmark	XS2210	Coastal	Y451TKN	The King's Ferry	YG02FWA	Reading Buses
X118MGN	Flights-Hallmark	XS2210	GU52HJX	Y536XNW	British Airways	YG02FWB	Reading Buses
X151NGK	Flights-Hallmark	XSK144	Worth's	Y537XNW	British Airways	YG02FWC	Reading Buses
X167BNH	Menzies	XXI7357	Heritage Travel	Y594HPK	Reading Buses	YG02FWD	Reading Buses
X171BNH	Flights-Hallmark	XXI8968	Cardinal	Y595HPK	Reading Buses	YG02FWE	Reading Buses
X172BNH	Wight Bus	XYE101G	Black & White	Y637AVV	Buzzlines	YG52CDZ	Marchwood M'ways
X203APY	Accord	Y1HMC	Flights-Hallmark	Y638AVV	Buzzlines	YG52CEA	Marchwood M'ways
X2120NH	Flights-Hallmark	Y2HLC	Lucketts	Y639AVV	Buzzlines	YG52CEF	Marchwood M'ways
X2130NH	Flights-Hallmark	Y3BUS	Souls	Y675UUM	British Airways	YG52CEJ	Marchwood M'ways
X2150NH	Flights-Hallmark	Y3HLC	Lucketts	Y676UUM	British Airways	YG52CEK	Marchwood M'ways
X216AWB	Centra	Y3HMC	Centra	Y677UUM	British Airways	YG52CEN	Marchwood M'ways
X293AKW	Altonian	Y4HLC	Lucketts	Y678UUM	British Airways	YG52CLO	Marchwood M'ways
X294AKW	Altonian	Y4WMS	Worth's	Y679UUM	British Airways	YG52CLU	Marchwood M'ways
X307CBT	Safeguard	Y5BUS	Souls	Y748HWT	Safeguard	YG52CLV	Marchwood M'ways
X308CBT	Safeguard	Y5HMC	Flights-Hallmark	Y752NAY	McLeans	YG52CLX	Marchwood M'ways
X351AUX	MK Metro	Y5PBS	Buddens	Y758HWT	Safeguard	YG52CLY	Marchwood M'ways
X383VVY	Thames Travel	Y6BAN	Banstead Coaches	Y811KDP	Courtney	YG52CLZ	Marchwood M'ways
X385VVY	Centra	Y6BUS	Souls	Y812KDP	Courtney	YG52CME	Marchwood M'ways
X400MTT	Motts Travel	Y7BUS	Souls	Y828NAY	Regent Coaches	YG52CMF	Marchwood M'ways
X417BBD	MK Metro	Y8BUS	Buzzlines	Y829NAY	McLeans	YG52CMU	MK Metro
X418BBD	MK Metro	Y8CCL	Courtney	Y831HHE	Courtney	YG52DHD	Country Rider
X419BBD	MK Metro	Y10HAM	Ham's Travel	Y832HHE	Courtney	YG52DHJ	Courtney
X424WVO	Buddens	Y10HOF	Hellyers	Y834NAY	McLeans	YG52DHK	Courtney
X461KUT	Flights-Hallmark	Y10TTL	The King's Ferry	Y875TKO	The King's Ferry	YIB9078	Altonian
X462KUT	Flights-Hallmark	Y11HMC	Centra	Y877KDP	Thames Travel	YIB9079	Altonian
X471AHE	Parking Express	Y11TTL	The King's Ferry	Y918UKR	Kent CC	YIL2185	Wheelers Travel
X472AHE	Parking Express	Y12HMC	Centra	Y951GFG	Hotelink	YJ03PPF	Marchwood M'ways
X473AHE	Parking Express	Y14HOF	Hellyers	Y952GFG	Hotelink	YJ03PPK	Marchwood M'ways
X474AHE	Parking Express	Y15HMC	Centra	Y953GFG	Hotelink	YJ03PPU	Marchwood M'ways
X482AHE	Amberlee	Y32HBT	Kent CC	Y954GFG	Hotelink	YJ03PPV	Marchwood M'ways
X491AHE	Amberlee	Y47HHE	Parking Express	Y956GFG	Hotelink	YJ03PPX	Marchwood M'ways
X493AHE	Amberlee	Y48HHE	Parking Express	Y957GFG	Hotelink	YJ03UMK	Reading Buses
X498AHE	Eastbourne Buses	Y49HHE	Parking Express	Y958GFG	Hotelink	YJ03UML	Reading Buses
X500GDY	Rambler	Y52HBT	Kent CC	Y959GFG	Hotelink	YJ03UMM	Safeguard
X516OJN	Cheney	Y63RBK	Altonian	Y961GFG	Hotelink	YJ05JXU	MK Metro
X601AHE	RDH Services	Y81LJO	Pearce	Y962GFG	Hotelink	YJ05JXV	MK Metro
X602AHE	RDH Services	Y82HHE	Buddens	Y963GFG	Hotelink	YJ05WCA	Country Rider
X636GJU	Buddens	Y82LJO	Pearce	Y964GFG	Hotelink	YJ05WCC	Country Rider
X643DLH	British Airways	Y83HHE	Buddens	Y972GPN	Thames Travel	YJ05WCD	Country Rider
X657WYG	Country Rider	Y83LJO	Pearce	Y973GPN	Thames Travel	YJ05WCE	Country Rider
X698AGM	Buddens	Y84HHE	Buddens	Y979TOJ	Hertz	YJ05WCF	Country Rider
X751HVL	Courtney	Y113LTF	Countywide	Y981TOJ	Hertz	YJ05WCG	Country Rider
X752HVL	Courtney	Y133LTF	Countywide	Y982TOJ	Hertz	YJ05XMT	Courtney
X753HVL	Courtney	Y141HWE	Grayline	Y983TOJ	Hertz	YJ05XNA	Courtney
X754HVL	Courtney	Y161HWE	Safeguard	Y984TOJ	Hertz	YJ51JWX	Kent CC
X758LOK	Wight Bus	Y162HWE	Safeguard	Y985TOJ	Hertz	YJ51JXA	British Airways
X799AGM	Buddens	Y185HNH	Parking Express	Y986TOJ	Hertz	YJ51JXB	British Airways
X906RHG	Courtney	Y203JPM	Eastonways	Y987TOJ	Hertz	YJ51JXC	British Airways
X961BPA	Reading Buses	Y222PDY	Rambler	Y988TOJ	Hertz	YJ51JXD	British Airways
X962BPA	Reading Buses	Y224NYA	Scotland & Bates	Y989TOJ	Hertz	YJ51JXE	British Airways
X963BPA	Reading Buses	Y251KNB	Compass Travel	Y991TOJ	Hertz	YJ51JXF	British Airways

The South East Bus Handbook

YJ51ZVE	Reading Buses	YN03UWR	Menzies	YN05XZT	Kent CC	YOI8115	Crawley Luxury
YJ51ZVF	Reading Buses	YN03UWS	Menzies	YN05ZXJ	OFJ	YP52CUU	The King's Ferry
YJ51ZVG	Reading Buses	YN03UWT	Menzies	YN51MFZ	Hellyers	YPB834T	Grayline
YJ51ZVH	Reading Buses	YN03WRR	Menzies	YN51XMS	Flights-Hallmark	YR02UMV	Flights-Hallmark
YJ51ZVK	Reading Buses	YN03WRU	Menzies	YN53CHC	Parking Express	YR02UOE	Flights-Hallmark
YJ51ZVL	Reading Buses	YN03WRV	Menzies	YN53CHD	Parking Express	YR02YTD	Country Rider
YJ51ZVM	Reading Buses	YN03WXZ	Country Rider	YN53CHG	OFJ	YR02YTE	Country Rider
YJ51ZVN	Reading Buses	YN03WYH	Centra	YN53CHH	OFJ	YR02YTF	Country Rider
YJ51ZVO	Reading Buses	YN03WYJ	OFJ	YN53CHK	OFJ	YR02ZKV	Flights-Hallmark
YJ54UXA	Courtney	YN03ZWV	Menzies	YN53CHL	OFJ	YR02ZKW	Flights-Hallmark
YJI5277	Charlton Services	YN04AHC	Reading Buses	YN53EHZ	Weavaway	YR02ZKX	Flights-Hallmark
YJN166	Tourex	YN04AHD	Reading Buses	YN53ELU	Country Rider	YR02ZKY	Flights-Hallmark
YK05CDV	Country Rider	YN04AHE	Reading Buses	YN53GEU	Menzies	YR02ZKZ	Flights-Hallmark
YN03AWM	W&H Motors	YN04AHF	Reading Buses	YN53GEY	Menzies	YR02ZMY	Richardson Travel
YN03AWP	W&H Motors	YN04AHG	OFJ	YN53GFA	Menzies	YR02ZZA	Lucketts
YN03GHA	Menzies	YN04AHJ	OFJ	YN53GFE	Menzies	YR02ZZB	Lucketts
YN03GHB	Menzies	YN04AVL	Lucketts	YN53GFG	Menzies	YR02ZZC	Lucketts
YN03GHD	Menzies	YN04GOC	Lucketts	YN53GFK	The King's Ferry	YR02ZZD	Lucketts
YN03GHG	Menzies	YN04GOH	Lucketts	YN53GFX	Menzies	YR52MDV	Lucketts
YN03GHK	Menzies	YN04GOJ	Lucketts	YN53GFY	Menzies	YR52MDX	Flights-Hallmark
YN03GHU	Menzies	YN04GOK	Lucketts	YN53GFZ	Menzies	YR52MDY	Richardson Travel
YN03GHV	Menzies	YN04LXM	MK Metro	YN53GGA	Menzies	YR52OGY	Accord
YN03LUE	Accord	YN04WSY	OFJ	YN53GGE	Menzies	YR52OGZ	Accord
YN03LUF	Accord	YN04YJR	Accord	YN53GGF	Menzies	YR52OHA	Accord
YN03LUH	Accord	YN04YJS	Accord	YN53GGJ	Menzies	YR52OHB	Accord
YN03LUJ	Accord	YN04YJT	Accord	YN53GGK	Menzies	YR52OHC	Accord
YN03LUL	Accord	YN04YJU	Accord	YN53GGO	Menzies	YR52OHD	Accord
YN03LUP	Accord	YN05GXA	Reading Buses	YN53GGP	Menzies	YR52OHE	Accord
YN03LUR	Accord	YN05GXB	Reading Buses	YN53OZK	Reading Buses	YR52OHF	Accord
YN03LUT	Accord	YN05GXC	Reading Buses	YN53OZL	Reading Buses	YR52VFE	The King's Ferry
YN03NCF	MK Metro	YN05GXD	Reading Buses	YN53SVG	MK Metro	YRV256V	Black & White
YN03NEF	MK Metro	YN05GXE	Reading Buses	YN53VBX	OFJ	YS02YXU	OFJ
YN03UVM	Menzies	YN05GXF	Reading Buses	YN53VCD	Richardson Travel	YS02YXV	OFJ
YN03UVP	Menzies	YN05GXG	Reading Buses	YN53YGZ	Heyfordian	YS03ZKR	Menzies
YN03UVR	Menzies	YN05GXH	Reading Buses	YN54AEP	Reading Buses	YS03ZKT	Menzies
YN03UVS	Menzies	YN05GXJ	Reading Buses	YN54AET	Reading Buses	YS03ZKU	Menzies
YN03UVT	Menzies	YN05GXL	Reading Buses	YN54AEU	Reading Buses	YS03ZKV	Menzies
YN03UVU	Menzies	YN05GXM	Reading Buses	YN54AEV	Reading Buses	YS03ZKW	Menzies
YN03UVV	Menzies	YN05GXO	Reading Buses	YN54AEW	Reading Buses	YS03ZKX	Menzies
YN03UVW	Menzies	YN05GXP	Reading Buses	YN54AEX	Reading Buses	YS03ZLK	Lucketts
YN03UVX	Menzies	YN05GXR	Reading Buses	YN54AEY	Reading Buses	YS033Y	Rebound
YN03UVZ	Menzies	YN05GXS	Reading Buses	YN54AEZ	Reading Buses	YSU975	Cheney
YN03UVZ	Menzies	YN05GXT	Reading Buses	YN54AFA	Reading Buses	YTP749	Seaview Services
YN03UWA	Menzies	YN05GXU	Reading Buses	YN54AFE	Reading Buses	YUE338	Tappins
YN03UWB	Menzies	YN05GXV	Reading Buses	YN54AFF	Reading Buses	YV03UTX	Country Rider
YN03UWD	Menzies	YN05GXW	Reading Buses	YN54AFJ	Reading Buses	YV03UTY	Country Rider
YN03UWF	Menzies	YN05GXX	Reading Buses	YN54AFK	Reading Buses	YX03OUL	Eastonways
YN03UWG	Menzies	YN05HAE	The King's Ferry	YN54AFO	Reading Buses	YX04AXJ	OFJ
YN03UWH	Menzies	YN05HFK	Lucketts	YN54AFU	Reading Buses	YX05AVN	The King's Ferry
YN03UWJ	Menzies	YN05HFL	Lucketts	YN54AFV	Reading Buses	YX05AVO	The King's Ferry
YN03UWK	Menzies	YN05HUY	Safeguard	YN54AFX	Reading Buses	YX05AVP	The King's Ferry
YN03UWL	Menzies	YN05XZP	Kent CC	YN54AKF	The King's Ferry	YXI9256	Wheelers Travel
YN03UWM	Menzies	YN05XZR	Kent CC	YN54WDE	OFJ		
YN03UWP	Menzies	YN05XZS	Kent CC	YN54WWR	Richardson Travel		

ISBN 1 904875 51 3

© Published by *British Bus Publishing Ltd* , October 2005

British Bus Publishing Ltd, 16 St Margaret's Drive, Telford, TF1 3PH
Telephone: 01952 255669 - Facsimile: 01952 222397

www.britishbuspublishing.co.uk   - E-mail salesbritishbuspublishing.co.uk